To Tito Miotti
for his contribution to the
rediscovery and appreciation
of the castles of Friuli.

THE CASTLES OF FRIULI
HISTORY AND CIVILIZATION

CHRISTOPH ULMER

THE CASTLES OF FRIULI
HISTORY AND CIVILIZATION

photographs by
GIANNI D'AFFARA

KÖNEMANN

Edited by:
Andrea Barbaranelli

Graphics and layout:
Gilberto Brun

*The drawings of the castles of Zoppola and Villalta
on pages 230-231, 287, 290-291 and 296 are by:*
Michele Potocnik

The relief tables and plans are by:
Christoph Ulmer

© 1999 for the English edition
Könemann Verlagsgesellschaft mbH
Bonner Str. 126, D-50968 Cologne

Translators of the English-language edition: Caroline Higgitt and Janet Angelini
in association with Goodfellow & Egan, Cambridge
Editor of the English-language edition: Shayne Mitchell
in association with Goodfellow & Egan, Cambridge
Typesetting: Goodfellow & Egan, Cambridge
Project coordination: Jackie Dobbyne
for Goodfellow & Egan, Cambridge
Production manager: Detlev Schaper
Assistants: Nicola Leurs and Alexandra Kiesling
Printing and binding: Mladinska knijga tiskarna, Ljubljana
Printed in Slovenia

ISBN 3-8290-2257-3

10 9 8 7 6 5 4 3 2 1

Contents

Foreword

Tito Miotti's seven-volume work on the castles of Friuli might seem to make it very difficult to contribute anything new to the subject. However, this is not the case. Miotti's massive and scrupulous study of the known sources will—with the exception of the occasional incorrect quotation—remain fundamental for all future research. So thorough was his research that nothing of any real significance remains to be discovered in the archives.

If Tito Miotti's work has a weakness, however, it is in its scope: it pays hardly any attention neither to the architectural role of the castles nor to their political, economic, and social context. The few descriptions of buildings or ruins in the book—often written by outside contributors—do not provide an entirely accurate picture of the castles, nor of their function and significance. Nowadays, indeed, it would be impossible for one person above to provide an exhaustive treatment of the subject, since there are quite a few unresolved and complex issues that remain.

This is true not only of Friuli but of the whole of Europe. Over the last century, many preconceptions have been demolished, notably those concerning the defensive role of the castle. The paucity of sources makes the work of classification difficult everywhere; only rarely is it possible to date with certainty a particular architectural feature, or demonstrate that a construction was used for a particular function.

European castles share a number of common features. By comparing them with each other, we can isolate categories that would not be apparent if we limited ourselves to a more narrow regional perspective. In Friuli, however, this element has been ignored for too long.

This book therefore seeks to set Friuli within the European context in order to overcome a nineteenth-century conception of the castle that is still widespread. It is the result of research carried out over the last few years into the medieval castle, its origins, and its functions. A future study will examine the castle in the early modern period, analyzing the transformation of castles into palaces and the emergence at the same time of the fortress.

Ruins of the castle of Attimis. Frequently only fragments of wall remain of a castle, contributing to the myth of the castle and fostering an exaggerated idea of the form and scale of castles.

THE MYTH
OF THE
CASTLE

All of us carry within us an image of a castle, one that has very little to do with what we actually see when visiting ruins. When my three-year-old nephew visited me for the first time at Villa di Tissano, my sister had told him that his uncle lived in a real castle. Faced with the prosaic reality of the house, the little boy burst into tears and was consoled only when he found a tower in the garden behind. Without doubt the fairy-tale image of the castle takes root in our imagination early; it is a myth that has been created in the past, over a long period of time. This book will attempt to trace the origins of the myth.

From the castle to the myth of the castle

The creation of an image of the classic feudal castle in art began long before these castles became redundant during the period in which the nobility moved down to the plains and when political, social, and economic activity became concentrated in the towns. With this change, hilltop castles became part of the landscape backgrounds in prints and paintings.[1] The castle, perched on vertiginous crags of impossible heights, became a decorative feature. Only the nineteenth-century Bavarian castles of Ludwig II have more

Ruins of the castle of Solimbergo in a drawing by von Zahn. Representations of castles in art frequently exaggerated the size of towers and walls.

towers and pinnacles.[2] The architectural forms of a castle were already exaggerated in the late medieval period, which revelled in a desire to reach ever higher, using increasingly slender and pointed elements.[3]

From the seventeenth century, depictions of ruins become increasingly common. The castle comes to be resonant with symbolism and fairy-tale attributes.[4] Birds wheel around mighty towers that seem unreal creations from a distant past. The further away the Middle Ages become, the greater the divide between image and reality.[5]

Castles and towers came to be represented in drawings, paintings, and prints. Tableware, porcelain, and fabrics were decorated with images of romantic ruins—which themselves became models for architecture. Initially, small ruins were used in the grounds of noble residences until eventually ruins themselves were built.

After the Baroque period, neo-Gothic aristocratic residences were constructed in the form of castles. Moreover, starting from pre-existing small ruins in their grounds, entire new ruined castles came to be built, becoming ever greater in scale. Thus in the nineteenth century an insignificant artistic phenomenon—representations of castles—developed into a trend that was to become a dominant architectural style.

It is not clear why this rediscovery of the medieval castle should have occurred. The vogue for neo-medieval construction cannot be explained only by the romantic attraction of ruins. A decisive factor was the nationalism that exploded throughout Europe, a nationalism that saw the symbolic force it sought in the castle. In Germany this enthusiasm reached a peak with the reconstruction of the castle of Hohkönig, praised by Emperor Wilhelm II as "an important symbol of a gloriously revived empire, proclaiming the essence of the Germanic chivalric spirit of ancient times."[6]

Bodo Ebhard and Otto Piper, the leading scholars at the time, produced radically different proposals for the reconstruction of Hohkönig. It is no accident that the plan chosen was that which placed emphasis on the visual effect of the whole rather than on a scrupulously faithful reconstruction. It is evidence of how closely allied historical

study and the Romantic vision, and restoration and imitation, had become by this time.

The fairy-tale constructions of the nineteenth century corresponded in every detail with the image of the medieval castle formed by historians. This explains why the grandiose and plausible nineteenth-century restorations are still today the best-known and most admired "medieval" monuments. No visitor doubts their authenticity.

In France this movement is associated with Viollet-le-Duc, who not only directed restorations but, through his writings, contributed to the diffusion of a misleading idea of the castle, since it was only large and important buildings that were restored and

thus known. Publications about the castles of Coucy in France, Windsor in England, and Marienburg and Hohkönigsburg in Germany did nothing to contribute to an understanding of the medieval castle since these huge castles are entirely exceptional for any period. The same is true of Krak des Chevaliers, the remarkable Crusader castle unequalled in any period or place.

Hand in hand with the Romantic conception and historical ideology went growing nationalism. Outside Italy, historians glorified the age of the great medieval kings and the Hohenstaufen emperors. Nineteenth-century architecture looked back to the architecture of the age that had seen the birth of nation states.

Albrecht Dürer, St. Eustace (1501), detail. The size of the castle is exaggerated, making it more striking. Castles appear in the backgrounds of frescoes and paintings from as early as the 16th century.

Two striking frescoes from the salon of Villa Beretta in Lauzacco. Images of castles such as these were common in the decoration of porcelain, china, and textiles, particularly in the Romantic age.

Nowhere did more pronounced national architectural styles emerge than in those nineteenth-century buildings that reproduced medieval forms. This is particularly true of restored castles. Their exaggerated size was no accident. Both romanticism and nationalism glorified the past. To restore a castle was to create a symbol of national pride. The nationalist style is most apparent in the castles built in the nineteenth century. For example, nineteenth-century German architecture—when it was not influenced by chill neo-classicism—drew on Hohenstaufen castles, with their rustication.

It was only in Italy that this trend did not take hold. I know of no example of a nineteenth-century building which was influenced by medieval castles. This is because in Italy the quest for national identity sought its models in a more distant—and more glorious—past. Unlike the rest of Europe, nineteenth-century Italy saw no large-scale restoration of medieval castles; those which were restored in Friuli generally followed English models.

Miramare

The most important nineteenth-century castle in Friuli is Miramare, near Trieste. Trieste, situated close to Istria, split early from the patriarchate and thus from Friuli. In the fourteenth century it put itself under the protection of the Austrian emperor in order to free itself of Venetian interference.

Since Trieste and the Istrian coast always held a particular fascination for the Habsburg emperors, it was no surprise that Maximilian, the younger brother of Emperor Franz Josef and future emperor of Mexico, should have built himself a palace when he was sent to Trieste as commander-in-chief of the Austrian navy. Since the palace was not a state commis-

sion but a private initiative of the archduke, it did not need to function as an official Austro-Hungarian residence but was inspired entirely by Maximilian's own taste.

Maximilian chose a relatively unknown Trieste architect, Carlo Junker. In addition to the palace of Miramare, Junker was also responsible for another building—reminiscent of Miramare—in the port area. It might seem surprising that Maximilian should have chosen an architect whose obscurity was matched only by his lack of originality, as is apparent from the architecture of Miramare. It is especially surprising in view of the choice available to Maximilian in Vienna, where all the great architects of the time were engaged on the buildings of the Ringstrasse.

FOLLOWING PAGES:
Aerial view of the castle of Miramare, the grandest and most important example of Romantic architecture in Friuli.

PRECEDING PAGES:
Interiors at Miramare, in an eclectic style combining Baroque and German Renaissance. Portraits of contemporary rulers, mainly German princes, hang on the bedroom walls.

Probably Maximilian's choice of a local architect can be explained by his poor relations with his brother the emperor; on this occasion at least he seems to have wanted to make the decision for himself.

The architectural competition for the palace had produced a number of designs. One thing had been made clear: the plan had to be for a castle. Yet none of the proposed designs display nationalistic Austro-Germanic architectural language but resemble English stately homes, and Miramare's vicinity to the sea may also have suggested this.

Maximilian's apartment, reflecting the taste for the German Renaissance.

At Miramare the impression of a castle is conveyed by an ensemble full of variety, reinforced by corner turrets and castellation. The large windows are not medieval but derive from those of 16th-century English palaces.

Thanks to the use of the local Istrian limestone, the building fits harmoniously into the rocky coast. The general design is typical of its age: a complicated ground plan and richly decorated elevation suggest a castle, further emphasized by the elaborate battlements and turrets. Entirely unmedieval, on the other hand, are not only the generous living quarters but, in particular, the large windows, which are stylistically close, as has been suggested, to those found in English Renaissance palaces.

Miramare reveals nothing of the native Italian architectural tradition—which in any case was not used for nineteenth-century castles and was not desired by the client. However, Maximilian, a cautious man whose regard for national sensitivity explains his success as governor of Milan, also rejected an obvious Austro-Germanic architectural style. Miramare is a typical example of a contemporary vogue, a Europe-wide form of Romanticism that was restrained, diplomatic, and cosmopolitan. Neither bourgeois nor nationalist, the castle is as tactful as its patron.

All the greater, then, is the visitor's surprise on entering the palace: the interior is all German Renaissance. The craftsmen who carried out the work were summoned from Vienna, although this is not evident from the quality of the work: the choice of materials seems to have been dictated everywhere by economy. The interior recalls that of many German castles of the period, such as the restored castle of Heidelberg, where a fairly depressing and gloomy interior has none of the cosmopolitan air suggested by the exterior.

If the restraint and bourgeois parsimony of the salons of Miramare reveal an Austrian-German nationalist spirit, the emphasis on the German Renaissance in the salons, with the arms and portraits of German rulers, similarly reflects national culture. The interior suggests a prince surrounded by his peers. Such an interior could be found in any castle of the medieval or nineteenth-century German Empire. In Italy, however, it is an eccentricity.

The castles of Friuli and Italian nationalism

The relationship between the Romantic idea of the castle and nationalism has influenced research heavily. Friuli is no exception. When, at the end of the nineteenth century, interest in the castles of Friuli began to grow, von Zahn published his study of the Germanic castles of Friuli. The stress placed on the birthplace of the patrons and the origins of their names coincided with the struggle over national political boundaries. Von Zahn's book reads as a historical justification of Austrian rule in the region, serving to argue against the Irredentists (those who before 1918 wished to see the Trentino and Istria united with Italy), who sought to return to Italy a region which, according to von Zahn, had never belonged to it. Von Zahn's arguments collided with those of a school of history of diametrically opposed views but equally fervent nationalism (and thus equally lacking in objectivity and historical accuracy) that saw all Friuli castles, without exception, as Roman in origin.

Tito Miotti has upheld this school of thought, asserting that all external castle walls are of Roman origin and that the later feudal lords from north of the Alps were mere interlopers, cuckoos exploiting nests that they were incapable of making for themselves. According to Miotti, von Zahn could not have been unaware of the fact that virtually all these castles evolved from Roman or late antique fortifications, patched up and occasionally enlarged or marginally improved to make use of new techniques of attack and defence. In every case the changes were minor, and they remained so, except in rare cases, until at least the fourteenth century.

The idea that Roman walls and towers are to be found in all castles has influenced research in Friuli to such an extent that it is universally accepted as fact. Yet there is no historical evidence for significant Roman defences in Friuli, apart from city walls. Nor is there a single structure that reveals continuity of occupation between the Roman *castrum* and the medieval castle.

In Italy, the emphasis on Roman origins derived from the same enthusiasm as that

which in France led to the glorification of the Merovingians, and in Germany to the cult of the legend of Frederick Barbarossa's grave in the Kyffhäuser Mountains and the expectation of a return of the Hohenstaufen emperors and a restoration of the lost Empire. Only in Italy did the Middle Ages remain outside the dream of greatness and national unity. Indeed Italian nineteenth-century literature viewed the Middle Ages as the beginning of the subjugation of the nation to foreign

The castle of Gorizia, one of the most visited in Friuli, although few original features survive. The 1930s restoration reflects the fervent nationalism of the Fascist era.

powers. It was for this reason that, in their search for a national identity, nineteenth- and early twentieth-century Italians looked back to the classical Roman era, of which they felt the rightful heirs. Lessing, in the eighteenth century, had had harsh words for such illusions of grandeur.[7]

This political and historical ideology found its architectural expression in Fascist architecture. In Trieste, for example, the Roman theater was restored and a Capitol on the lines of that in Rome was created on the castle hill next to the cathedral. Here, fake ancient ruins combine with marble inscriptions of classicizing verses by Irredentists and supporters of national freedom to form an ensemble which blends Italian late Romanticism with Fascist propaganda.

RIGHT:
The entrance to the castle of Gorizia. The huge lion of St. Mark was placed there in 1919.

BELOW:
Two pre-1930s views of the castle of Gorizia, revealing how much was altered in the restoration.

The restoration of Gorizia Castle

The most important castle restoration project in Friuli, that of Gorizia Castle, grew out of the same spirit. The extraordinary falsifications carried out elsewhere in Europe in the nineteenth century have an important epilogue at Gorizia, with a markedly late Italian variation of aggrandizement and nationalism. As elsewhere, visitors can have no conception of how little of what lies

before them corresponds to the original. The restoration and presentation of this classic example of Italian Fascist culture is impeccable and intriguing. However, a glance at a photograph of the castle from before the First World War and consideration of the drastic reconstruction and additions over the centuries, reveals how few of the original medieval parts survive.[8]

From the very beginning, the restoration was intended as a symbol of Italy's success in liberating the town and duchy of Gorizia, long subject to a foreign power.[9] Before work was even started, a huge lion of St. Mark was hastily placed over the castle entrance. It remains there today, its presence leading many guides to attribute to Venice a major role in the construction of the castle in reality, in the 800 years of its existence, it was under Venetian control for only a few months.[10]

There was intense debate on the form the restoration of Gorizia castle should take. Annalia Delneri, in her excellent article on the history of the castle, expresses it in a

Even the gateway and windows, none of which is original, reveal how the near-total reconstruction of Gorizia robbed it of its original features.

The kitchens in the castle of Gorizia. While most rooms were lavishly restored and retain little of the medieval, the tiny kitchens would have been inadequate for the requirements of an important court like that of the counts of Gorizia.

nutshell: "In a postwar age marked by strong nationalist sentiment, it is easy to understand why restoration should have opted to emphasize the Roman origins of the culture of the region." Unfortunately, within the city limits, the only Roman remains that could be found were the top of a funeral altar. "This Roman fragment was immediately moved into the castle and placed—almost like a cornerstone—on the foundations of the medieval keep."[11]

The total absence of Roman remains in the castle concurs with the archival evidence, according to which in the early Middle Ages there was only a small unfortified settlement, described as a *villa*, on the hill. The main castle—the most important fortified site—was elsewhere, in Salcano; even in the later medieval period, the church of Gorizia Castle came under the authority of the parish church of Salcano. Despite the unequivocal historical context, the foundations of a tower uncovered in archaeological excavations near the old Salcano gate are still claimed as Roman, an example of the persistent desire to claim ancient origins for medieval castles built by feudal lords who were not even necessarily Italian.

Disappointment at this failure to find any evidence of a pre-medieval, Roman fortification that could be used for nationalist propaganda led to several decades during which interest in restoring Gorizia Castle waned. Eventually, in the 1930s, the way was free for restoration based on aesthetic grounds—but in which the same nationalistic interests were still discernible. A report by Guido Cirilli, the architect in charge of the restoration plan for the Cultural Ministry in Rome, summarizes the new attitude to reconstruction. Cirilli writes that before 1914 the castle was a

> massive, uniform, and dull building on top of the hill where the earliest settlement of Gorizia originated. The building had been used as a barracks and Austrian military headquarters for more than fifty years since the Austro-Italian War of 1866. The main building had no notable features: a high perimeter wall, pierced with a large number of rectangular windows of varying sizes placed all around with oppressive monotony ... The splendid sixteenth-century Venetian outer wall, enlivened at intervals by round towers and rendered austere by centuries of darkening, was overshadowed by the vast barracks, a discordant note in so incomparable a setting—a typical example of the poverty of the military imagination.[12]

In order to emphasize the Italian element of "so incomparable a setting" (in contrast to philistine militarism—a surprising criticism for the Fascist period), Cirilli suggested that "flowerbeds of native Italian species should be placed in front of the over-narrow entrance in the Venetian wall, giving life to the stone."[13] As for the restoration of the castle itself, since the lack of finds made it impossible to justify a reconstruction of a Roman building, the choice of style was left to the architects who were given free rein. Cirilli wrote:

> The fundamental principle of the restoration of the castle is an awareness of all architectural and stylistic elements of any significance which have come to light. Where individual buildings are concerned, the dominant original character must be restored, renewing every part of it as far as possible, and completing the various buildings in a similar way, with new additions, so as to create a coherent and harmonious appearance.[14]

On the basis of these criteria, a sixteenth-century castle was created, whose sole medieval element is the large Romanesque-style windows of the main hall, now called the "Count's Hall".[15] Visitors see a space that in all its non-medieval grandeur is certainly impressive, but which lacks any authenticity. A visit to the castle of Gorizia thus confirms the widespread myth of the medieval castle, one which—precisely because of its seeming authenticity—plays a part in reinforcing its essential inaccuracy.

The military myth of the castle

A further reason why our image of the castle is incorrect arises from the fact that the first to study the history of castles were army officers and military engineers. Given their professional interests, they tended to exaggerate the defensive role of the castle, seeing it as part of a logical development from the Roman *castellum* to early modern fortifications, and judging it from a modern strategic and political viewpoint. In other words, they regarded the castle as a means for the defense of territory, although to do so is to presume a centralized power and organization that did not in fact exist in the Middle Ages.

Only rarely did castles contribute to border defense. Studies of the concept of borders show that in the medieval period the idea of linear borders did not exist. Instead the prevalent notion was of wide, vaguely defined, areas of dominion which were focused on a castle. The idea of protecting a border with a line of fortresses is modern. Obviously castles had some defensive function, but this varied from castle to castle. Emperor Frederick II's celebrated Castel del Monte in Puglia, for example, is almost indefensible, yet it assured his power; this was its true function. Dominion was guaranteed by the appearance alone of these daunting constructions, endowed with an architectural strength that appeared to defy time, suggesting that their power would last for all eternity.[16]

Nineteenth-century assumptions have left their mark not only on historical studies. Our idea of castles has also been shaped by nineteenth-century illustrations in fairy stories

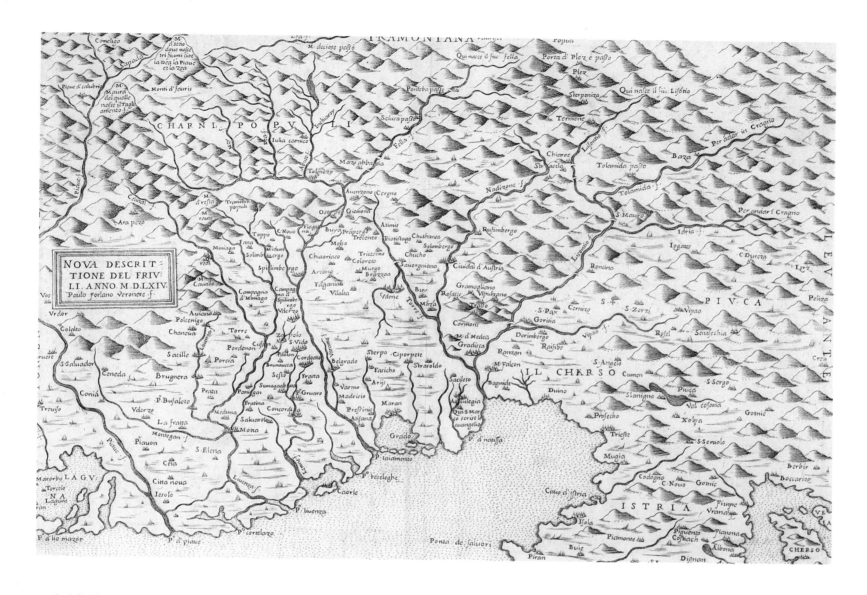

Nova Descrit:
tione del Friv:
li. Anno. M.D.LXIV.
Paulo forlano Veronese f.

and chivalrous romances that have little to do with the reality of a normal noble residence in the Middle Ages. In Friuli, a region populated by feudal lords who were less well-off precisely because there were so many of them, poverty was the rule. We need to pay attention to such people. A book about castles should also be about the feudal lords, only a very few of whom enjoyed the splendid courtly and chivalric life that has come down to us through so many works of literature. We know little of the harsh living conditions of the average rural noble, whose life was one of constant struggle against more powerful lords, his equals or his superiors, putting up a desperate resistance so as not to slip once and for all into the indistinct mass of the population from which he was separated only by the fact that he lived in a castle and possessed

certain rights, exercised by virtue of his position as his lord's representative. The prevailing image of the castle is of a carefree life of wealth and luxury. Ruins are transformed into sumptuous fairy-tale structures, the architectural setting for the myth.

16th-century map of Friuli. Castles are scattered all over the area but are particularly dense on higher land.

29

FORTIFICATIONS

In his study of the castles of Friuli, Tito Miotti includes a large number of highly diverse buildings, revealing a persistent uncertainty—one that is shared by other historians of Friuli—about the manner in which to distinguish a castle from other types of buildings. This is clearest in relation to other contemporary constructions of a defensive type, rather than in the definition of a castle (though this is admittedly difficult) in the context of classical or medieval aristocratic residences in the countryside, medieval estates, or the villas and country houses of the early modern period.

All fortifications offer protection but the various types of fortification vary according to the importance of the person being protected. This is perhaps the most insoluble of the problems posed by the castle, the defensive function of which is not always clear. The castle could be a place of refuge for the local population, who found protection within its walls, although the central area was often too small to accommodate many people for long. It could offer real protection only to the feudal lord—whose person was, of course, what really mattered.

The castle was a highly individual structure that, in a complex and stratified network of relationships, could not be separated from the feudal lord. It was the home as well as the center of power of the feudal lord and his family, independently of the privileges he might enjoy and the position he occupied. The privileges with which he was invested were held personally by the lord and were connected so closely with ownership of the castle that they could not be separated from it.

This is why it is important to emphasize the uniqueness of the feudal castle in order to distinguish it from other defensive structures. Apart from castles, there is a great variety of other kinds of fortified sites comparable to, but different from, castles. It is important to examine the juridical status of each fortified site, whether village, town, or monastery. From such an analysis it becomes clear that military function is relatively insignificant in the definition of the castle.

Strongholds and fortified churches

The original purpose of every defensive structure is as a refuge, a natural or artificially created stronghold which in times of danger can provide the local population with a safe retreat for themselves and their most valued possessions, above all their animals. Such places of refuge were already found in prehistoric times and until recently were widespread. In Friuli, besides the fortified hill villages excavated by archaeologists, a large number of *cortine*, fortified villages, are recorded, providing an idea of the most basic form of defense. In late antiquity and the Middle Ages such structures were called in Latin *castrum* or *castellum*. Castles to which there are very early references, such as Duino, were perhaps originally simply *cortine*, fortified villages. Otherwise, if they had no defensive *vallum* or ditch they would have been called simply *ville* (settlements).

Cortine normally consisted of platforms raised artificially not more than five meters (15 feet), surrounded by a *vallum* and ditch, with a diameter of, on average, one hundred meters (330 feet). The *cortine* were protected, in the simplest examples, by a wooden fence or hurdles (as is apparent from many records), in some cases by substantial palisades, and even, exceptionally, by walls. Such defenses were generally of a basic kind and in much of Friuli they became villages that still exist today and are still called *cortine*. In very rare cases they were nothing more than fortified places, the area within the walls used only as a refuge. The *cortina* at Codroipo is described in documents as virtually a small village, while to the east of the county of Gorizia a whole series of so-called *Tabor*, small fortified villages, survives, such as that at Vipacco.

Even today a number of churches enclosed within walls survive. However, while in other parts of Europe exposed to danger or close to borders, fortified churches were often imposing buildings that may have had a real defensive function, the same cannot be said of those known in Friuli. Important examples, comparable to similar constructions elsewhere, are found only in Tarvisio and in the valley historically linked with Carinthia.

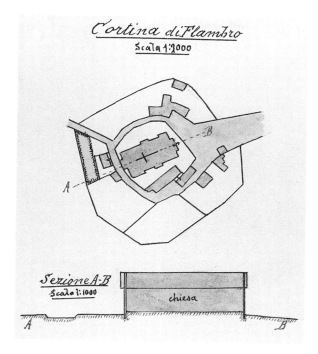

Cortina di Flambro
Scala 1:2000

Sezione A-B
Scala 1:1000
chiesa

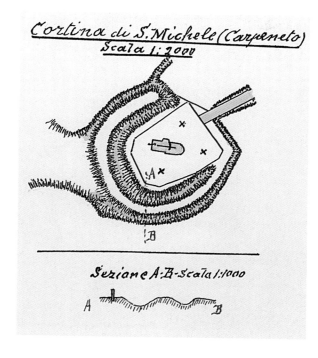

Cortina di S. Michele (Carpeneto)
Scala 1:2000

Sezione A:B - Scala 1:1000

Early 20th-century sketch-maps showing the forms and size of three of the few remaining cortine in Friuli.

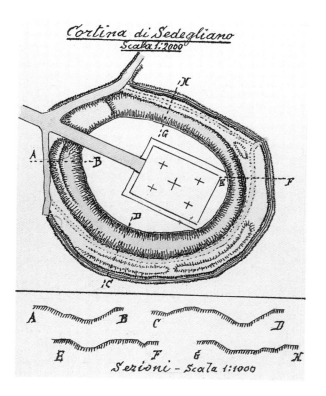

Cortina di Sedegliano
Scala 1:2000

Sezioni - Scala 1:1000

A drawing exists of the *cortina* of the church of San Michele in Carpeneto, near Pozzuolo, showing it in a better state of conservation than today. In the center of the typical arrangement of *vallum* and ditch around a flat area surrounded by a more recent low wall is a sixteeth-century chapel with high Gothic windows and a brick frieze below the roof. The old *cortina* is now the village cemetery, which is why the restored surrounding wall, only one meter (three feet) high, does not seem out of place, pierced only at the entrance.[17] San Michele's importance as a fortified church can be seen from this drawing, for it shows an arrangement looking much more like a fortified space than we see today.[18] At the entrance is a tower that stands higher than the chapel. A bridge can also be made out, leading from the tower. The complex is surrounded by a wall already showing signs of disrepair. The fact that other *cortine* do not have such walls may mean that they had simple wooden palisades.[19]

The *cortina* provided villagers with a small defensive structure that was generally built by their own efforts. The chapel with its liturgical vessels, the most precious objects in the village, was the building most worthy of protection since it was often the only stone construction. Placing their trust not only in the building but also in God's protection,

Prospectus Ecclesia Veteris Sⁿ Michael de Carpeneto

Drawing of the cortina of San Michele at Carpeneto. The cortina, today the village cemetery, is reminiscent of a castle.

The view of the cortina from the surrounding fields reveals its characteristic elevated position.

villagers would take shelter in the church in the hope that any enemy horde would pass by without stopping. Such constructions were not strong enough to withstand an attack by any but the smallest band of robbers.

Given the constant threat of attack, as described in history books, it is hard to understand why better defenses were not built. However, when I asked the medieval historian Aldo Settia whether this could be acccounted for by the low population density, he pointed out that the question was wrongly posed. As far as Friuli is concerned, there is nothing in contemporary records to suggest a particular threat from enemy hordes, whether Hungarians or Ottoman Turks, despite the claims by local historians over the last hundred years, each handing on the myth to the next generation. If we confine ourselves to the sources, it is apparent that the risk of invasion on the plain of Friuli was about the same as in the rest of northern Italy, which in general enjoyed peace, if a somewhat fragile one. It is not surprising then that in Friuli fortified places of refuge and *cortine* should be similar to those elsewhere in northern Italy. This one example demonstrates how, in the study of castles, it is easy to reach conclusions based on false assumptions.

Unlike the castle, the *cortina* was not permanently inhabited and was not the residence of a feudal lord. It was nothing more than a simple structure, having no overlordship function. Lacking such symbolic function, the *cortina* never had the imposing walls we admire in feudal castles. On the other hand, so far as defensive capacity was concerned, the castle was little better than the *cortina*: it too was not strong enough to withstand a serious attack. The most important difference between *cortina* and castle lay, however, in their juridical status. I know of no case of a *cortina* which had feudal privileges.[20] *Cortine* enjoyed no privileges and played no part in the organization of the state; they had no political role. From this, we can conclude that, unlike the castle with its various and complex functions, the *cortina* had only one function, the most basic: the defense of people and possessions.

Fortified villages

Fortified villages are much rarer in Friuli than the small *cortine*. Here too we are dealing with a primitive form of fortification which has existed in all periods. It was known in antiquity as a *castrum*. One of the very few examples in Friuli is the village of San Martino, in the Slovenian part of Collio. The village stands on a ridge that falls away on three sides while on the fourth side a small saddle connects it to another hill, which rises steeply. The site is not particularly secure and yet as late as the seventeenth century the village was able to withstand a Venetian siege despite the enemy's modern weapons and the village's unprepossessing fortifications.[21] The best defense, as San Martino demonstrates, is the will of the besieged to survive.

The village comprises around thirty houses and a church on the highest point. The biggest house belongs to the parish priest and was used, in the past, by the representative of authority, a *gastaldo*, or steward, of the monastery of Rosazzo, under whose jurisdiction the village came.[22] The defensive structure today consists of a few stretches of wall

The gate of the fortified village of San Martino, in the Slovenian part of Collio. San Martino is one of very few examples of such ancient fortifications still surviving.

Although the arch of the gate and the walls are not typical of early defensive construction, in general San Martino retains the structure of a medieval fortified burg.

with a rampart; most of the rest of the town wall has been used to form the backs of the houses built up against it. There are three simple gates, apparently of more recent date and now having the appearance of no more than symbolic archways. The most striking feature is the solid corner towers whose form is transitional between medieval and modern: they are no longer tall, narrow defensive towers with narrow arrow-slits, but are still too small to be proper circular bastions designed to withstand artillery. Except in a case of emergency, these towers probably had no roofs.

The difference between San Martino and a feudal castle is obvious. San Martino was a fortified place with a permanent population but, like the *cortina*, it had no administrative or juridical functions. The feudal rights and obligations were claimed by the monastery of Rosazzo; the representative sent to the village did not receive the village as a fief and had no individual political power. The military

importance of this village was, however, as can be seen from the outcome of the war of Gradisca, exceptional, greater than that of any of the other fortifications in the area.[23] Thus its defensive function is something that makes San Martino different from, rather than more similar to, the true medieval castle.

Fortified towns

The distinction between fortified village and fortified town is slight and quite difficult to define. An example is the small town of

Marano, one of the oldest fortifications in Friuli. Marano's position in the twin lagoons of Marano and Grado gives it natural defenses. Like other centers in the lagoons of north-eastern Italy, the origins of the settlement can be traced to the period of the barbarian invasions. In 589–590 a Church council was held there, attended by the most important ecclesiastical representatives of north-eastern Italy.[24]

Most probably Marano was a small settlement at the time, with an important church; this is the most plausible explanation of why it is described as a *villa* (settlement) in the earliest records.[25] Although Marano continued to be described as a *villa* until the

Thanks to its site in the Slovenian hills, in the 17th century the fortified village of San Martino was able to withstand repeated Venetian sieges.

thirteenth century, its economic importance must have increased. In 1287, for instance, it was evidently worth the Venetians' while to pillage the town and loot "every single thing." Venice did not tolerate competition in the Adriatic, which she regarded as "her" sea. From that time onwards, Marano underwent a series of repeated reinforcement and capture, in turn by the patriarch, by Venice, and finally, above all, by the emperor.

A glance at the map shows that this remote town had absolutely no strategic

itself by levying tolls on the road to Marano, to the annoyance of Venice.[27] Maranutto had justified its existence.

A fortress such as Marano had in common with a castle the essential function of symbolic power. It was a pawn in the regional power game, not because of any commercial importance, but merely by virtue of its existence, particularly because of its fortifications which in reality protected nothing more than a political claim. It was for this reason that only those who had no such claim were

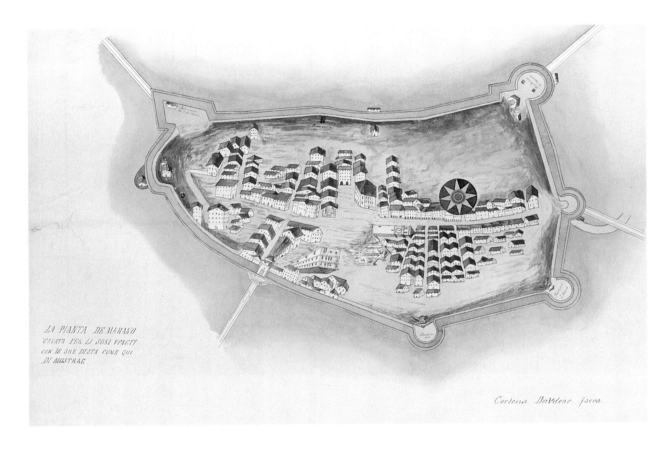

LA PIANTA DE MARANO
CAVATA PER LI SOSI VENETI
CON LE SUE DISTA COME QUI
DI MOSTRAE

Cortona DaValene facea

Map of Marano, one of the oldest fortified towns in Friuli, protected by its position in the lagoon.

importance; the surrounding area lacked even a navigable river. With Marano, it was solely a case of fostering or destroying a rival. When Austria finally lost control of Marano, in 1542, it built a small "counter-fortress" on Austrian territory and called it Maranutto, a modest construction never considered of any importance.[26] With a garrison of nine or ten soldiers, Maranutto did not represent a threat to be taken seriously, and it was in fact unceremoniously destroyed during the war of Gradisca. But it had cost the Austrians nothing, paying for

interested in the town; in itself Marano was of no significance.

The walls of Marano witnessed every change in the fortifications of the region but have unfortunately been demolished. Only a corner bastion still stands. A first circle of walls,[28] among the best examples in Friuli, was built here in the time of the patriarch Poppo. In the fourteenth century four attempts by the Venetians to capture Marano were repelled. In 1514 Venice tried again, unsuccessfully, to take the town with "fierce battles, on land and at sea." Marano fell twice into enemy hands, but only through treachery and betrayal.[29]

From the military point of view, then, Marano was superior to all the other castles in Friuli. The history of fortifications has always exaggerated the importance of castles and has

Once again, it is juridical status that is crucial. A town with municipal privileges was an independent political entity, owing allegiance directly to the emperor, to the patriarch, or to a feudal lord, as in the case of Spilimbergo. Any town could obtain feudal

The clocktower in Spilimbergo. The steady expansion of the outer limits of the burg of a castle might lead, as here, to its development into a town.

omitted to take into consideration the fact that towns, even when they were small and insignificant like Marano, were already in the Middle Ages the real military focuses. A close reading of the history of Friuli in the period of incessant disputes between the patriarch and the feudal lords makes clear the importance of towns such as Udine and Cividale. Their economic power, greater number of inhabitants, and better supplies of food (for sieges) meant that it was the towns that were the key links in the feudal system. They resembled a castle much more than did a town such as Marano.

privileges, invested with them for their particular merits or simply by purchasing them. In this way towns could acquire land, estates, villages, even castles. Every town could have its own jurisdiction, exactly like that enjoyed by a castle, and have a seat in the parliament of Friuli.

In addition to this common juridical status, towns had a decisive role to play in the struggle for power between feudal lords. Such struggles decided the political situation of the day. Despite its imposing walls, Marano played no part in such matters. Cividale, on

from the town of Spilimbergo, where it is difficult to disinguish the castle from the surrounding town. The town developed gradually out of the castle, as the boundaries of the burg were constantly enlarged. At a certain point, it is hard to be sure whether we are dealing with the burg of a castle or a newly formed town. They can be distinguished only from a juridical point of view: if the inhabited center, or greatly enlarged burg, acquires its own municipal privileges and the majority of inhabitants become independent of the feudal lord, then it is valid to speak of a town. If, on the other hand, the feudal links between the lord and the inhabitants of the burg remain strong, then the whole inhabited area, however large, must still be called a castle.

the other hand, was active in the struggle for power and for centuries sought, for example, to maintain control over the walls of the monastery of Rosazzo, with some success, even though its adversary was the abbot, one of the greatest landowners and most powerful feudal lords.[30]

The status and growing confidence of the towns were reflected in their appearance. Just as a powerful lord would display any increase in his power or wealth by extending his castle and building a higher tower, so the towns constructed walls, gates, and, in particular, towers as evidence of their power. Even more than in the case of towers on castles, military explanations for the shape, height, and number of towers built in towns are unsatisfactory. Towers should be seen purely as status symbols. Thus towns borrowed from castles not only the notion of territorial domination but also that most visible sign of power, the tower.[31] Marano, as a small, well-fortified town, had no ambitions to build such towers because it had no pretensions to power. Nor did it attempt to compete with the feudal lords since it had no role to play in this political system.

It is logical, therefore, that a study of castles should examine towns, and the differences and similarities between castles and towns. Such an examination should not stop at walls and towers, however. This is clear

Fortified abbeys

Of all fortified constructions, those which most closely resemble castles are the abbeys, which possess other attributes besides the juridical privileges shared with the towns. In Friuli there are four large monastic complexes, which are always included in studies of the castles of the region. They are the abbeys of Sesto al Reghena, Moggio, Rosazzo, and of course—the classic example— Castelmonte. Castelmonte's dominant position and resonant name (mountaintop castle) give it pride of place and allow us to overlook its obvious weaknesses.

Castelmonte

The abbey of Castelmonte, which still has a resident community of monks, is situated in the mountains above Cividale. Visible from far away, no other castle in Friuli has as splendid a site and makes such an impression. Unlike the other three abbeys, Castelmonte gives the impression of being a well-fortified complex which gives a good idea of the original construction. In reality, however, the abbey has undergone a number of major reconstructions. The first thing the visitor sees is the huge parking lot carved out of the side of the hill. The

monastery buildings have also been brutally adapted to modern requirements, to the extent that they are effectively new buildings. As for the church, the ugly 1930s façade is a preface to the appearance of the interior. Here, the main feature is what was originally the small crypt, where extensive stuccowork by Giovanni da Udine and frescoes by his followers make the crypt effectively a lower church.

Underneath the monastery are the remains of a much earlier building. Excavation work to enlarge the lower church revealed late Roman *opus signinum* pavements. The first mention of a fortified monastery is in 1296, when the chapter of the monastery of Santa Maria in Valle, to which Castelmonte was subject, "repaired the castle and church."[32] Even at this date it must have been an important place of pilgrimage, because it was one of the wealthiest monastic houses in the region. In 1253, a

portico was erected in front of the church to provide lodging for pilgrims.[33]

However, the building history of the monastery and church falls outside the scope of this work. What is of interest here is the defensive role of Castelmonte. The implications of this in connection with armed conflict are significant, and it is surprising that no record of any siege has come down to us.[34] There is only a brief allusion to war damage in 1419 and no reference to damage inflicted by the Ottoman Turks; the only references are to improvements to the fortifications.[35] War seems to have left Castelmonte unscathed.[36] It is clear that strong walls in themselves did little to frighten aggressors, since richer and more powerful abbeys such as Rosazzo were affected in every conflict. It is likely that Castelmonte was never attacked because it had no political importance.

Despite radical alterations in the 1950s, the great monastic complex of Castelmonte, with its strategic and dramatic position, is still the best-known fortified abbey in Friuli.

Although the peasants of nearby Premariacco and Risano were subject by feudal obligation to work for the abbey and to defend it with arquebuses and halberds,[37] these were not privileges conferred on Castelmonte itself, which was subject to the chapter of the mother church in Cividale. Because it was administered by Cividale, Castelmonte differed from the other great abbeys in having no feudal privileges and no direct revenue. Furthermore, since it was not the residence of an abbot, the abbey never aspired to power.

Castelmonte lacks buildings which might have given it an imposing appearance. The only construction of any presence that has been spared by the monks—at least as far as the façade is concerned—is the building with a ground-floor loggia at the lower end of the burg, begun in 1640 and completed in 1675. Its fine architecture reflects its use as the meeting place for the chapter delegation and as a guesthouse for important visitors.[38]

Despite the existence of this building, however, the abbey, with an originally much smaller church, looked more like a modest village, distinguished only by its elevated site. Its defensive function differed little from that of a *cortina*. Biasutti notes that the abbey gates were shut each evening to prevent the entry of thieves or the bands of robbers that roamed this lonely border region in large numbers. For this purpose, a guard lived near the gate. This house was used as a prison after 1765; the iron bars on the windows can still be seen today.[39] The existence of a prison might seem an indication of feudal power, but in fact it was used for petty thieves picked up during pilgrimage as well as for "a place of solitude and spiritual retreat" for monks guilty of some sin. One of the last inmates was indeed a priest, brought up the mountain in 1765 in a cart.[40]

The only element typical of a castle is the burg. Even today, with its small houses, it is the most attractive part of the ensemble. The houses originally belonged to private owners who provided services for the abbey, ran the inns, or worked in the fields. Life around the monastery would have been animated and markedly rural, with cows and pigs wandering freely around the church. These condi-

The entrance to the great monastic complex of Castelmonte, flanked by obelisks, in many castles a symbol of the owner's aristocratic birth.

tions improved only gradually, with the acquisition of the houses by the chapter of Cividale. Nevertheless, the monks obviously had to be provided with food and drink. Sometime before 1724, in the area that is now the parking lot, a new farmhouse and cattleshed were accordingly built, so that the livestock and dungheaps might be removed to a more respectful distance from the church.[41]

The provision of food and water was always a problem for castles situated on hills or mountains. Although Castelmonte was not a castle, it experienced the same practical difficulties. The daily life of the monks, living and working amid peasants and animals, exposed to the biting wind, and always needing water, was hard, much like that of the feudal lords.

The great abbeys

No building—fortified church or walled village, town or fortress—more resembled the castle than the great abbeys. The abbeys shared many features with the castles of the nobles, which we shall describe here only briefly, without going into the long history of the three great Friuli abbeys, which goes back to the early medieval period. Sesto al Reghena is probably the oldest of these abbeys, founded by the Lombard kings.[42] Over the centuries all three abbeys grew rich through donations and bequests, resulting in their owning more land than any castle in the region. After the patriarch, the abbots were the most important feudal lords.

Unlike the fortified places discussed so far, abbeys had the same privileges as castles. An abbey could obtain possession of a castle and hand it over as a fief or administer it itself.

Tommaso Gerometta estimated the possessions of Sesto al Reghena at more than fifty villages and castles. However, this estimate is unreliable, and it might be more accurate to say that Sesto owned property in that number of places.[43]

At Moggio, the abbot received the fief from the patriarch in a ceremony *per vexillum et gladium* (with standard and sword), as was the practice for only the most important feudal lords.[44] He had "jurisdiction with simple and mixed power including *jus sanguinis*" over penal law. The unique position of the abbots of Moggio and Rosazzo corresponded to an unusually high aristocratic title: both abbeys were linked to the title of marquis and therefore had precedence over other feudal lords in Friuli.

Like castles, monasteries had outbuildings, animal sheds, and barns, just as we have seen at Castelmonte. Sesto al Reghena still has a well-preserved burg, an inhabited area close to the monastery, surrounded by its own wall. This burg is what today makes Sesto appear similar to the great castles of Spilimbergo and Porcia. As well as their juridical similarities, castles and abbeys had in common their appearance: abbeys, like castles, had not only a burg and a farmyard, with their typically rural mixture of peasants and animals, but also walls and towers.

The documents relating to the monastery's privileges and property were kept in the chancery. They were valuable: to lose them could mean that it was impossible to prove ancient privileges. In 960, after a fire, the abbot of Sesto had to present himself before Emperor Otto I in order to have the abbey's ownership of all its possessions confirmed.[45] At Sesto al Reghena, the chancery, an impressive structure with Romanesque windows, is the only building of the old abbey still standing.[46] At Moggio, the chancery did not have the same importance and was housed in two narrow rooms near the entrance leading to the cloister.

Written sources suggest that these abbeys were well defended. As late as the sixteenth century, Girolamo di Porcia described them as *castelli* (castles).[47] Today this is hard to imagine, although Rosazzo still has the appearance of a castle even though little remains of its wall and towers.

Sesto al Reghena, encircled by the river Reghena, had seven towers.[48] Only the entrance tower still stands today. The magnificent coat of arms that now decorates it dates from a restoration of 1541 when the abbot was Giovanni Grimani, whose coat of arms it is.[49] As well as serving as an entrance to the monastery, the tower had great significance for the abbot, who made it a monument to his position and his person. It is probably for this reason that it has survived. It is an indication that towers were still regarded as important in the sixteenth century, long after they had lost their defensive function.

Similarly, at Moggio the entrance tower is today part of the wall that has survived longest. Above the entrance was "a room for the use of the guard", a lookout. As at Castelmonte, the gate was always closed at night for reasons of safety. The danger from thieves and robber bands was great and the Moggio granaries, which were outside the wall, were raided several times.[50]

Inside the wall were the church and monastic buildings, a stone tower in front of the church, and "other associated buildings giving on to the courtyard, cemetery, orchards and gardens."[51] From this description it would appear that such a wall could not have had a strictly defensive function: its circumference was too great to allow

OPPOSITE:
The abbey of Sesto al Reghena. All the important buildings, from the chancery to the abbot's house, are situated in the square in front of the church.

The entrance to the abbey reveals the alterations that over the centuries have contributed to its present picturesque appearance.

Entrance tower of the abbey of
Sesto al Reghena, decorated
with the arms of the abbot,
symbolizing his power which
survived into recent times.

OPPOSITE:
The Benedictine abbey of
Rosazzo. Very little remains of
the walls and towers that made
this one of the most strongly
fortified abbeys in Friuli.

Interior of the church at Rosazzo. Damaged by the 1976 earthquake, it has been restored and the stonework left bare.

OPPOSITE:
The imposing western tower of Rosazzo, the last surviving symbol of feudal power.

it to be defended by the few armed men in the monastery and the peasants who might come to assist them. At Rosazzo too, although it continued to be described as a stronghold,[52] we find mention of a series of robberies and break-ins.[53]

In other words, these monasteries could not be defended effectively. The walls and, in particular, the towers, had above all symbolic political force, enabling the abbots to take part in the political intrigues in Friuli. Just as with the castles, here too towers symbolized political power and feudal privilege. They do not need to be interpreted as defensive towers, watchtowers, or places of refuge.

In this context, there is no justification whatsoever for the often-repeated view, found almost without fail in the literature on the subject, that the belltower at Sesto al Reghena was originally a lookout tower. The wall decoration, following Ravenna models, clearly reveals the ecclesiastical origin of the architecture, also found in the baptistery at Concordia and in the apse of the cathedral at Caorle, but never in castle towers.[54] All the same, the symbolism of the tower is similar: a highly visible sign of feudal power, to which its use as a belltower lent even greater prestige. It was not for nothing that victorious enemies would remove the bells from towers, silencing them. It is also likely that in troubled times a watch might be sent up the tower to keep a lookout.

Of all the similarities between castle and abbey, the most significant was political power, its exercise, and its agents. From a comparison with the abbey of Castelmonte, it is clear that it was precisely their political power that provoked the repeated attacks on the abbeys. Spurning the peace of the cloister, the abbots, almost all of whom came from aristocratic families, involved themselves in worldly power struggles and intrigues. Their ambitions were political, seldom spiritual.

The most strongly fortified monastery was Rosazzo, which had a significant role on account of its preeminent position in the Friuli parliament. Although the monastery had the most property, the strongest defenses, and the stoutest wall, it was nevertheless involved in wars right up to the seventeenth century and was repeatedly razed precisely because of its dominant role, just like a castle.

OPPOSITE:
The cloisters at Rosazzo.
Abbeys grew rich over the
centuries from gifts and
bequests, as a result of which
they owned more land than any
of the castles in the area.

Arms of the commendatory
abbots, painted in the
cloisters. After the patriarch,
abbots were the most
important feudal lords. An
abbey might own a castle or
grant it in fief to a vassal.

In order to increase the monastery's power and privileges, the abbots had insisted to the pope that they be freed from the overlordship of the patriarch to become dependent directly on the pope himself, as bishops were.[55] They thus gained autonomy within a feudal framework, with the possibility of exercising their ecclesiastical power over the temporal powers. When the nearby town of Cividale attempted to bring the abbey of Rosazzo under its control as a fortified center, it was opposed by the abbot, Pileo di Prata, who, supported by his patron Pope Boniface IX,

threatened excommunication of the town.[56] It was an effective threat, and one that the feudal lords of the area no doubt envied.

The political importance of the abbots is also apparent in a contrasting example. When Rudolph IV, duke of Austria, attempted to conquer Friuli, he was supported by a number of powerful lords who hoped for power and influence. The abbot of Rosazzo became involved in the power struggle on the opposing side to his patriarch, Lodovico della Torre, but was on the losing side. The abbot did not escape punishment: "imprisoned and

FOLLOWING PAGES:
View of the valley below
Rosazzo Abbey, used from
the mid 18th century by the
archbishops of Udine as
a summer retreat.

51

The abbey of Moggio. The abbot, who also held the title of marquis, was considered the most important lord of Carnia. He had received the fief from the patriarch in a ceremonious investiture.

tortured by the patriarch's officials, he falsely denounced as accomplices many Friuli nobles and commoners ... On 4 April 1364, in the main square in Gorizia, he retracted what he had said against them."[57]

A complicated mix of functions characterizes the three abbeys: the residences of feudal lords with regional, political, and juridical power. But such status was clearly not sufficient for medieval abbots, who became embroiled in political and military struggles

to the extent of destroying themselves. The encircling abbey walls reveal the complexity of the defensive structures. Their erection was a sign of political power. In reality they provided little protection, even against incursions by robbers—and yet they were essential for anyone wishing to participate in the politics of the region, thereby indirectly increasing the wealth of the abbey. An architectural element which highlights the similarity between monasteries and castles can be found at Moggio. It is a small stone building resembling the base of a tower. This construction, which originally had a third storey, was previously assumed to be the remains of a Roman watchtower. In fact it was the abbot's house, similar in form, construction, and position to a *palas* (dwelling place of the lord within the castle).[58] The house was once an imposing building, facing the church and representing the temporal power of the abbot of Moggio as feudal lord of the valley. At this time, only very few of the castles of Friuli could claim such a splendid *palas*, an unusual example of a claim to personal power by an abbot.

What distinguished an abbey from a castle? Simply the fact that a castle was not a monastery. Any book on castles must take the great Benedictine abbeys into consideration. All the same, it is important to distinguish between fortified monastery and medieval castle; the castle is the seat—and, most importantly, the symbol—of a noble family or lord, such as the patriarch of Aquileia, in his role as duke of Friuli.

19th-century watercolor of Moggio. The abbot's house can be clearly seen. At one time, with an additional story, it was an imposing building, symbolizing the abbot's temporal power.

The abbot's house as it appears today, without the top floor recorded in the watercolor. Mistakenly believed to be the remains of a Roman guardtower, the building is an impressive medieval dwelling.

THE ROLE OF THE CASTLE

Castles must be understood not as works of engineering which were intended for defense, but rather as architecture which expresses the ideas of power and domination. In modern political discourse we speak of three powers—legislative, executive, and judicial power—which are exercised by different bodies. The idea of the separation of powers is an achievement of more recent centuries; it certainly did not exist in the Middle Ages. In medieval times, legislative, executive, and judicial power, the mark of secular power, was conferred by the ruler on the feudal lord, who was given great and wide-ranging authority. As well as this authority and power, feudal lords had other rights and privileges which increased their influence. As landholders and as those who controlled labor, they held economic power and wielded great influence over the people under their authority.

However, the importance of the medieval castle did not lie only in the fact that it was inhabited by the holder of such authority. It is more the case that the rights and privileges of power were so intimately connected to the castle that it was frequently impossible to determine whether the authority belonged to the castle itself or to the lord of the castle.[60] Castle and power were one and the same, yet power and authority was granted to an individual who was bound by feudal allegiance.

The administrative and judicial center of the domain was the dwelling of the feudal lord. This did not necessarily have to be a castle: it could be a tower, a house or farm, a town, or an abbey.[61] To gain possession of a castle was to acquire the privileges that went with it. These could be bought, inherited, or granted—or simply appropriated. Often the new lord took on the name of the new acquisition, which means that great caution is required when compiling medieval genealogies.[62] The result is that domain, castle, and feudal lord were one seamless entity, the elements of which are hard to separate out.

The defensive role of the castle

Power, in its most basic form, is violence and force. From the military point of view, however, castles are defensive structures. Built on hilltops, of imposing appearance, they could have no military influence on events taking place in their vicinity because of the considerable distance between them and the nearby village, road, or river. Although it is certainly true that a castle can dominate a valley, this dominance cannot be directly exercised.

Both topographical considerations and the construction and techniques of contemporary weapons made it impossible for the surrounding territory to be controlled from a castle. If a village in the valley was attacked by an enemy, a counterattack meant leaving the safety of the castle. It was only when the castle itself was being attacked that it could use its strength. If a village was being attacked, a great deal could happen in the time taken to reach it.

Thus a hilltop site meant that the holders of the castle could not intervene in anything occurring in the village or valley below, or on the road. This is a difficult concept to grasp and it is an aspect not generally commented on. Frequently it is simply taken for granted that castles must have provided a degree of protection; otherwise, it is argued, castles would not have existed.

Castles and borders

Only a very few examples exist in Europe of castles that were built to defend a country from foreign enemies. While we find defenses at the entrance to valleys (as in Bellinzona and Chiusaforte), such structures were not castles in the usual sense of the word. North of the Alps, castles might be built against the specific threat of the Hungarians in the ninth century or the Vikings, but these castles were essentially constructions that were intended to provide a place of refuge and which covered a large area. They were not, at least in origin, intended to be lived in by a feudal lord and

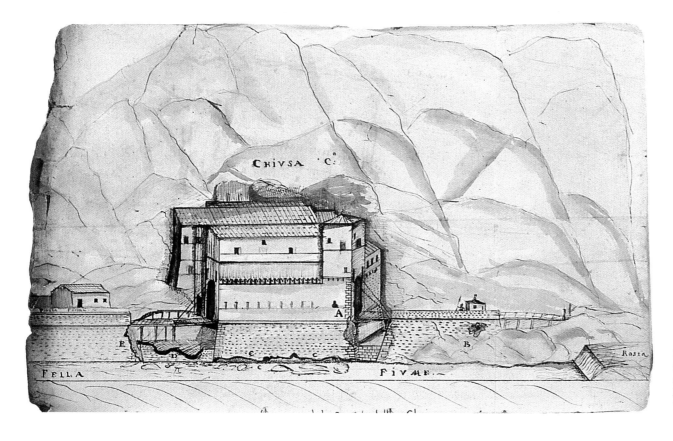

Chiusaforte Fortress, one of the few examples of purely military fortified architecture. It marked the gateway to Venetian territory.

they did not enjoy any of the conventional privileges associated with a feudal lord that were typical of the castle. Their purpose did not go beyond that of providing an immediate place of safety for the local population.

The idea that in Friuli the patriarch or some other central power protected the region by building a chain of castles to defend the border is entirely without foundation. To believe this is to assume the existence of an organized state with a central administration and ruler. Such a state did not exist in Friuli in the Middle Ages. The misconception reveals a fundamental misunderstanding of the medieval political world.[63]

It does not take long to understand that the idea of protecting territory with one or several chains of castles is quite absurd. If even modern defenses are incapable of stopping an army, it is very unlikely that the small garrision of a medieval castle would have been successful.

Even more implausible is the theory that the towers of castles were used to warn of imminent danger. Not only are many of the castles in these presumed chains situated on hilltops and thus cannot be seen from the

valley, but such a system presupposes the reliability of every single link of the chain. In Friuli this was never the case: it was common for many of the feudal lords having possession of castles to ally with the invader in the hope of gaining something for themselves.

Finally, although there are many castles in the foothills in Friuli popularly believed to form part of a defensive system, very few castles are to be found in the west. Yet it was from here that the lords of Camino made frequent and enthusiastic attacks, assisted by the lack of natural barriers.

Castles and roads

While it is often asserted that castles were used to defend borders, others maintain that they were built to defend or control roads. It is suggested, for example, that the castle of Strassoldo was built at the junction of two important roads in order to control the Stradalta route, as a bulwark against invasion by the Hungarians. This idea too is implausible. Quite apart from the doubts cast by experts on the extent of the Hungarian threat

to Friuli[64]—and even setting aside the obvious fact that Strassoldo would never have been sufficiently strong to block passage through the plain to invading hordes—the castle stands several miles away from the road and could have had no influence over what happened there. Furthermore, it was hidden away in a marshy, wooded area that was difficult of access. If the hordes from the east had decided to advance on the plain by this route, Strassoldo's position made it possible to hope that the enemy would not notice the castle—or if they did, that they would not bother to attack and capture it.

The relationship between castles and roads is thus much more complex than initially appears. What is clear is that the reason for building castles was not the defense of the roads, which in any case were for the most part controlled by the ruler, while castles were generally privately owned.[65] The interest that the lords of the castle had in the roads was quite different. Since they had the right to exact tolls, noble families—who were always struggling financially—could demand money from travelers and to some extent gain from the profits of trade. According to the rules of escort, a vassal was required by his feudal lord to protect travelers; he made up for this by collecting tolls.[66]

A well-documented case is that of the castle of Duino. Duino, on the important trade route between Friuli and Istria, began to demand excessively high tolls. The partiarch often had to intervene in defense of the road and of the free movement of merchants.[67] It is telling that the old castle of Duino, in use until the mid fourteenth century, has no view of the road; even here it is not possible to speak of direct control. It was only with the building of the new castle of Duino that it is possible to see a deliberate attempt to control the road to Trieste. In 1371 Duino was charging tolls two or three times higher than those at Monfalcone, and the patriarch had to fight long and hard to force the powerful lord of Duino to lower them. A compromise was eventually reached: the patriarch would mend the road around San Giovanni and repair the decrepit bridge at his own expense, while the lord of Duino would reduce the tolls.[68]

Control of a road by a castle was thus exercised for two reasons. First, it brought in

The old castle at Duino, on a spur of rock high above the sea and connected to the mainland by a narrow isthmus. It was not possible to control the important road to Trieste from here since it was hidden from view.

revenue. A family like that of the lords of Duino, constantly in debt until the fourteenth century, could not afford to give up this income. Second, it allowed the lord to disrupt travel and traffic, giving the lords of Duino an excellent opportunity to irritate Trieste, their eternal rival.

Rustication at the castle of Moruzzo. The high technical quality of construction of medieval buildings has sometimes led scholars to consider them Roman.

Military architecture

Historians have sought to explain every aspect of castle architecture in terms of defensive function. For example, the blocks of rusticated stone which are found in many walls have been interpreted as a defense against siege ladders, the protruding stones preventing rapid ascent.[69] In reality, from a practical point of view such protrusions instead disadvantaged those inside the castle, making the stonework weaker than a smooth surface would have been, and the wall easier to climb. Moreover, rustication is never found in those places where the use of siege ladders was most to be feared, whereas it is to be found in the most visible parts of the building, on the gateway and tower. On the outer wall, it was often only the most conspicuous

part that had rustication. In other words, rustication had a decorative function. It had a symbolic function as well, since a wall built with it appeared more solid and imposing, dissuading potential assailants. Roman buildings had used rustication in the same way, on gates for example, and this usage became common in the Middle Ages.[70]

In sieges, the psychological element was important. Those inside the castle were quite ready to throw their last remaining provisions down to the besieging force, sapping the besiegers' hopes for a surrender dictated by hunger. Similarly, a besieging force sought to demoralize those inside the castle and to force them to surrender.[71] For this reason, besieging forces had to look as daunting as possible and had to give the impression of being numerous.

If a besieging force was renowned for invincibility or particular savageness, less resolute defenders were quite capable of destroying their own castle in order to avoid siege. This is what occurred when Bishop Ulrich II of Constance was threatened by the count of Bregenz.[72]

In general, victory went to the side with superior morale. A determined force could hold a weak position for an extraordinarily long time, while even the strongest of castles might surrender within a few hours if the will to fight was absent.

In England, as late as the seventeenth century, an ancient motte defended by nothing more than a small rampart and palisade was able to resist attack by Parliamentary troops, even though the besieging force used weaponry which was undreamed of in medieval times.[73]

Examination of castles should therefore never restrict itself to considerations of the defensive role of individual elements. A tower might be situated at a point where it could help to guard a particularly vulnerable entrance—but equally it might be found where it best enhanced the appearance of the whole building.

The height of towers was essentially a question of prestige. Although stones thrown down from a height gain force as they fall, they have to be carried up the tower in the first place. A high tower certainly offered greater safety, yet although a height of ten to

twelve meters (thirty to forty feet) would have been entirely adequate, many castles have much higher towers.

The most common errors with regard to the interpretation of castle structures derive in general from an over-emphasis on their defensive capability. Accustomed to the scale of modern armies, it is all too easy to forget how small medieval armies were. When on 14 April, 1306 the patriarch moved against Buttrio, he mobilized an army which had been raised from all the feudal lords and had been reinforced by contingents from the towns. This totalled an exceptional 1,200 men, who marched against a well-armed castle that had had plenty of time to prepare for the attack. The castle surrendered after three days, a relatively long time, and the entire garrison of one hundred men was taken prisoner.[74]

Even if today these numbers seem absurdly low, they were exceptional for the time. The lord of Buttrio was in no position to keep a hundred men under arms on his own and he was obliged to call upon aid from other feudal lords. The garrison of a castle needs therefore to be seen in a different light.

A knight required around a hundred peasant households to pay for his own defense. A typical Friuli castle such as Brazzacco would not have had much more than this. On nearby hilltops lived other feudal lords with their possessions. The territory around Brazzacco, moreover, was divided between two castles, each of which belonged to a number of lords. The paltry revenue available thus scarcely sufficed to finance even a meager force. No lord was able to afford a proper feudal army.

It is probable that the average garrison of a

Tournament armor.
Suits of armor such as
this are quite untypical.

OPPOSITE:
16th-century armor
of exquisite workmanship,
very unlike the usual plainness
of medieval armor.

castle seldom exceeded six men: a porter to open the gates, perhaps a second porter to take over at night, a couple of servants, and, only where the lord did not live in the castle himself, a castellan who was responsible for defense. Further support came from the peasants, who originally had been under a feudal obligation to contribute to the defense of the castle. However, their weapons were so primitive and their enthusiasm to fight in these petty feuds understandably so slight that this system did not last long. As a result, feudal lords had recourse to men bound by contract, obliged to defend the castle. Such men did not necessarily live locally and would come to guard the castle only when danger was imminent.[75] In exchange they received payment, though not all lords were in a position to pay.

It is not surprising then that the few surviving documents concerning the garrisons of castles mention absurdly low numbers. The castle of Spies, a well-defended den of thieves near Bayreuth besieged in 1397 by King Wenzel, was so well defended that instead of the usual couple of men there were at least twenty-four.[76] Similar numbers are recorded at the castle belonging to the knight Paul of Wichenstein at Plankenfels, who had "a giant" professional soldier, a bailiff, a servant, and two herdsmen.[77]

Weapons, which were expensive, were in short supply. There were, of course, always stones, which could be dropped, boiling liquids, and waste from the privies. Unfortunately there are no records concerning weapons in the conventional sense of the word until the fifteenth century, and even then it is clear that weapons were few. A castle in Germany, for example, possessed six arquebuses, four of which were so heavy that it took several men to use them, but the garrison had too few men for it to do so. The nearby castle of Leinfels had at least two working arquebuses and two hunting guns.[78]

The castle armories we see today, with their impressive arrays of weapons, give a totally misleading impression. They display almost entirely arms that were used, if at all, in tournaments, and which date from no earlier than the fifteenth and sixteenth centuries. Similarly, the splendid suits of armor found exhibited in the corridors of

castles were not objects for normal use but were made by master craftsmen for display on festive occasions.

Evidence that arms had above all symbolic value is provided by an event that occurred at Castelmonte during the insurrections of 1848, when the occupying Austrian military authorities confiscated all the weapons in the region, including halberds and muskets, despite the monks' protests that these had been used for centuries as "decoration for ordinations or anniversaries of ordinations."[79] Again, it is clear that the importance of the military significance of castles should not be exaggerated.

The advent of firearms changed the situation little. If anything, castles lost yet more of their role—already doubtful—in the defense of the surrounding area. On the other hand, as fortified houses they were able to continue for centuries in their role against bands of robbers and brigands, even though they had at their disposal only a handful of firearms.[80]

The blood feud

Although castles may have had no special defensive role, they are crucial to an understanding of the medieval juridical system. This is a system in which the blood feud had a central role. The blood feud was not the same as war. War—in theory at least—was not possible within Christendom. The use of violence was justified only in defense of law and peace, in other words, in the blood feud.[81] Since there was no concept of the sovereignty of the state in the Middle Ages, nor of nations in the modern sense of the word, a declaration of war between kings was the same thing as a blood feud between knights. These concepts gradually changed until the blood feud came to mean a small-scale and personal vendetta, while larger military actions became known as wars.

The word *feud* is Germanic in origin, as is the concept of the blood feud itself. Among the oldest words indicating a blood feud, that

is, antagonism and hostility, is the Germanic *werra*, which became *gwerra* in medieval Latin and the Romance languages, and *war* in English.[82]

From the very beginning, the Germanic peoples regarded the blood feud as a binding duty. While it was possible to free oneself from this duty by paying compensation, such a course of action was not regarded as just or appropriate. An Icelandic saga tells the story of a man who refused to give up the idea of avenging his father's death in exchange for money, saying that he had no wish "to carry his father in his purse."[83]

The blood feud was possible and necessary not only in cases of grave injustice but also in cases of offense to authority, and thus to honor. Though the idea of revenge was of course a contradiction of Christian values, it gradually began to take on the meaning of a struggle for what was right.[84] If it was not possible to support a claim to justice before a judge or in a court, then the claim had to be affirmed by force. Otherwise, to renounce one's own claim would be to renounce honor.[85] Recourse to arms was thus essential in order to obtain and maintain not only one's own rights but also those of others.

The influence of the blood feud made itself felt in every aspect of life. To understand this, it is necessary to take into account how the contemporary feudal system functioned: the feudal lord provided a house, farmyard, and land; the peasant, in exchange, gave tribute and services. The lord owed the peasant protection; in return the peasant owed the lord work. It was a relationship which lay at the heart of the medieval political system. The lord had to protect the interests of the peasant before the law and in a blood feud, which is to say that he had to protect the peasant's possessions and his person.[86]

If feudal lords quarreled among themselves over any kind of authority or power, they began a blood feud. Those most affected by this were the peasants, whose fields and animals were the first to be burned and stolen. If the lord called them to arms, thus involving them directly in the feud, they were no longer able to protect their villages. Their only remedy was to come to an agreement with the enemy and arrange that they should be spared, offering in exchange money and goods in kind.[87] Thus it was the peasants who all too often bore the brunt of the blood feud, suffering looting, burning, diminished harvests, and epidemics.[88]

The feudal lord himself might suffer from the consequences of the blood feud. When damage was inflicted on the property of those under him, he would have to agree to reductions or postponements of payment in cash or kind, sometimes over a period of several years. Alternatively, if he had failed to take measures to protect his peasants, or had been remiss in his duties towards them, they might go so far as to repudiate him, since failure to observe the duties of protection released them from their obligations. Peasants who had left the village and renounced their feudal obligations might refuse to go back and would look to a new lord for protection.[89] Whole villages were thus abandoned: in many areas, depopulation in the later Middle Ages coincided with the period when the blood feud was at its height.

One of the first written codes of laws in the West, the *Schwabenspiegel*, articulates this relationship: "We are required to serve our lord so that he will protect us. If he fails to protect us, legally we do not owe him any service."[90] The departure of his peasants could mean economic ruin for the lord, and consequently politcal and social ruin. There was much uncultivated land and it was difficult to find people to work it. In order to maintain his power, a lord therefore had to fight for the rights of his peasants. His success in this fight was less important than the fact of his being prepared to engage in it.

It is clear, then, that a castle could protect a village, but it does not follow that it could succeed in saving it from destruction. The castle safeguarded the rights of the peasants, since the landowner who lived there was ready to fight for them. The castle was therefore the most important instrument in such matters, its position providing a highly visible indication of the extent of the lord's dominion. Anyone invading this territory had to reckon with a potential blood feud from the lord. The more imposing the castle, the more imposing did the lord appear. An impressive wall might protect an entire village from attack.

The normal form of the blood feud was the knightly feud, where nobles fought over rights and demands, or over presumed offenses. In such blood feuds, a lord of a castle would make a move against another, with sieges taking place that might end in the conquest of a castle, its destruction, and the capture of the lord.

Very strict rules were laid down to govern the blood feud.[91] It could not be exercised inside a dwelling because dwellings, as places of peace, were immune. Churches were carefully protected. Women and children, clerics, free peasants, merchants, pilgrims, entertainers, and Jews could not be involved in blood feuds, nor could peasants at work in the fields.

The king or ruler, as the feudal superior, had to guarantee the observance of truces and of the rules of engagement, just as was the case, at a lower level, between lord and peasant. Offenses against law and order were severely punished by the ruler, as in the case of Buttrio. The highest feudal lord (in Friuli the patriarch) was also responsible for resolving disputes, in his role as high judge. If he was unable to bring about an agreement, he was obliged to allow the blood feud to proceed. If someone persisted in an unauthorized blood feud, the lord had to prevent it.

The punishment for a lord who broke a truce was, in the words of the *Sachenspiegel*, "death" to the castle, that is to say, destruction. The castle and the lord were thus punished together and the lord, representing the castle, had to swear an oath of purification or fealty on its behalf.[92]

The destruction of a castle did not mean that it was razed to the ground. It might be burned, which would make it uninhabitable but would not damage the structure. The ruler normally confined himself to "breaking" the castle. Since he usually had the right of entry to a castle, he exercised this right symbolically by breaking down its gates, by making a breach in its walls, or by removing the ramparts.[93] Since the act of opening up

the gates of a castle in this way was essentially symbolic, alterations and rebuilding around the entrance gate are visible today in many castles.

Only very rarely did hostility towards the castle and its lord lead to destruction such as that which occurred at the castle of Villalta. Having locked up the lord in the dungeons, the government of Udine sent men to demolish the castle. The present state of the walls reveals, however, that not even in this case were the walls razed to the ground, since the remains of the old walls still stand to a height of over a meter (three feet). In cases where at least the base of the walls remained, and if the stone blocks were in good condition, the castle could be rebuilt as before without great expense and relatively quickly.

The endless quarrels and outbreaks of fighting that mark the history of Friuli were all essentially the outcome of the classic blood feud. The lords in their castles might not recognize the election of the patriarch and would declare a blood feud against him. Or the patriarch might distribute fiefs and privileges, which would be perceived as an abuse of power by those who were passed over. Or the patriarch might ignore the claims made by these lords, who would respond to this slight by declaring a blood feud.

The ruler was able to control and dominate this system as long as he was in a position of strength. Although his sources of wealth and the number of soldiers in his service were far greater, he nevertheless needed the castles to guarantee his power.

The history of the blood feud and that of the castle go hand in hand, and the importance of their reciprocal relationship is only too obvious. After the dissolution of the centralized Roman state in late antiquity, the Carolingians had succeeded in creating a new order with judicial organs endowed with extensive powers. They were established to keep in check the lords' tendency to exercise justice themselves.

In the twelfth century, the attempts by the Holy Roman Emperor and the rulers to bring about general peace and reconciliation suffered a serious setback with the advent of the blood feud. It is no coincidence that this came about at the same time as the flowering of the castles.

From now on, rulers were unable to prevent the blood feud; they could merely hope to keep it under a degree of control and

Detail of a fresco in the crypt of Aquileia Cathedral, with a knight armed with a lance pursuing a mounted archer.

to restrict it to the nobility. They made every effort to control the blood feud, seeking to replace it by penalties and compensation, and by creating a rule of law and authority stamped with their personal guarantee.

The formation of organized territorial states with their own rulers marked the end of the Middle Ages. In this new world, castles gradually lost their importance. Their diminishing role has therefore nothing to do with the technical developments that were occurring in warfare. The castle, as a symbol of the medieval juridical order and the blood feud, had quite simply become superfluous.

Castles and power

Castles made it possible for their owners to convert their power and dominion over people into power and dominion over territory. The castle marked the lord's rights over the territory and assured his authority.

Once a lord had succeeded in building a castle on an area of territory, it was difficult to remove him, even if he had no right to be there or if his rights to the territory were unclear. It was possible to expel him only by force of arms.[94] The building and acquisition of a castle, and the feudal privileges that came with it, served to augment the territory controlled and it reveals the hunger of the aristocracy for power and for land.[95]

A good example is provided by the strategy of the counts of Gorizia. They made use of their favorable economic situation and an already strong position to increase their power in relation to the patriarch, seizing one castle after another, that is, one territory after another. Through this policy of acquiring castles and territory, they created a vast domain which became increasingly independent of the patriarch.

Not only the counts of Gorizia but also other families in Friuli sought to increase their zones of influence through the acquisition of ever more castles. The counts of Porcia extended their lands to the south and west of Pordenone, taking over the castles of Torre di Pordenone and Santo Stino near

Livenza. The counts of Spilimbergo created a domain between Valvasone and Spilimbergo, which to the north reached as far as Solimbergo. North of Udine, the counts of Colloredo created an entire ring of castles around their seat at Mels, including a relatively new one that was to become the new family seat of Colloredo di Montalbano.

If castles could increase the power of their owners, the highest feudal lord had to try to keep castles under control if he was not to see the whole territory slip out of his power. Thus it very soon became necessary to regulate the construction of castles. There are no records referring to the right to build fortifications from the period of the barbarian invasions and the Merovingians, since at that time castles were of very limited importance. Only in the edict of Pitres of 864 do we see this right referred to as a royal privilege, with the order to destroy all fortifications built *sine nostro verbo* (without our authorization).[96]

In the eleventh century, laws governing the construction of castles were passed, while in 1080, in Normandy, the edict of Lillebonne stipulated that no one could dig ditches, erect ramparts, or build any other type of fortification.[97] Thus the right of fortification was transferred—little by little and grudgingly—to the ruler.

It was not until the twelfth century, however, that rulers obtained it officially, though the new laws were doing no more than recognizing what had been the practice for a long time. Rulers on their part had to defend their monopoly against the lower nobility, which they did by issuing further laws of their own.[98] Any fortifications erected without the ruler's permission could be seized and destroyed, or alternatively sanctioned and integrated into the existing system.[99] Near the castles of disloyal feudal lords such as the counts of Gorizia, other castles would be built in order to neutralize them. In particularly contentious areas, this led to a proliferation of castles.

The prince's power could thus be seen in the way in which he exercised control over the construction and ownership of a castle. In most of the Holy Roman Empire, the great lords challenged the power of the emperor and the lower feudal nobility, in this way succeeding in enlarging and making permanent their own domain. The fact that the patriarch did not succeed in this in Friuli is the reason why the entire state collapsed.

The decline of the patriarch

Almost all regional histories of Friuli attribute the end of Friuli's political independence in the fifteenth century to the total collapse of law and order as a result of constant warfare between the feudal lords. They regard the history of Friuli and the patriarchate in the last century of its existence as one of almost permanent warfare, with

continually changing battlelines until finally Venice occupied a region which had long been marked by anarchy.

All the same, it may be useful to examine the reasons for the political collapse of Friuli in order to clarify the role of the castles and the feudal lords in these events, while keeping in mind events elsewhere in Europe. It is particularly important to do so in a book on the history of the castles of the region.

The collapse of the patriarchate meant an end to the longstanding and significant political and cultural influence of northern Europe in Friuli. This influence had started at least as early as the advent of the Lombard duchy and had soon led to political autonomy and a unique culture. The strong sense of regional identity felt by the people of Friuli (today recognized constitutionally by Friuli's status as an autonomous region within the Italian state) has its origins in these medieval centuries, when Friuli had political independence. From this early history also derives the fascination not only with the Lombards and with the patriarchs, but also with the castles, whose history still today has a political resonance and glamor.

The decline of the patriarch as lord of Friuli can be explained by the differences between this region and other territories within the Holy Roman Empire. Throughout Europe, the later Middle Ages saw a gradual strengthening of the position of the feudal lords, who eventually asserted themselves over the king or emperor and over the petty feudal nobility. Their success was generally linked to a policy which effected itself through castles. If the lords were successful in acquiring a large number of castles, or at least in controlling them, they could impose their power throughout an entire territory, establishing a strong domain.

Contrary to what was generally thought in the past, the typical feudal castles did not offer much resistance,[100] since they were already subordinate to the lord. A more serious threat to the lord's territorial power came from the allodial castles, that is, from those castles that belonged to the lord himself. In a region such as Bavaria, where the house of Wittelsbach was particularly active and successful, the proportion of allodial castles seems always to have been about half. Such castles had to be incorporated into the feudal system by political treaties, or simply by destroying them by force of arms.

Compared to other parts of Europe, Friuli had a surprisingly low number of allodial castles and families of free nobles. Almost all the castles were subject to the patriarch and ninety percent of the feudal lords were *ministeriales* (retainers) of very limited means.

Initially, the situation of the patriarch, who was seeing the gradual stabilization of his authority, was therefore much more favorable than that of, for example, the lord of Bavaria. The patriarch had the right of entry to almost every castle; it would have been unwise for any of his vassals to have refused this. He derived significant revenues from his position, which he used for the maintenance of his castles and for his own requirements. If the patriarch, despite these distinct advantages, was the only one of the great lords within the Holy Roman Empire who failed to consolidate and extend his sphere of influence in the later Middle Ages, there must have been other reasons for failure which could not be attributed simply to the power of the local lords.

A comparision of the situation in Friuli with that prevailing in other areas of Italy reveals significant differences. Not only in the Veneto and in Lombardy, but also in Tuscany and elsewhere in central Italy, the most powerful towns had prevailed over the surrounding countryside and had come to control it. The feudal nobility had to move into the towns if it wished to retain any political power, since in the countryside the only role remaining was that of landowner. The subjugation of the surrounding countryside had already begun in the early Middle Ages and it continued in the wars between cities as they struggled for power in the countryside.

Yet this process did not occur in Friuli. The reason is that in Friuli there was a divide between city and country right up to the eighteenth century, a divide similar to that in northern Europe, where urban culture, in all its political, social, and juridical aspects, stopped at the city wall, while in the countryside the feudal system prevailed.

This is not to say that attempts to extend the political influence of the town were not made. Udine carried on a campaign against the lords of the surrounding castles, and succeeded in controlling them, including the important abbey of Rosazzo.

To sum up, neither trend came to fruition in Friuli. The towns failed to dominate the countryside, as the Savorgnans had hoped, but equally, the feudal lords were unable to sustain their plans for power against the towns that were, quite simply, too strong for them. Only someone who had the backing of the towns, in particular Udine, would have been able to influence the outcome of a war. On the other hand, Udine on its own was not strong enough to subdue either the feudal lords or Cividale, its chief rival.

Presiding over this stalemate was the patriarch, the lord of Friuli. His capital was Udine, the dominant power in the region. As if that were not enough, he also had possession of the majority of the castles. It should have been possible for politically astute patriarchs with experience in diplomacy, who survived in office for a sufficiently long time, to increase their power and to take advantage of the rivalry between feudal lords and towns.

The end of Friuli independence in 1420 thus came about for a number of different reasons: a series of weak characters who held office for too short a time, the continuing growth in importance of the city state, and the increasing pressure from external powers, which all the parties involved tried to turn to their own advantage. The feudal lords and their castles had no impact in the final period since they neutralized one another through their constant feuding instead of defending the common interest against a threat that they had clearly not noticed.

With the conquest of Friuli by Venice began the decline of the castles. They were destroyed not by artillery or by the modern art of war, but by the centralized bureaucracy of Venice.

The "justice column" at the ancient fief of Santa Maria la Longa. At one time justice was administered under this column.

Castles and territorial organization

No function of the castle was more important than that relating to its role in the government of the surrounding territory, which made the castle the center of administrative and judicial organization. When everything is taken into consideration, the military aspect of the castle was only a means of guaranteeing the exercise of important political functions. The rise and fall of castles cannot be satisfactorily explained in terms of defense and military techniques. Instead, they occupy an important place—and a place that hitherto has been neglected, in European history—in relation to the growth of the territorial state. The claim, now commonplace, that a castle dominates a valley or village is not an invention of the modern scholar but derives rather from

real past experience. However, the exercise of power was more indirect, taking place on different levels and at a degree of complexity which embraces the whole intricate political situation in the Middle Ages.

Castles and justice

Although we think of a castle as a place where justice was administered, the reality is more complicated. The conference on castles held in Marckburg in 1996 made it clear that the castle was indeed a place of jurisdiction, but that justice was rarely administered there. The castle was, first and foremost, the seat of the holder of the right to administer justice, a right which had gradually passed from the town to the castle.[101]

With the transfer of the *ban*, the defensive structure acquired a new and decisive function, one that it had never before exercised: it became the administrative center of authority over the territory and the holder of the juridical organization. This was a slow and painful process, and one which ended only in the late Middle Ages.

Earlier, in the Carolingian period, the most important unit of territorial organization was the county. "Count" was not yet a noble title; it simply indicated a high-ranking functionary whose principal task was to administer justice in the name of the king. The process which transformed this Carolingian officeholder, who often resided in the town, into the relatively independent noble living in a castle and enjoying a number of inherited privileges, was slow and complicated.

In Bavaria and Austria, for example, castles did not become centers of juridical organization until the thirteenth century, when they began to act as tribunals, taking the place of the towns. Through the acquisition of estates belonging to noble dynasties, the archdukes of Bavaria created the conditions for peace and a juridical organization based on the castles and including the entire state. The limits of this administrative power corresponded to the limits of the territories belonging to the castles. Those who were allowed to administer justice were the *ministeriales*, who were installed in castles by rulers in order to guarantee and reinforce their authority over the territory.[102]

Coins from the time of the patriarchs Volchero (1204–18) and Bertoldo (1218–51). Like rulers, patriarchs, the prince-bishops of Friuli, had the right to mint coins.

Friuli was similarly divided into judicial departments. Those responsible for these areas lived in the castles, which served also as chanceries and centers of juridical ruling. Cases, however, continued to be tried in places traditionally intended for the administration of justice, and which induced suitable awe: at gateways, under porticoes, even under a tree. Ancient columns survive in Friuli around which the court of justice was once accustomed to meet. Such ancient sites survived despite administrative reorganization and despite the transfer of the judicial administration to new functionaries.

Early administration

The castle also served as the administrative center of a jurisdiction. It was a way of using its space, and reinforcing its authority.[103] One should not imagine, in the Middle Ages, an efficient and capable administration; this would be to suppose a vast increase in the size of the population and the territory, something that was reached only in the early modern period. Strictly speaking, the concept of administration is not appropriate to the medieval period.

Every aspect of authority over the surrounding territory depended on ownership of the castle. It was the castle itself that was the holder of these powers, not the lord, whose power lay in the fact that he owned the castle, with which he identified himself. The word castle was thus often used as a synonym of domain or territory. When a domain was sold, the documents speak in terms only of the sale of the castle, or of the castle and its attached properties.[104]

The noble *ministeriales* were those most closely identified with the castle, since their economic, political, and social status depended entirely on possession of a castle. In the medieval system, the lord of the castle and the castle itself assumed, along with the judicial functions exercised in the name of the ruler, responsibility for defense as well as territorial organization. They also had a regulatory role in the appointment of the church hierarchy.[105]

To this administrative role can be added the economic responsibilities performed on behalf of the state, in which the castle anticipated a system of taxation, having the right to collect tolls and dues on roads, for water rights, and for the right to hunt. Finally, castles enjoyed bailiffship or patronage over churches and religious houses, as well as many other lesser privileges concerned with everyday life which also provided revenue.

Since he was not in a position to maintain a centralized administration, in this way the lord transferred all the essential tasks of administration to his *ministeriales* or to independent counts who, in the later medieval period, lived in the castles. Such a system of decentralized government was exercised by the castles, while the lord traveled through his land in his capacity as the supreme representative of control. He had the right of entry to any castle, meaning that he would be admitted immediately wherever he went.

A castle like that of Maniago went so far as to provide a special house for the use of the patriarch. But every ruler had his favorite castles that had not been handed over to *ministeriales*, being assigned instead to trustworthy men. Such men had, furthermore, a right to live there deriving from the *fief of habitation*, and they thus contributed to the maintenance of the castle.

We find that almost all surviving documents were drawn up in these more important castles where, over the years, a large number of clerks and chancery assistants collected, adding to the lord's increasingly large retinue. Given its by now sizeable proportions, the court moved about less and less frequently until finally it settled down in one or more castles that can already be described as capitals.

In Udine, the castle of the patriarch developed into a veritable town. Along with the patriarch and his court, space was needed for his household as well as for the families of those in the retinue, for the staff serving the clerks, and for the craftsmen who came to work there.

In the early Middle Ages, because of the form of government, focused on the character of the ruler, the towns had given way as capitals to the royal courts or to the most important castles. In the later Middle Ages, by contrast, the administrative system based on large chanceries with specialist staff gradually brought about a renewed need for capitals. These generally grew out of a feudal castle, unless they established themselves in an already existing town.

Castles and rulers

The history of castles spans the entire period from the Carolingian Empire, still reflecting late antique attitudes to the exercise of power, to the dawn of the early modern era, with the definitive establishment of the territorial monarchical state.

The Merovingians had revived the late antique title of *comes* (literally companion, later count). The administrator who bore this title was the highest judge in his area, but he also had the role of a military commander, with powers of prevention, repression, and financial jurisdiction. This *comes* gained the right to build a castle, which was to be the focal point and the center of power for his area, although the power that came with it clearly diminished as the distance from the center increased.[106]

In this period it is not possible to speak of territories clearly defined by borders. Instead there was a central focus, where power was strongest, and marginal areas, less clearly defined, where authority was weaker, scarcely exercised, or dominated by other powers, or where it was absent.

The Carolingian period saw a noticeable diminution in royal power. Aristocratic lords attempted to copy what the counts had done,

A 19th-century model of the castle of Maniago. The patriarch's house is on the top right, separate from the main castle complex.

that is, to transform the title of their position into an inherited noble title, regarding the territory to be administered as their own possession. The new lords' confidence in their own importance was reflected not only in the process of construction of castles, and hence in the usurpation of an ancient royal privilege. The construction of a castle also meant setting up an independent domain. Rulers were only partly successful in controlling this process and in the late Middle Ages, were forced to make significant concessions.

This process was reflected not only in the greatly increased building of castles by the highest nobility and *ministeriales*, but also in the failure of the idea of a general peace, or truce, guaranteed by the king, which was made almost impossible by the increasing popularity of the blood feud. The Empire

split up into a number of small domains, joined to one another by increasingly fragile bonds. At the heart of each domain was a castle, although it is not yet clear how its functions as center and place of government were exercised. Whatever the case, whole regions were governed by the castles and were given the same name as them.

Castles thus became the central element in the political framework of the late Middle Ages.[107] Around them, from the thirteenth century, developed functions that were entrusted to magistrates. In this way they were transformed into components of the administration of the country.

The issue of sovereignty is emblematic of the medieval world. Unlike the Roman emperors, the Carolingians, or even Otto the Great, the late medieval ruler was responsible

Coats of arms of the families, ecclesiastics, and towns that made up the parliament of Friuli. Feudal lords made up the overwhelming majority of this assembly, which was presided over by the patriarch.

for every part of his state. It was possible to oppose him legally, because he was not in fact sovereign. Law alone, according to scholastic philosophy, was sovereign, and therefore untouchable, and then only as long as it did not go against God.[108]

The parliament, common throughout the Empire, existed in Friuli too. It reflects accurately the position of the ruler in the Middle Ages. The so-called Friuli parliament represented all those bodies that participated in power, exercising it as small independent powers on behalf of the patriarch. Sitting together with the few great abbeys and towns in the region, the feudal lords made up the overwhelming majority of the members of the assembly, which was presided over by the patriarch. The right to take part in the parliament depended not on the castle as a valuable material possession but on the fact that the feudal lord, by virtue of his possession of a castle, was part of the military power and government of the country.[109]

If the process of the disintegration of the centralized state was gradual, the trend in the opposite direction was equally slow. Now it was the rulers who, little by little, were centralizing and concentrating power. The limits set on the role of the provincial states as a result of Maria Theresa's attempt to create an absolute monarchy, and the protests of the nobility, by now practically powerless, in the France of Louis XIV and Louis XV, are symptoms of the same phenomenon. Both occurred, and not by accident, in a period when the decline of the castle was at its greatest; the gradual loss of its governing powers signified its end.

The establishment of a central bureaucracy went hand in hand with the recovery of a peace guaranteed by the sovereign. The blood feud was restricted and controlled and, eventually, though not until after the sixteenth century, prohibited. The background which made this possible was the development of a common penal code and a well-ordered judiciary, with the sovereign as guarantor of order. Absolutism was an important and necessary step on the path to the modern state: it brought an end to the medieval system and, in addition to this new judicial order, established a central bureaucracy and security against internal and external enemies, guaranteed by the central power in the person of the monarch.

Against this background, castles and their owners saw severe restrictions placed on their privileges and functions. The end of the castle must therefore be seen in relation to the changing system of power as a whole. Castles came into being at a time when the nobility was emerging as the dominant power. With this, they had their period of greatest prosperity, becoming the very symbol of the nobility.

Castles had immense political significance, much greater than their role in the defense of the territory.[110] Our idea that a castle dominates a village or a valley is essentially correct. The only problem was how to defend them. The castle walls protected the holder of privileges, as well as the documents that proved these privileges; they protected his dominion.[111] Thus the defensive capability of the castle is an element that contributes to the formation of the political, social, and economic whole that is the medieval castle.

It would be wrong to see the castle as a medieval version of the strategically important fortresses of other ages. While some castles may of course have had this function, they were exceptional. From the tenth century to well after the sixteenth, the castle was crucially important as a form of private defense, revenue, and home. It was the seat and focal point of the domain, the center of political unity, fulfilling functions that were political, military, economic, juridical, and administrative.

Above all, it had social importance, for in it was apparent the high status of its owner or whoever lived in it. Its importance for the medieval ruling class, whose identity it established, and hence for the European elites at their birth, explains why even today castles represent the architecture *par excellence* of the aristocracy, and why they continue to fascinate architects, poets, historians, and their readers.

LIFE IN THE CASTLE

Many ruined castles and noble dwellings still stand in the area around Kyburg. Within a radius of a mile I could show you some seventy ancient castles that belonged to noble families who were for the most part in the service of the counts of Kyburg. Yet these people most certainly had a style of life that was anything but luxurious—quite unlike the nobility of today—living as they did in the midst of their animals and fields. If these nobles had indulged in the same luxury that is commonly found among our nobility, the soil of this region could not have supported them.

This passage from the *Chronicle* of Johannes Stumpf,[112] written in 1548, makes clear how unreal our stereotypical image of daily life in a medieval castle is. Idealized descriptions in chivalrous romances as well as the habit of nostalgia for past times have projected on to the medieval period the way of life of the aristocracy of the early modern era. The situation described by Stumpf is confirmed by the work which has been carried out in recent years. In the majority of cases, the castle was home to not more than ten people, all of whom had to work hard to earn a living.

The castle as farm

In the early Middle Ages, the great lords and landowners were still to be found on their large country estates, the *curtes*. Here they lived and here they involved themselves personally in the management of the estate. The estate ensured the survival of the family and its continued wellbeing and was the basis of its power.

It was only with the rise of feudalism, and thus the increased income from payment in money or kind from the peasants, that the lords were able to emerge from the restricted environment of the village and move into castles. These castles, perched on hilltops and symbolizing the newly emerging ruling class, now made the difference in status between lord and peasant very obvious.[113]

In a period when the practice of the blood feud was continuing to increase in

frequency, improvements to siege machines and fortifications went hand in hand with the economic and social changes that were the indispensable conditions for the development of the castle.[114] The customary exaggeration of the military importance of the castle, in contrast to its economic importance, has come about not only as a result of the written sources. Physical evidence is also lacking: hardly any traces survive of the farm buildings which would have been found around castles, since they were generally outside the walls and were constructed from wood.[115]

Moreover, in many cases dwellings for the noble family and their household were later built on the site of the former farmyard. At Artegna, for example, the houses which are found today below the castle mound enclosure, clearly not built as defensive constructions, may lie over earlier structures. The noble residence might be moved into the burg because it offered easier access to the village, or simply because the castle had been destroyed and the old farmyard had buildings in a good state of repair.

Normally the farmyard was a burg that stood next to the main castle or a farm below the castle, on the slope of the hill or on flat land at the bottom. Today the farmyard at Villalta is a good example of a castle with a burg, although it dates back only to the sixteenth century and thus represents the more recent part of the ensemble.

The examples of farms which are situated below the castle all date from the early modern period: the farmyard at Rocca Bernarda, a little below the fortress which was built as an aristocratic home around the middle of the sixteenth century; and the farmyard at the foot of the castle mound at Fontanabona, the date of which is uncertain, but which was already in existence, albeit smaller, in the sixteenth century. Documents from that period mention stables as well as buildings which would have served for a number of the activities that went on within the castle proper.[116]

Every noble castle needed land, title, and a fief, that is, an estate that the lord administered in person and that he set his peasants to cultivate. Castles had kitchen gardens where vegetables, herbs, and flowers were grown. Medieval poetry frequently mentions

"gardens with trees," which may have been used for shade in the summer.[117] In literature these gardens appear above all as places for private conversations and dalliance.

The story *The Nightingale* describes a garden which as well as flowers had vegetables and sweet-smelling herbs, and in which the owner of the castle had constructed an arbor. "It had been built so that the lord of the house could sit there to take his meals. He believed that food eaten there did him good."[118] The shady garden was also a suitable place for amorous trysts, as we find in *Tristan*,[119] where Isolde prepared a bed there

The old farmhouse below the castle of Fontanabona.

before sending for her lover.

Even with the obligatory tributes made by the peasants, the feudal lord's personal efforts to maintain his family were much more important than has generally been admitted. The peasants' contributions were as a rule made in kind, but they were never adequate.[120] The lord was therefore dependent on the availability of a number of orchards and vegetable gardens, and on cattle-rearing and grazing.

Fields, orchards, and meadows were so important that in order to defeat an enemy it was not essential to destroy the castle itself. In 1309 a small group of soldiers who attacked the castle of the lord of Gramogliano "cut down the vines all around and destroyed the gardens that had been expertly tended, without the besieged being able to demonstrate their valor".[121]

The feudal economy was based essentially on livestock and cereals. Large stores were built for grain, since selling in the towns provided an important source of income. Even so, a poor harvest could still benefit the lord, since his finances were based on a surplus with which he could pay for the services of outside craftsmen such as the expensive armorers. When the price of cereals was high, the lord made considerably more money.

As well as the sale of cereals, the raising of livestock for meat was important, and was carried out on the spot.[122] Animal-rearing predominated even in those geographical areas where sheep might be expected. Animals were not used only for milk; sheep-rearing, for example, was geared to the production of wool and mutton. The large numbers of animal bones found in archaeological excavations show that consumption of meat was high.[123]

Within the economy of the castle, which was based on self-sufficiency,[124] there were a number of people able to produce crafts and tools for everyday use—carpenters to make furniture, spinners, weavers, and leather tanners. In the castles of the lower nobility, which were occupied by a maximum of some twenty people, it would appear that everyone, even the youngest children, must have participated in domestic and agricultural work as well as contributing to skilled craftwork.[125]

Things were different in the big dynastic castles, particularly those belonging to rulers. Not only did the life of the court dominate—corresponding to some extent to the modern stereotype of castles—but members of the ruling family did not have to work in the fields or involve themselves with any other such manual work.

Even in the very early Middle Ages craftsmen were to be found in castles, following their specialized trades. There were furnaces for the production of iron and forges which produced highly skilled work.[126] The earliest evidence for metalworking comes from the *castrum* at Invillino, where in late antiquity craftsmen's workshops were to be found in the vicinity of a noble castle.[127]

Crafts contributed to making the castles important centers around which towns might develop, as we can see in the cases of Udine and Gorizia, as well as Spilimbergo and Porcia. We know of the presence of a number of artisans in the burg of Strassoldo, and the town undoubtedly performed an important function before the construction of the new town of Palmanova.

The geographical distribution of castles shows how important agricultural income was for the feudal lords. The apparent chain of fortifications in western Friuli, from Maniago to Spilimbergo and south towards Valvasone, the alignment of which could be mistaken for a defensive line along the border, is in fact evidence that the choice of site for castles was based on very different criteria. The chain marks out the narrow strip of the best agricultural land, the sole explanation for the castles' wealth. The strongest proof of the importance of the economic basis for the castle is that the site of the castle was above all dependent on the nature of the land. This may also have been a determining factor in the cases of the towns of Udine and Gorizia.[128]

Everyday life

> The life of pleasure I once lived I'm now paying for in full, stuck under one roof, in my castle ... At Ratzes on the Schlern I live against my will in my castle, which increases my desolation ... my sole diversions are the braying of the donkeys and the screech of the peacocks.[129]

The autobiographical poem of Oswald von Wolkenstein, a feudal lord from the South Tyrol who died in 1445, is one of the earliest sources which gives us a realistic picture of everyday life in a castle. In contrast, the stereotype of the elaborate and splendid world of the medieval castle is based essentially on the instances of medieval literature in which the chivalrous ideal is so magnificently represented, such as the legend of the Holy Grail, with its exalted vision of chivalry.

The scarcity of information on everyday life in the Middle Ages has always encouraged historians to draw on the few accounts to be found in medieval literature. But we need to question the value of such passages as evidence. In his book on medieval court culture, Joachim Bumke quite rightly assesses the problem:

> The question of the value of works of literature as historical evidence cannot be resolved theoretically. It would be reasonable to conclude that theoretical considerations do not permit us to draw direct

July, from the 15th-century fresco cycle of months of the year in the Torre dell'Aquila (Eagle's Tower), Castello di Buon Consiglio, Trent, a rare example of secular art from the main period of castle-building.

conclusions about medieval life from works of art and imaginative literature. Yet such questions of methodology have been entirely ignored in writing on twelfth- and thirteenth-century court culture.[130]

Whether or not literary evidence can be considered a reliable source of information about court life, it is most certainly true that we cannot expect to find realistic descriptions of everyday life in the smaller castles in such sources.

Our image of the Middle Ages goes back a long way, even in matters concerning material culture. In 1793–94 a work by Christoph Meiners was published with a highly revealing title: *A Historical Comparison between the Customs and Decrees, Laws and Trades, Commerce and Religion, Science, and Educational Institutions of the Middle Ages and Those of Our Own Age, in Relation to the Advantages and Disadvantages of the Enlightenment*, a work that, as was common at that time, emphasized the negative aspects of the past.[131]

With the Romantic era and the nineteenth century, however, the image of the Middle Ages changed radically. This was not the result of new historical research, but was derived entirely from works of literature. The gallant heroes and amorous damsels of medieval poetry were regarded as evidence of a more romantic past; fiction was taken as reality. Bumke stresses the lack of realism in medieval literature:

> In place of the grim, dispiriting reality of medieval life, court poets offered an image of society which had been cleansed of anything that made life difficult and oppressive. Political conflict is absent; people strive towards moral and social perfection. This highly unrealistic image of society was clearly conceived in opposition to reality, and it must be interpreted in this way … The principal mistake of earlier social and cultural history-writing was to fall for this poetic construct and take it for an image of reality.[132]

Just like the mystical quest for the Holy Grail, that symbol of purity and sacred chivalrous service which has as its center, on the threshold of the supernatural, the castle of Monserrat, so life in the castles as described

by Wolfram von Eschenbach is a free poetic rendering of medieval ideals. His sumptuous castles with their great halls, hundreds of knights, and precious furnishings never existed. The much-quoted descriptions of the glass in the windows and the wax candles in the candelabra indicate that these aspects of daily life were often only an expression of what people in general did not have.

We know nothing of everyday life in castles in the early Middle Ages. However, there is no reason to suppose that conditions worsened in the later period, from which all the evidence dates. If complaints increase in the late Middle Ages, this is either because more sources survive from this period or because rural areas saw no improvement in conditions, whereas in the towns and the great feudal castles a way of life was developing that differed markedly from that of earlier centuries.

Within the Holy Roman Empire, the aristocracy had struggled with economic hardship throughout the later Middle Ages, to reach finally a higher standard of living. But tribute from the peasants, the lord's main source of income, remained at the same level, while the value of money steadily fell and expenses grew enormously.[133]

Moreover, these economic difficulties were increased by the absence of primogeniture and by the custom of dividing up inheritances. In 1349, for example, Nicolò di Brazzacco sold to the Colloredo family his third share in the upper castle, while his sister sold her sixth share.[134] The inheritance of the siblings was meager because the tiny territory of the domain of Brazzacco had already been divided between two castles. It was broken up permanently as a result of such divisions into smaller and smaller fragments, approximating to little more than a couple of farms.

Alongside the owner's family in the castles of the lower nobility lived a few servants—rarely more than ten—who worked in the kitchens and fields and might be required to help defend the castle. At Berwertstein in 1411 there was a steward who collected and looked after the finances, a man responsible for transporting firewood and provisions on donkeys, two porters responsible for the gate, a shepherd, a scullery-boy, and a female servant. This was a typical household.[135]

Given the few servants, members of the family were obliged to work. In 1462 the wife of the feudal lord of the castle of Altspaur is recorded as working in the kitchen garden and in the house and kitchen, although she had a cook, a female servant, and a maid.[136] In turn, the lord of the castle would be responsible for the livestock, as we know from the record of a dispute from Tagstein in the Grigioni, where the peasants were trying to stop the lord of Tagstein castle from bringing his animals to graze on the common land.[137]

Thus, despite the *corvées* (labor services) and tributes which were due from the peasants, the lord of the castle had to work too if he wanted to survive. It is true that in order to protect the dignity of his rank he could not perform manual labour, and certainly could not engage in trade, but he might have an interest in a merchant's business and sell products from the castle lands at market: horses, cattle, pigs, vegetables, wine, grain, wax, leather, and crafts. Agriculture played so crucial a role in the survival of the feudal lord that despite the proximity of the enemy, knights in the army often had to ask their leader for permission to return home to cultivate their fields.[138]

Even at the time, contemporaries commented on the extraordinary gulf between the idealized life of the knight in literature and reality, which was a great deal less luxurious.

In the fifteenth century, the *Seifried Helbing* tells the story of a page at the court in Vienna who was astonished to overhear two knights talking. Instead of conversing on the subject of beautiful ladies and magnificent tournaments, the knights swapped advice about how to rear animals and how to make a cow give more milk, and discussed the progress of the harvest and how much profit could be made from that year's wine.[139]

Life in the castles of the rural nobility was very different from that in the splendid castles of counts and dukes. Large castles benefited from the growing affluence of the urban bourgeoisie and could profit from the flourishing trade in towns. Such castles offered the possibility of leading a genuinely courtly life, one in which even lesser knights could take part.

To disburden himself of economic difficulties, a feudal lord needed to enter into the service of his feudal superior or take up military service. The life of Wilwolt von Schaumberg, written around 1500, provides a typical example. Having fought as a young man in the French-Burgundian war in 1474–76, he returned home to find his castle virtually stripped bare. At his death his father had had a considerable number of children, some of whom had been obliged—and with a significant outlay of money—to enter the Church. Having no inheritance, Wilwolt presented himself at the court of the margrave Albrecht Achilles von Brandenburg, whose magnificent princely court was famous. Here he proved himself as a military commander of extraordinary ability and rose to the rank of imperial captain in Friesland.

Eventually Wilwolt was in a position to take honorable retirement from military and administrative service. With the fortune he had acquired, he bought back the family castle, which had fallen into the hands of creditors, and built a new residence on the ruins. His biographer speaks of fine walls, towers, moats, ramparts and bastions, great heated halls, and, lastly, the chapel, dedicated to the memory of his parents and his ancestors, who were thus to be remembered for as long as the castle stood. This, it turned out, was not to be for long, as the castle was destroyed in the Peasants' War in 1525. Today it is clear from the ruins that it must have been a large and splendid construction, very different from other, and decidedly more humble, castles.

In Friuli, the case of Duino is similar. Here two castles stand next to each other, one a ruin on a rocky spur above the sea, the other still inhabited. The old castle is a typical late medieval construction. To take maximum advantage of the lie of the land and natural defenses, a site was chosen that was suitable for the modest requirements for space at that time. During a short siege water could be collected in cisterns. The whole construction provided an extraordinary and impregnable residence for the patriarch's administrator.

The castle itself, however, was tiny and could accommodate only a limited number of people. Furthermore, its position meant that it was impossible to get access with wheeled

Aerial view of the new castle at Duino. The abandonment of the original small fortress and consequent change of site are indicative of the owners' economic prosperity.

vehicles, which would have made supplying the castle particularly difficult.

The choice of site for the new, larger castle is an indication that the owners had entirely different circumstances in mind. The highest point of the site was chosen for the new building. Not only did it have a good view of all the surrounding area, but it made the castle clearly visible from all directions.

Although we have no information about when work started or who commissioned it, the scale of the castle, much bigger than all other castles in the region, makes one wonder how, in the whole history of Duino, there could have been a lord so rich as to undertake such an expensive project. Comparison with

parallels elsewhere in Europe would suggest that it must have been commissioned by a ruler, since only a ruler would have had available the means needed for such an enterprise. But the lords of Duino were vassals of the lord of Friuli, that is, the patriarch. Moreover, the castle was not allodial and thus did not belong to the family. Its territory, above all, was not extensive.

Although scarcely in a position to do so, the lords of Duino nevertheless attempted to play the role of independent lords. They broke their oath of allegiance to the patriarch on more than one occasion, allying with the counts of Gorizia and with the Hapsburgs. Throughout the twelfth and thirteenth centuries, none of the lords of Duino enjoyed a secure financial position. Indeed, the documents relating to the history of the family published by Pichler give a picture of constant debts and distraints of possessions, not unusual for the feudal lords of the time.[140]

An attempt to improve family finances can be seen in the peace treaty made with the patriarch, Bertrando. Under the terms of this typical example of a treaty between lord and vassal, Giorgio of Duino declares his independence of the counts of Gorizia, swears fealty to the patriarch, and confirms the patriarch's customary right of entry as feudal superior to the castle (which in any case he was obliged to yield in return for the right to occupy the castle). In exchange, Giorgio received an annual pension—1,000 pounds in Verona *piccoli*—and certain duties within the power of the superior authority, conferred on him in the interests of the prince. The patriarch promised "to defend, maintain, and aid the inhabitants of the castle and their possessions. Should Giorgio suffer any loss, he will be compensated."[141]

It was under one of Giorgio's successors that the Duino family reached its greatest splendor. Ugo VI revived the anti-patriarchal stance of his ancestors and sided with the Hapsburgs. Assisted by quarrels and murders in the family of the counts of Gorizia, this unusually able lord of Duino acquired an enormous quantity of titles to add to his originally modest position: marquis of Istria in 1373, captain of Treviso and of the imperial possessions at Pordenone in 1383, and, from 1383 to 1388, captain of the duchy of Carniola.[142] Any one of these positions would have been sufficient to remedy his financial difficulties. As it was, Ugo assembled a collection of offices that made him exceptionally wealthy. Moreover, these new riches enabled him to pay out of his own pocket for the restoration of the castle of Trieste for the emperor.

Although the architecture of the medieval parts of the castle at Duino suggest a date between 1200 and 1250, construction of the castle has to be linked to Ugo VI. Only a man as rich as he, who was acquainted with emperors and dukes and must have had a suitably large retinue, was in a position to abandon the old castle on top of its crag to build a

new one, worthy this time of a king. Such a dating would coincide with the first mention of the existence of two castles at Duino, in 1363, a date which fits the beginning of Ugo's rise.

The new castle at Duino, in which a degree of courtly ceremony must have prevailed, is not representative of everyday life of feudal lords in the fourteenth century. Ugo's contemporaries continued to live in their more modest castles, the size of which was comparable to that of the old castle of Duino.

The example of Duino shows that it is impossible to generalize about everyday life in the castles of Friuli. There was a huge difference between the great feudal castles such as the new castle at Duino and the simpler and plainer dwellings of the lesser rural nobility. The homes of the rural nobility, which were in the majority, were little different from the homes of more prosperous peasants.

Living quarters

Although farm buildings and outer walls were important, the real center of the castle was the lord's residence. Initially, this was the tower, inside which were a few rooms, one per floor. Over time, however, accommodation requirements increased, to the extent that the restricted space in which lord and servants were forced to live together was no longer sufficient.

A remarkable description, written by Lambert von Ardres in about 1200, gives us an indication of how simple a noble castle could be, although compared to many others this was considered luxurious. Lambert describes a spacious inhabitable tower of the type found in Flanders. On the ground floor were storerooms for grain, with chests, barrels, troughs, and tools and utensils of all kinds. The two floors above had rooms and a hall, which was shared by all the inhabitants, as well as storerooms for provisions and a large room where the lord and his lady slept, with the rooms of the female servants and pages adjoining. The kitchen was attached to the main dwelling house at first-floor level. On the top floor were attic rooms where the lord's sons slept, if they wished. Daughters were obliged to sleep there, because it was considered proper for them to do so. Here too lived the guards and servants who kept watch over the castle and were on guard when the nobles slept.[143]

The number of rooms should not lead us to imagine that the building was large. All the rooms on each floor were contained within a roughly square area of tower with sides of not more than 20 meters (65 feet). Rooms were consequently small and dark by today's standards. Even in this castle, the inhabitants

The tower at Partistagno, once the nucleus of the castle, combined the functions of tower and living quarters.

must have lived in fairly cramped and disorderly conditions.

A particularly good example of living quarters is the *palas* of Partistagno. Today the remains of a tower can still be seen on a small shoulder on the side of a hill. Given its size—the base measures eight meters by nine (26 by 29 feet)—it must have contained living quarters. It was probably surrounded by an outer wall, the remains of which can be seen in the supporting walls below the castle.[144] This kind of construction corresponded, therefore, to the architectural typology of the old tower castles, evidence for which exists

from the twelfth century. A date earlier than 1100 is impossible for Partistagno, and as implausible as the theory of a Roman origin for the tower.[145]

In the later medieval period, the dark and cramped tower at Partistagno was considered inadequate and the grander *palas* was built. This is often known as the lower castle, a misleading name[146] since it merely integrated the older nucleus with more modern and up-to-date living quarters. The site for the new *palas* was chosen so that the original tower, although not very high, still rose above the strong walls of the new *palas*, allowing the concentration of architectonic mass and providing a unifying effect, a characteristic of the later Middle Ages. It is possible that the new building was constructed on top of an earlier building. Whatever the case, there are a number of irregularities in the walls which indicate successive alterations. The new *palas* looks out over the valley and has fine Gothic mullioned windows.

The new castle of Partistagno had all the advantages and disadvantages of a noble dwelling of the time. Inside there was enough space for the lord's rooms, which would have been on the upper floors, with the more elegant windows. Provisions and materials were kept on the ground floor, as was customary in towers. The prisons are likely to have been on the upper floors so as to avoid unpleasant smells rising from below.[147]

In contrast with the lack of light in the first tower, the interior of the new *palas* was bright. From the typical Gothic windows, with their window seats, the lords could enjoy a magnificent view over the countryside—though only in summer and when the weather was warm. At other times, especially in winter, having daylight also meant having cold air and drafts. Glass was not used in castle windows until the late Middle Ages and there is no evidence of window frames at Partistagno. Glass, and its installation, was expensive and initially only a few patricians in the towns could afford such a luxury.[148]

At Partistagno modern wooden shutters are now installed. This may have been one of the methods used in medieval times to close off the window opening, though there is no convincing evidence that this was the system used here. An animal bladder, or piece of thin parchment, tightly stretched over the window would have allowed in a little light. Usually, however, windows were closed in winter with wood or leather, sealed with straw or wool, or even stuck down with pitch or tallow.[149]

Castles were therefore either cold and drafty or dark and smoky. However, Zeune is right to point out that this was true of every kind of dwelling at that period. Such conditions would not have seemed particularly unpleasant or unusual.

Lighting in the rooms—which in winter burned rapidly and were much more expensive. Just how much they were regarded as a luxury can be seen from the description given by Wolfram von Eschenbach of the castle of the Holy Grail: in a hall with 400 knights in it 100 lamps blazed forth, as well as countless little candles on the walls.[150]

Just as important as light was heating. The most common form was the open fireplace and chimney. The Italian word *camminata* and the German word *Kemenate* came to indicate not only the fireplace itself but the

The palas at Partistagno, the new residence built in the late Middle Ages with fine Gothic mullioned windows. Despite the cold and lack of light in the winter, this palace was a response to the desire for a more comfortable lifestyle.

would have been dark—was provided by resinous wood or by torches, which burned for longer but were smoky and dirty, spreading soot everywhere. These were placed in rings attached to the walls or in metal candelabra that stood on tables.

Another common form of lighting, found in great quantities in archaeological excavations, was the oil lamp. Made from terracotta, and used from classical times, these employed a wick floating in tallow. They produced little light and a lot of soot but lasted for a longer time.

No one could afford wax candles, which whole of the family's living area. More recently, the words came to indicate a lady's room. The importance of heating is shown by the example of the castle of the lord of Tyrol, where Elias, the servant in charge of the fires (*fornarius Elias*), appears, with his 11 assistants, at the top of the list of the servants.[151]

However, open fireplaces were not a particularly efficient method of heating. References to tiled stoves are recorded from as early as the eleventh century in Germany. Such stoves not only gave out more heat and reduced drafts but were much safer, significantly reducing the danger of fire. Despite

Next to the storerooms and living quarters, even in the Middle Ages every castle required sanitary arrangements, the most important being the latrines. A common version took the form of a recess built into the thickness of the wall over a chute that continued down to the foot of the wall, where on the outer side a small arch was opened to allow the accumulated waste to be removed from time to time. Examples of such arches can still be seen at the castles of Gorizia and Cormons.

The most interesting example that I have found is at Rocca di Monfalcone, where the visitor is immediately struck by the ten latrines visible on the exterior, positioned at regular intervals around the outside of the imposing round castle building. Considering that many modern sports stadiums, with their thousands of spectators, have only a few toilets, it seems unlikely that the large number of latrines at Monfalcone served a genuine need. The most plausible explanation for this eccentricity is that the intention was to impress the enemy with the size of the garrison. This would make this one of the rare cases in castle architecture where latrines were given symbolic meaning to express strength, and hence to intimidate.

The arches at the foot of the wall latrines, which are very common, have often been misinterpreted. Miotti, for example, thought that the arch at Cormons was the remains of an earlier entrance to the castle.[153] While the suggestion is absurd, there is an element of truth in it: there was always a risk that an intrepid—and, needless to say, extremely agile—enemy might climb up one of these chutes. The assault on the castle of Gaillard in 1204 was certainly not the only time that this occurred.[154]

This was one reason why the *Erker* form of latrine was frequently preferred[155]. Here the excrement fell directly to the ground or was channeled down wooden tubes. For obvious reasons, *Erker* were built above the less frequented parts of the castle, preferably where there was a stream which could carry the waste away.

The function of these small *Erker*, like the arches at the foot of the walls, has often been misinterpreted. Although it is possible to deduce from its placing whether an *Erker* was used as a drain or as a latrine, amateur

their advantages, however, tiled stoves became common only in areas where the German nobility were found.[152] Today in Friuli it is still possible to find fine examples, but only in the area of the former county of Gorizia.

Another solution to the problem of heating was to build out of wood a small room within a larger room. Thick wooden or lattice walls held the heat coming from a fire or brazier much more effectively than stone walls. Such rooms, found even in important residences such as Karlstein Castle near Prague, must have inspired the wooden panelling that was so commonly used until very recently. One such easily heated wooden room is recorded in 1461 on one of the lower floors at Arcano: "in stuffa parva inferiori" (in the small lower *stufa*).

Even if no bathroom survives, we know that even smaller castles had them. It was often the only room in the building that could be heated at all.

This is the background to the medieval story of the servant who was sent to look for his master in the bathroom. Delighted at the unexpected opportunity to have a warm bath, he stripped and went in, only to find his lord and his entire family fully dressed, huddled over the fire.[159]

The interior of the castle

As well as the above-mentioned fireplaces and large windows, which can still be seen today, there were of course other ways of making these bare rooms more comfortable. Floors on the ground floor were of stone, as they might also be on upper floors if these were supported by vaults; otherwise, floors were wooden. Decorated tiles are found from a very early date.

During the winter the cold floors were covered with skins or rugs. Poorer nobles made do with straw and moss. To control the constant problem of insects and bugs, sweet-smelling herbs were strewn and, on special occasions, flowers.[160] Walls were white-washed for reasons of hygiene. Exceptionally, they might be decorated with frescoes, as we shall see in the next section.

Unfortunately, we know almost nothing about the actual furnishings of a castle. To illustrate the furnishings of a medieval castle in a book, or even in exhibitions, as Fiaccadori and Grattoni have done, is, when all is said and done, to do more harm than good to a general understanding of the castle. All the furniture and furnishings that are illustrated date at the earliest to the Renaissance, a time of radical change, when city culture was becoming predominant in Italy and exceptional masterpieces were being produced.

German historians regard the end of the Middle Ages and the beginning of the modern era as marked by the Reformation or by the fall of Constantinople (1453). In Germany such a date, of around 1500, does

In the 13th century latrines were usually built with waste chutes that terminated in an arch opening to the exterior, as in the castle at Cormons. Such arches have often been mistaken for the entrance to the castle.

historians are often convinced that they were used to throw pitch and boiling water down on to the enemy,[156] an explanation often encountered in Friuli.

Although ideas about personal hygiene were certainly very different from those of today, medieval people still liked to wash and take a bath. Following the model of the public baths in the towns, many castles had a bath-house, or at least a bathroom. Bathrooms were situated on the ground floor and had vaulted stone ceilings, since dampness and condensation might cause the beams of a wooden ceiling to rot.[157]

Unfortunately, the large number of bath-rooms mentioned in inventories and accounts from the thirteenth century onwards, particularly in the later centuries, is in sharp contrast to the number of examples which survive.[158]

indeed coincide with the beginning of a new era, one of the culmination of bourgeois culture and, with the affirmation of the central power of the prince, the creation of the modern nation state. It therefore marked the end of the medieval system of decentralized power, based on castles. But in Italy, where this process began earlier, it makes little sense to consider the Middle Ages as a single entity up to the year 1500. It is not acceptable, therefore, to reconstruct life in a medieval castle on the basis of Italian fifteenth-century furniture.

The reconstruction of the interior of a castle is further complicated by other problems. Daily life underwent considerable changes between 1200 and 1500. While these changes were most noticeable in the towns, they were also felt in the castles. If we are to be strictly accurate on the subject of the furniture and furnishings of a castle, we would have to present not a static picture but a series of developments through time. However, given the lack of evidence this is obviously impossible.

Even if it were possible, however, it would be further complicated by the need to distinguish precisely between completely different situations. Life in a typical big castle was entirely different from that in a smaller castle. Nor can life in a castle be deduced by looking at the daily life of the inhabitants of a town. A town house in the late Middle Ages or early modern period existed in a unique environment, its relationship to the castle one of reciprocity evolving over time.[161]

Can anything be said then about castle furniture and furnishings? Clearly, castles were not bare and empty. Some were richly decorated and furnished, like the nineteenth-century reconstructions discussed by Grattoni in his exhibition catalogue. But how many were like this? Were they exceptional, or are they typical of the medieval castle?

Nowadays historians agree that daily life in the castle was bleak. This view is supported by the complaints of castle-owners of the late Middle Ages. Two centuries earlier, when castles had been a new phenomenon, life in them must have seemed pleasant enough. This was not because the nobility lived more comfortably—on the contrary, the rare reconstructions of the first castles show that in the eleventh and twelfth centuries living space was restricted and cramped, often consisting of a few rooms above each other in an almost windowless tower. And yet the nobility were happy with these dwellings, which were comfortable, even luxurious, compared with those of most people at that time. At the time when castles first began to appear it is likely that life in them, together with the ideals of chivalry, had an influence on urban culture in the towns, which were then beginning to grow and were centers with rarely more than 1,000 inhabitants. Any town citizen with ambition and aspirations chose to live in a tower looking very similar to a castle, as can be seen from a number of examples in Cividale.

Little can be said about the furnishings of this early period, since no evidence survives. It seems likely that in the thirteenth century, before the rapid expansion in the fourteenth and, particularly, fifteenth centuries, furnishings would have been of a stark simplicity, impossible to imagine today.

As for the late Middle Ages, it is possible to speak of a period of transition. Both towns and court life were flourishing. Thanks to expanding trade, wealth was increasing, while the ideal of chivalry determined secular culture and made its influence felt even on the bourgeoisie. It was a period when modest town houses were turning into the first palaces, when dwellings began to diversify, and for the first time it was possible to talk of the art of living.

Castles shared in this development, as can be seen from what remains of them. From the later Middle Ages, the family's private living accommodation became increasingly important. Castles became better lit, welcoming rather than severe, and much more spacious. An outstanding example such as Castel del Monte, built in the mid-thirteenth century, has many large halls, making it possible to accommodate a sumptuous court.

However, it is not at all clear how these rooms were furnished. Given the evidence from churches as well as from contemporary secular manuscripts and dress for the taste for bright colors and multicolored ornament, there seems little to support the view that Frederick II's castles had the austere and bare appearance we see today at Castel del

Monte. However, without evidence about furniture and original furnishings from that period, we are scarcely in a position to make any definitive statements about what would have been there.[162]

Only from the late Middle Ages is there evidence which allows us to hazard a guess at how castles were furnished. It was at this time that a fundamental shift occurred in cultural life. For the first time, towns reached an unprecedented level of development, thanks to the growing prosperity brought about by flourishing trade. This made possible specialized labor of great skill by different craftsmen, while precious materials began to be imported from the East. At the same time, the arts of furniture and furnishing were carried to new heights, involving a great outlay of money. The style of life in the towns became the model for those living in the castles, as we have seen in the case of bath houses, and which now became true for houses and furnishings.

This is the economic and social background to increasing complaints about the primitive way of life which still prevailed in the castles. Such complaints should not be attributed to a worsening of conditions. Rather, the nobility envied the life of the rich merchants, a life that they themselves could not afford.

It is no surprise then to find a large-scale move of the nobility out of the countryside into the towns, as occurred in Udine. At first the townsfolk opposed the tendency, afraid that the feudal knights might cause strife and disorder. After the first positive experiences, however, the feudal lords were accepted. They eventually built their own palaces, contributing to the appearance and prosperity of the towns.

It was not uncommon for knights to give in to the temptation to earn money through bourgeois pursuits, as happened in the case of the Montegnacco family. The truth was that the small income available from land and feudal dues was rarely sufficient to cover the costs of life in a town.

The Montegnacco family was divided into three branches. One branch of the family lived in the castle of Cassacco and Montegnacco and as early as 1270 belonged to the nobility of Udine,[163] receiving citizen-ship in 1380.[164] The two other branches of the family settled in towns, in Udine and Gemona. The Gemona branch, with the second name of Fantoni, by the fourteenth century was already involved in the spice trade. The Udine branch, with the second name of del Pozzo, became goldsmiths.[165]

For the most part, however, feudal lords had to give up hopes of wealth in order to concentrate on preserving their social status. Rather than moving into the towns, they were obliged to stay in their castles, although they did not have enough money to furnish their castles richly or comfortably. Poor compared with their contemporaries, they had good reason to complain of the harshness of their life, a life that was nothing like the ideals of chivalry as described in the courtly romances. Their circumstances must have seemed to them to have worsened compared with past times, and so they yearned nostalgically for a lost past, a literary commonplace which goes back to classical times.[166]

Furniture

Very little remains to give us an idea of what castle furniture looked like. The chests, benches, and tables that we think of, which appear in the catalogue of the exhibition devoted to furnishings in late medieval Friuli, belong instead to the lifestyle of the upper nobility. Such pieces of furniture would have been found in large castles at this time or in houses belonging to the urban patricians; they are not representative of castle furnishings, or even of medieval furniture in the widest sense.

The few pieces that do survive seem primitive when judged by modern tastes, yet they would have been exceptionally luxurious for their time. To have an idea of what might have been found in an ordinary nobleman's castle in the Middle Ages, we need to imagine household objects that were much simpler, even crude and primitive. People sat on benches at simple tables that could easily be moved, the top often resting on trestles or other moveable supports. The simplicity of such furniture is proved by the fact that it has not survived; doubtless it was not worth preserving. The lack of examples of medieval furniture from castles is matched by the absence of any mention of furniture in contemporary literature. Furniture was unimportant and was not a desirable luxury object. Had it been, it would have been referred to in the descriptions of splendid halls in poetry.

We can only guess at what furniture was available. Chairs, stools, and cushions for sitting on were definitely rare. There were no cupboards; instead, chests were used to store and protect precious objects, crockery, and, above all, documents, the written proofs of the lord's rights. Niches in the walls may have contained wall tables, the primitive ancestors of shelves.[167]

The interior of Duino castle, with a mixture of pseudo-medieval and 17th-century objects which give the impression of a sumptuously furnished castle.

The late twelfth-century Falkenstein codex, with the earliest inventory of a noble residence, is evidence of the austerity and poverty of castle furnishings. This is an inventory of the castle of Neuburg, the seat of the counts of Neuburg-Falkenstein, one of the most important families of the middle-ranking nobility.

The scribe records no items of furniture but lists six silver goblets with lids, five silver chalices without lids, three silver glasses with lids, four without lids, and two silver spoons. Other items of interest are fifteen suits of armor, eight metal jambs, sixty lances, four helmets, six trumpets, and, finally, three gaming tables, three games boards and ivory pieces, and twenty quilts.[168]

Beds are the only piece of furniture that receives any mention in written sources. Evidence of their great value is that in 1189, before leaving for the Crusades, Emperor Frederick Barbarossa received a gift from the queen of Hungary of "a bed furnished with a magnificently ornamented bolster and a splendid coverlet, together with an ivory chair with a cushion to stand beside the bed."[169] Such beds are described in contemporary poetry and are visible in paintings.[170] The mattress was given a flexible support by stringing cord across the frame.

Only from 1500 onwards is it possible to have a more detailed picture of life in a castle. From Franconia, for example, a detailed list of the losses caused by the Peasants' War survives. It lists many pieces of cloth, particularly tablecloths and bed linen.

Beds must have been comfortable in even the most modest castles, to judge by Christoph von Seckendorff's "lazy bed," for example, which consisted of a thin feather mattress, a pillow and a "bench cushion," perhaps another mattress. He also had a quilt and twelve pairs of sheets, a total value of sixty-two florins, the value of a small farm. We should not imagine, however, that all castles had such expensive beds. In any case, the majority of the inhabitants, and certainly the servants, would have slept on straw pallets on the floor.

In only six of the fifty-eight castles in Franconia listed as damaged on the Peasants' War list are books mentioned. In one case, the library consisted of a Bible, a text on canon law, a herbal, a collection of legends, and a volume of poetry.

We should not make the mistake of imagining that the situation at any point in the Middle Ages resembled that of the early sixteenth century. Until then, conditions were much simpler, if not to say primitive, particularly in the castles of the ordinary feudal nobles, which formed the great majority.

Art in the castles

What has been written on the castles of Friuli is also not particularly helpful on the subject of art. Bergamini's article in the sixth volume of Miotti's *Castelli del Friuli* is typical: he claims as examples of medieval castle art the frescoes in the abbey of Sesto al Reghena and in the churches of Buia and Brazzacco. The only examples from actual castles that he provides are from the early modern period, namely the Renaissance frescoes at Spilimbergo, Giovanni da Udine's work at Colloredo, and, finally, the painted decoration in the central hall of Udine castle by Pomponio Amalteo. This last example makes clear, however, how this palace, built in the sixteenth century for the Venetian governor, should be regarded as an example of Venetian taste; the decoration has nothing to do with the art found in castles. Indeed Bergamini begins his article with these words:

> The castles of Friuli … are not the sumptuous romantic constructions with a magical air which are found elsewhere in Italy and Europe. They are not, and never were, imposing edifices, the splendid dwellings of celebrated lords. Rather they are—for the most part—modest fortified houses used by the minor nobility of the region. And since art usually reflects not only the cultural level but also the level of available wealth, it follows that the commissioning of work for castles in Friuli was in all periods of little importance.[171]

The chapter could well have ended with this sentence. More recently, in the above-mentioned work on late medieval furnishings in Friuli, Gian Camillo Custoza has written about the furnishings commissioned by those of the nobility who had the right to sit in the parliament of Friuli. Where medieval work is concerned, we find that Custoza's reference is, once again, to the abbey of Sesto al Reghena. While Bergamini, an art historian, included Sesto al Reghena among the castles because, though an abbey, it is fortified, Custoza makes the mistake of including the abbot of Sesto among the castle holding nobility.

We should not look for parallels between religious art and secular decoration, even if there are exceptional instances of work that was commissioned by members of the same family.[172] In noble families it was common for younger children to be put into religious orders and they would therefore

Medieval fresco in the chapel of Duino old castle.

FOLLOWING PAGES:
The vibrant frescoed façade of the castle of Spilimbergo. Such frescoed façades were fashionable for town palaces at this time.

have grown up in a particular cultural milieu. The relationship with secular art was, in the Middle Ages, very different from that with religious art, which had much greater importance and value. Thus the frescoes in the chapel at Duino—oddly not mentioned in any of these studies—which must have been commissioned by the lord of Duino himself, cannot be cited as proof that the living quarters of a castle had similar polychrome frescoes.

What is true of medieval furnishings in general holds good for wall paintings: it is impossible to reach any conclusion about the interior decoration of the castles of Friuli in the Middle Ages. We know of no examples of secular painting and there is nothing to indi-

cate that there ever were any. The only exception is the castle chapels, which, however, should be seen in the context of religious art in general, rather than as examples of mural decoration in castles. There are some examples of late medieval painting in the castles of the upper nobility and in patrician houses in the towns,[173] but it is hard to draw any conclusions about artistic activity in the castles of the region from these.

The problem can only be resolved if we keep in mind the relationship in the later Middle Ages between town and castle, between a bourgeois culture and an aristocratic one, though the fundamental shift that took place in this relationship has not yet been fully analyzed. In the Middle Ages, the aristocracy as well as their castles were an important model for the burgers and patricians in the towns. This is apparent not only from the tournaments held by towns, and from the towers that patricians built for themselves, but also from contemporary literary and artistic works, where courtly and chivalrous themes are always prominent and are

such work with the nobility of the castles. Nor is it possible to assert that such works "clarify the precise role played by the aristocracy of Friuli in the context of the fifteenth-century world," or to conclude that "it is above all in the castles of the most eminent families of the land that the most significant artistic works are found."[174]

Late Renaissance decoration with a hunting theme in the castle of Villalta.

used as subject matter in room decoration.

It was only with the Renaissance that new themes, emerging from humanistic circles, begin to appear. This is another reason why it would be unwise to regard the Middle Ages as continuing up to 1500, since in the mid fifteenth century an entirely new period begins, one in which castles and their inhabitants lose both political power and their dominant role in culture.

The frescoes in Palazzo Altan at San Vito al Tagliamento, the most important fifteenth-century secular cycle in the region, are a good example of this artistic rebirth. Yet the artistic Renaissance had its origins not in the castles of Friuli but in Florence. It is not possible, however tempting it may be, to associate

The fertile imagination of those who continue to seek evidence of rich furnishings in castles derives from the same romantic view that a century ago led to the extraordinary vogue for reconstructing and restoring medieval castles. As the settings of chivalric culture, castles had to correspond to the glamorous image which surrounded them, and with which they were represented in medieval literature. In reality, it is absurd to regard them as places where poetry and court culture flourished, if for no other reason than the fact that the castles generally date to much later than the celebrated literary models.[175]

Only in the case of the patriarchal palace in Udine castle, the residence of the patriarch, is it possible to suggest with any certainty that

The frescoed ceiling by Giovanni da Udine in the western tower of the castle of Colloredo, one of the best-known examples of Renaissance art in the castles of Friuli.

there existed rich medieval decoration of any artistic merit. The decoration of the patriarchal palace must have been similar to that at other contemporary courts. The great public rooms would have been decorated with frescoes or with the hangings and tapestries we know about from the few surviving examples and from written sources.[176]

Shortly after 1066, the famous Bayeux tapestry was made. In the Middle Ages, many parts of Europe saw the rise of workshops specializing in the production of tapestries.

As well as having a decorative function, tapestries also prevented drafts and were a source of entertainment, for they illustrated the epics and ballads of the day. In a world as lacking in visual images as the Middle Ages, where ordinary people could see art only in church, secular art had a much greater importance that we can imagine today.

The themes used in tapestries are interesting: illustrations of stories were popular, along with historical subjects and images of everyday life. Sometimes there was a reference to the person who had commissioned the tapestry.[177]

The poet and bishop Baudri de Bourgueil, who died in 1130, left a description of a whole cycle of precious tapestries which decorated the walls of a lady's day room, and which had been executed under her personal supervision. On the first wall was depicted the Creation, the Garden of Eden, and the Flood. The second wall showed more scenes from the Old Testament, and the third showed scenes from classical mythology and history, the siege of Troy, and the foundation of Rome. The fourth tapestry, which was particularly elaborate, decorated the alcove where the bed stood. It showed the Battle of Hastings and the conquest of England by William the Conqueror. On the ceiling was a representation of the night sky with stars, planets, and the signs of the zodiac, while the marble floor was transformed into a map of the world with all the rivers, mountain ranges, and cities.[178]

Such a cycle is more or less what we might have expected to find in a castle, if we are to believe the descriptions in medieval literature. However, the woman whose room was decorated with these tapestries was the countess Adele de Blois, daughter of William the Conqueror and one of the most important women in France. Obviously, it would be wrong to imagine that the furnishings of a castle belonging to a noble family in Friuli might be similar to those of the chateau of Blois. Not even the patriarch knew such luxury. The culture and magnificence of French courts was the highest to be found at the time, a model that Friuli castles could not hope to rival.

Tapestries depicting similar themes were also to be found in the palaces of the Holy Roman Emperor. At the castle of Hagenau, Frederick Barbarossa had a cycle which depicted the history of the world, following a tradition based on Carolingian models.[179] According to Petrus de Ebulo, Henry VI, Barbarossa's son, had six rooms in his imperial palace decorated with paintings showing the history of the world from Creation, as well as Old Testament kings. Frederick Barbarossa's journey to the Crusades and his death in the waters of the Saleph were the subject of the paintings in the last room.[180]

The best-known examples of frescoes in a castle are those at Trento. In the Torre dell'Aquila (Eagle's Tower) are frescoes depicting the months of the year, a popular motif at that time.[181] In the fifteenth century, this theme, one frequently found in manuscript painting, was adopted for the frescoes of the Palazzo Schifanoia in Ferrara. In Palazzo Schifanoia, the medieval model was reworked in a particularly complex way, with humanism and philosophy providing many details of the cycle. It is clear how much had changed from the period of the restrained decorative painting in the earlier court style.

In this context, it is equally difficult to categorize the paintings of the months in Casa Antonini-Perusini in Udine. Their date, to judge from the few remaining fragments, cannot with any certainty be established as late fifteenth century.[182] It is possible to imagine similar decoration in Udine castle, which would have rivaled anything to be found in patrician houses.

The many examples of fifteenth- and sixteenth-century decoration in Friuli show quite clearly that bourgeois urban art and the chivalric art of the castles used the same themes and forms. Courtly scenes dating from almost the same period can be found in Valvasone castle and Palazzo Richieri in Pordenone, "inspired by episodes in medieval epics and romances."[183] Throughout Europe at this time, the model was the chivalric romance, influencing not only furnishings but also tournaments and also the choice of first names.[184]

In addition to the depiction of court life inside castles, an important role was played by the decoration still seen on the outside of castles and palaces, such as the remains of frescoes which still survive at the castle of Valvasone.

We have, therefore, good reason to think that in the sixteenth century, even fairly small castles had rooms which were comfortable and decorated, with decoration of some artistic merit. However, by this time it was not possible to distinguish between paintings in town houses and paintings in the country. The chivalric culture associated with the castle was at an end, even if the works now being produced put everything that had come before in the shade.

A good example is the new residence built for the Partistagno family, which in the second half of the fifteenth century abandoned its old castle to build a new palace on the plain below, still known in Belvedere as the *domus magna* (big house). The new palace is in fact an early version of the villa that was to become common in the Veneto. The internal decoration is of good quality and must therefore have been among the most up to date in the region. Although it was the feudal lord who commissioned the building, it cannot be considered an example of feudal art in Friuli. New themes were incorporated, without the family realizing that their adoption spelled the end of chivalric culture. Nor did they appreciate that after the military conquest of Friuli by Venice, they were now helping the Venetians to destroy their local culture as well.

It was not for a century that the aristocratic families of Friuli became aware of the resulting loss of a sense of identity, when they began to stand up against a triumphant bourgeoisie. In Germany, the bourgeoisie was forbidden to participate in tournaments; in Friuli the feudal nobles built new castles, or at least villas that could pass as castles.

Sala del Parlamento, Udine Castle, with frescoes by Pomponio Amalteo, Giovanni Battista Grassi, and Giambattista Tiepolo.

OPPOSITE:
Elaborate gilded coffered ceiling with allegorical paintings dating from the 16th to the 18th century in the Sala del Parlamento, Udine Castle, one of the richest interiors of the castles of Friuli.

THE ORIGINS OF THE CASTLE

The earliest castles

The tower of Villalta. The large ashlar blocks at the base, often thought to be Roman, are a fine example of medieval workmanship.

The whole history of the Middle Ages can be seen in castles. Castles were the focus of political and jurisdictional activity as well as the centers of culture and territorial organization. At the same time, they were also symbols of the social position of their owners. Castle, feudal lord, and state, the political structure and feudalism, all were part of an indivisible unit.

Since the castle is so closely connected with its era, it is logical to connect its genesis to the emergence of those characteristics which typify the medieval period. A book on the castles of Friuli ought really to begin with the Carolingian era. However, this is not possible since in Friuli it is widely believed

that the origins of castles go back much earlier than this.[185]

All the same, two further reasons justify an examination of the period preceding the birth of the castles. Historians agree that in Italy, the Iberian peninsula, and France (in southern Europe) feudal castles generally have a rectangular ground plan, while in northern Europe they are predominantly round. It has often been assumed that this rectangular ground plan was a survival from the Roman *castrum*.

Normally, different ground plans do not allow typologies to be created, but the choice of either a rectangular or a round plan is significant. Although Friuli belonged to the Roman world—it was part of the Roman Empire for a longer time than Spain or France—castles in the eastern part of Friuli are as a rule round, while those in the west are mainly rectangular, adhering to the typical Italian castle type. The castles of Zoppola and Porcia are good examples.

Friuli can therefore be viewed as divided into two distinct areas, with two different typologies of castle. Various explanations have been offered for this. Eastern Friuli may have been less influenced by the Roman world, and thus lacking in Roman *castella*. The *castella* may have all been destroyed. Roman culture may have disappeared so completely as a result of the Germanic invasions that the models changed. Alternatively, circular and square ground plans may have nothing to do whatsoever with Roman and non-Roman tradition. Of all the questions surrounding the form of medieval castles, this is one of the most important. Friuli, with its typological watershed, is an intriguing case and one that gives much food for thought to those who study castles.

Looking at the Roman defensive tradition can help us understand later developments. It is my firm belief that the medieval castle was not so much a military construction as a political, feudal, and cultural center. If we trace the evolution over time of the seats of power within the region, we can see that when the modern state began to emerge, with its centralized and impersonal administration defended by anonymous standing armies, there was a move from castle to villa. At the same time, the towns were transformed into fortresses.

This dual development shows events moving in precisely the opposite direction from that at the breakup of the Roman Empire and its administration and the beginning of medieval feudalism. We shall attempt to trace this process over time.

Roman defenses and the medieval castle

As early as 1654, Matthäus Merian suggested that the towers of the castle of Dreieichenhain were Roman. It was in the nineteenth century, however, that the enthusiasm for discovering Roman work in castles reached its peak, with von Haller claiming that every tower with rustication was Roman. Innumerable works appeared, culminating in 1859 with Krieg von Hochfelden's *History of Military Architecture in Germany from Roman Times to the Crusades*.[186]

Apart from a few isolated cases of the reuse of the walls of the many border *castella* in Germany after a period of some thousand years, it has not been possible to prove any influence of Roman military architecture on medieval castles.[187] And yet Roman *castella* continue to be cited as the precursor of the medieval castle.

The Roman military author Vegetius gives us a detailed picture of Roman fortifications through the eyes of an educated man living in the fourth century after Christ. He also provides information on military camps.

In times of war, fortified towns are not always available for a stay, whether longer or shorter. However, it would be imprudent and dangerous to allow the army to encamp for even a short time without protection … It is not enough just to choose a good site for the camp … The area of the encampment should be firm and without bumps and hollows, since the arrival of the enemy could make a rapid departure awkward. Furthermore, the enemy should not be able to attack the camp from above. When you have made sure of this, build the camp in the form of a square, rectangle, or circle, according to the terrain. In itself, the form has no bearing on the suitability of the camp, but camps where the long side is longer by a third than the

short side are considered to be particularly pleasing aesthetically.[188]

This passage from Vegetius would suggest that Roman camps had for some time departed from the classic rectangular form in which they are always shown today; the rectangular form appears to have been more of an aesthetic ideal. It is also clear that sites which possessed natural defenses from the lie of the land were preferred, although hilltops—later to be typical sites of castles—were excluded because their narrow and steep approaches made access to the valley below—the theater of battle—quite slow and also very difficult.

Vegetius notes too that in peacetime towns offered the best accommodation for troops for longer periods. It was only on the *limes* (boundaries), on the border of the Roman Empire, which was defended for centuries, that camps were built as permanent quarters for the frontline troops. There are well-known examples of camps built in stone, evidence of the desire to build permanent places of defense. The most impressive examples are the forts of the Saxon shore in Britain, a chain of fortifications along the south and east coasts of England, from modern Hampshire to Norfolk, which were begun in the third century after Christ. Nine of them have survived the ravages of time.[189]

All such fortresses, constantly cited and described in the literature, are to be found on what was the border of the Roman Empire. Yet there is not a single example in Friuli. Here, soldiers were billeted in the towns. It is not a question of mistaking the term *castrum*, a term which recurs constantly in the sources: a *castrum* is a settlement that is not yet a town. The only difference between a *castrum* and a *castellum* is that the *castellum* was smaller, but in late antiquity the terms were interchangeable.[190]

We do not know precisely when people began to fortify ancient settlements. Roman towns of the first centuries after Christ had no fortifications. Security was guaranteed by defenses on the border of the Empire, far from Italy.[191]

Besides the *castrum*, however, other types of military architecture existed, which should be taken into consideration as possible precursors of the medieval castle: the watch-

tower and the *burgus*. We know of their existence from numerous written sources. Cicero records their use as ancient. Caesar describes their use in the war in Gaul for transmitting messages with smoke or fire, and Irzio indicates a similar procedure in his *De bello africano* (The War in Africa).[192]

All the sources imply that this was a practice that went on at the battle front. It is improbable that the whole of Italy could have been covered in watchtowers and signaling posts. In fact, it is much more likely that the towers were part of a system of staging-posts that provided for a change of horses along the road and for the sending of news. These staging-posts were unlikely to have been fortified.

In Friuli, then, it is not possible to speak of constructions dating from the early Empire that could have been precursors of the castle, because there was no such thing as Roman military architecture.

Late Roman defenses

As is well known, with the first barbarian invasions life in the Roman Empire changed forever. After a century and a half of peace, in northern Italy the sense of security ended with the wars of the Marcomani in the years around 170 AD. It is not hard to imagine the psychological impact these events must have had on the Romans, accustomed as they were to a peaceful existence.

Localities which are described as *castra* were now surrounded by a *vallum*, which provided a degree of protection, and even large cities had walls built around them.[193] In Friuli, the focus of defense and the site of the principal battles was Aquileia, whose walls were constantly repaired and improved.[194]

The external threat coincided with internal power struggles and with ever more frequent raids from bands of robbers. The typical inhabitant of Italy must have felt such robbers as an oppressive and constant threat during this period.

We do not know whether, or to what extent, the small guard-posts and larger military stations along the Roman roads were fortified against such attacks. It would have been relatively simple and cheap to build walls strong enough to keep out bands of robbers. However, given the flimsy nature of any such constructions, it is very unlikely that they would have been in a condition to be reused a thousand years later as the nucleus of a new castle. What is certain is that not a single one survives.

If other kinds of defensive structures for guarding the territory did exist, Vegetius does not refer to anything of the kind. He mentions no fortified places apart from the towns and the regular camps.[195] Either such places did not exist or they were so insignificant that they were not worth mentioning.

This is confirmed by the lack of resistance encountered by the emperor Maximinus when he came south over the Alps to invade Italy in 238, penetrating as far as Aquileia. According to Herodian, all the towns were abandoned and their inhabitants took refuge with all their possessions in Aquileia.[196] Even the *castrum* at Gemona, situated on Maximinus's route, was abandoned. It is clear that people felt that only cities could provide significant protection.

The situation on the borders of the Empire was different.[197] Where there was a permanent and fixed frontier, with its *vallum*, there developed military defensive structures that varied according to position: small *castella* and peasant settlements organized on military lines near the border, larger *castella* along the roads, and small *burgi* between them.[198]

Given the tremendous efforts made to protect the northern border of the Empire, historians have always supposed that something similar must have existed to provide an internal defensive line for the immediate protection of Italy itself. Some historians have suggested that under the emperors Honorius and Constantine there was an extensive campaign to create great defenses for Italy, the *tractus Italiae*, led by a *comes Italiae* (count of Italy), who was responsible for its organization and maintenance.[199]

It is possible that this *tractus Italiae* was in fact an administrative reorganization within the army, parallel to the creation of fixed points for reinforcement. In all probability, there was never a system of fortifications to resemble that of the *limes* along the Danube or in Britain.

Traces of late Roman fortifications have been found in the more remote Alpine valleys, while many others have been discovered in Slovenia.

One of the most impressive examples is the *castrum* at Aidussina, the walls of which measure 215 by 154 meters (705 by 505 feet). It was ringed by twelve round towers. Aidussina was completely destroyed, however, as early as 394.[200]

Even if they had existed, such fortifications would not have been an obstacle for invaders. In 401 and 403, the Visigothic leader Alaric met no resistance from the fortified towns on the plain. The same is true of the successive barbarian invasions, up to that of the Goths.[201] If the fortifications of the *tractus Italiae* ever existed, they must have been so weak that Vegetius did not even think it worth mentioning them.

Although many historians have combed the entire Friuli area in search of Roman fortifications, the present state of knowledge suggests that the region never had a system of defense for the plain at the foot of the Alps and the Alpine valleys. The only exceptions are local fortified shelters which, given their remote and elevated sites, could never have subsequently seemed suitable sites to build castles.[202] These structures were never part of the military organization of the Roman state. Rather, they are the result of local initiatives, buildings which were intended to meet immediate and pressing needs and which have nothing whatsoever in common with the daunting constructions that were built to protect the northern border of the Roman empire.

Gothic and Longobard fortifications

The history of the Goths in Italy was recorded by contemporary historians, who noted even the details of court life. Byzantine histories give us in turn an idea of the military tactics employed by the Goths, and the weaknesses of their equipment. We know nothing, however, about Gothic fortifications. Theoderic, king of the Ostrogoths, spent large amounts of money on repairing the walls of the cities,[203] realizing that their retention or loss meant victory or defeat in war.[204] Even in this field, the Goths reveal themselves as preservers of tradition.

There is one source which records an extension of the *tractus Italiae per alpes* (in the Alps). It is however, so brief and in such generalized terms that it is not clear what is being referred to. It may mean no more than *castella*, understood as barracks for border troops, or a system of barriers across the Alpine valleys to dissuade other peoples from invading Italy. In this period, the construction of strong defenses does not yet mean actual military organization. "Until at least the Longobard period, defenses are a response to a dynamic and broad strategic concept; they can therefore be taken as the work of a central power."[205]

Similarly absent is any archaeological evidence of building activity. Only at Doss Trento, a natural stronghold high above the valley of the river Adige, has the discovery of a number of coins suggested the existence of a Goth garrison.[206] As is the case with other strongholds that appeared in the mountains in the late Roman period, this was used only as a fortified place of refuge. The sparse remains at Doss Trento indicate that the construction was of little significance.

In the 1960s, Vetters suggested that at the time of the Alemannic invasions fortified refuges were built, designed by the Roman army and constructed using local labor.[207] It is possible that a recent, and extraordinary, archaeological discovery in Friuli might confirm this hypothesis.

Tito Miotti and the Longobard *limes*

On the hills around Nimis, Tito Miotti has discovered a complex network of roads and small defensive constructions that deserves intensive archaeological examination since it could shed light on the debate about continuity or otherwise of Roman and medieval fortifications. If these constructions date from the period of the Longobards or the Goths, or even earlier, they could well be examples of the fortified refuges which were described by Vetters.

Around Nimis there are more than a hundred small constructions, between 20 and 100 meters long (65 and 330 feet). Their size corresponds to that of a flat area that in places still has the remains of a surrounding drystone wall or ditches and earthworks. Some of the constructions have the foundations of stone structures which, to judge from their small dimensions, could have been the bases for wooden towers protecting the entrances. More than a hundred such buildings, scattered over an area of only five square kilometers (two square miles), were connected by a dense network of roads.

It is difficult to explain this remarkable discovery. The complex network of constructions would seem to suggest a sophisticated system for border defense which would also have served as protection for the plain behind. But its position on the hilltops seems to suggest a broad area for retreat, since these supposed defense works could not have impeded access to the plain in any way. It is possible that farming may have destroyed some of the buildings, and Miotti himself played a part in the destruction of some of the remains he discovered. However, it is difficult to see why fortifications closing off the valleys should have co-existed with such a large number of refuges in the mountains. All in all, the creation of such a labyrinth of tiny fortifications seems futile, since there is no doubt that a few stronger constructions would have been more effective.

The apparently haphazard construction of all these small *castella* would seem to have been the uncoordinated work of numerous isolated groups hiding in the forests, who wanted to provide themselves with some sort of basic protection. And yet contradicting this hypothesis is the fact that the connecting roads are paved. This suggests an organized program of work, but it would also have made the presence of those wishing to remain hidden only too apparent to the enemy.

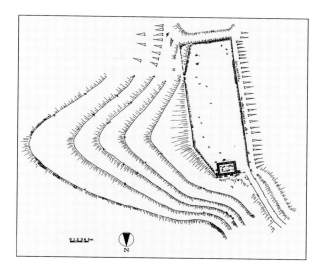

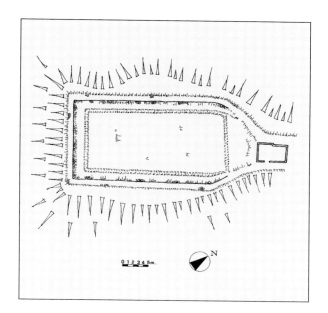

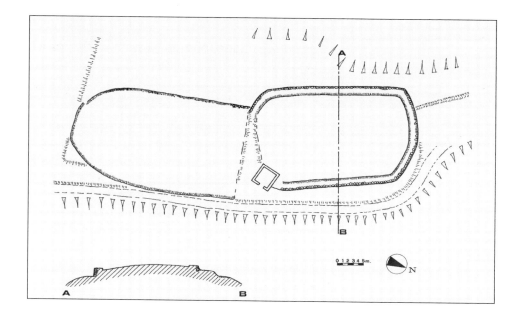

Plans of small buildings and enclosures found on earthworks in the hills around Nimis.
TOP:
The most simple form, adapted to the contours of the hill.
CENTER:
A rectangular, more sophisticated, enclosure, with the foundations of a small stone building at the entrance.
BOTTOM:
Double enclosures, reminiscent of the earliest castles north of the Alps, with their division between village and castle.

The situation is further complicated by the fact that several kinds of defensive structure are visible at Nimis. The first and most basic type, and also the smallest, consists of a simple flat area, without any walls, or with walls which follow the contours of the hill. The intermediate type consists of a construction following the lie of the land, forming a kind of burg. The third group comprises rectangular constructions which almost always have the remains of a structure beside the entrance.

The entrance to the castrum at Invillino, still used for access to the cemetery and to the via crucis (stations of the Cross).

It is tempting to assign these three different types to three different phases in the construction of the *tractus Italiae*. In fact, the rectangular constructions do seem to belong to the older, Roman tradition, while the other constructions are more akin to Germanic fortified refuges.

However, Aldo Settia has suggested that the drystone walls could date from prehistoric times, though this would have to be proved by archaeological investigation.[208] If this is the case, all the structures described might be nothing more than constructions connected with agriculture, such as animal pens, similar to those which have been found in Istria or on the coast of Croatia.

Miotti believes that the seven *castra* mentioned by Paul the Deacon are all associated with a defensive line, and that together with it they formed a *limes*. He has not, however, found any other site with a similar density of small defensive constructions, although remains of paved streets have come to light.

Interpretation of the complex at Nimis remains inconclusive. Archaeological investigation would be required to ascertain whether the sites bear out Vetters' theory that from the late Roman period up until the Longobards much energy was devoted to building fortified refuges.

Whether this is true or not can be disregarded, as such a development would have had no significance whatsoever for the development of the medieval castle in Friuli. The models for the future centers of the feudal system would certainly not have been constructions that were intended only for temporary shelter and which had been built by the local community.[209]

Invillino

Invillino, to the west of Tolmezzo, is an example of a late Roman or early medieval *castrum* that has received considerable attention from the archaeological point of view. It is almost certainly the *Ibligine* referred to by Paul the Deacon as impregnable on account of its location.[210]

There are two distinct areas at Invillino: Colle di Zucca to the west, where the foundations of an early medieval church have been excavated;[211] and the high natural mound above the present village, now with only a cemetery on it. Although no evidence remains of the archaeological excavations carried out in recent years, they revealed a *castrum*, a typical example from the period between late antiquity and the early Middle Ages, which attracted international attention. A summary of the findings, which were published in two volumes, follows.[212]

The mound, consisting of conglomerate or pudding-stone and 55 meters (180 feet) high, stands almost sheer above the plain of the river Tagliamento. The present access was opened up only in modern times. The old entrance is still used as a Via Crucis (stations of the Cross) to the cemetery chapel.[213] The ancient track, which in places is cut out of the rock itself, was protected by a tower. The base of the tower had walls a meter (three feet) thick. Next to it was a passage nine meters (thirty feet) wide.[214] The absence of any trace of a surrounding defensive wall is surprising but can be explained by the fact that at the edge several feet of rock, where the ground is loose and friable, have fallen in a landslide.[215] The original *castrum* must have extended over the whole summit of the mound, as no dividing walls are apparent and archaeological finds useful for dating were found over the whole area.[216]

Four main phases can be identified in the history of the site: two from the main period of the Roman Empire, one late Roman, and one Byzantine-Longobard. There is evidence of Iron Age occupation, and a permanent settlement was probably established, at the latest, by the middle of the first century after Christ. We should not visualize this as a military construction with any kind of defensive work. It is probable that the position of the mound high above the valley, safe from the risk of flooding, encouraged the development of a supply station in connection with the Roman road.[217] Between around 100 AD and 350 AD it had a modest settlement of just two simple, rather insignificant, buildings with mortar walls. The excavation report suggests that these buildings may have had an agricultural function.[218]

In a second, brief, phase, towards the end of the fourth century, evidence of occupation increases substantially. Next to the two main buildings rose smaller secondary constructions. Production of glass and iron begins, and for the first time objects manufactured in other parts of the Roman Empire appear.[219] The settlement here, on Colle Santino, may have been the result of the fear felt as a result of the growing threat of Germanic invasions. Just as elsewhere in similar circumstances,

According to Paul the Deacon, Invillino was one of the castra most easily defended, thanks to its impregnable position. Only a cemetery chapel remains on the site of the settlement.

people responded by retreating to naturally defended strongholds.[220]

In late antiquity, around 500, a construction was added with the appearance of a villa. This was modified and extended several times and there is evidence of occupation over a considerable length of time. At the same time, a fortification was built, of which only the bases of three towers survive. Older buildings from the first and second phase were demolished and replaced by a single type of construction in wood on dry-stone foundations. To judge from the objects they used, the inhabitants, now numerous, still had a Roman language and culture. The economy continued to be based on the products of artisans, although many more goods were now imported.[221]

By the eighth century, burials are to be found among the buildings, suggesting that the settlement had been abandoned. We do not know the reason, but it cannot have been as a result of an attack since there are no signs of destruction. The settlement was finally abandoned during the relatively peaceful period of Longobard rule.

Invillino is the best-recorded example of a *castrum*, showing continuity of occupation from Roman times to the period of domination by the Goths, Byzantines, and Longobards. The Germanic occupation of the region left no recognizable material evidence. The presence of the Goths is unlikely—and cannot in any case be proved—but it is possible that the Longobards may have stayed in Invillino for short periods.

The decisive change at Invillino occurred around the year 400, when the site acquired greater importance as a result of the end of peace and security in Italy. Since after the construction of the villa-like building there appear to have been no other major changes, we can, with Paul the Deacon, agree on the name of *castrum* to designate the structure that lasted for three centuries, from 400 to 700.[222]

The fact that Paul the Deacon describes the site as impregnable is only in seeming contradiction with the insignificant remains of defensive structures today. The word *castrum* need not imply the existence of imposing walls. In any case, Paul the Deacon is referring only to the favorable position of the site itself. The Longobards may have taken refuge on the mound during the Avar invasions and may have defended the site, together with the inhabitants.

The excavations at Invillino thus revealed that the Longobard *castrum* was not a fortification but a late Roman settlement. There is a clear parallel with a fifth-century structure in Vranje, which similarly has two towers, one on each side of the entrance, and no surrounding walls.[223] Unfortunately, it is no longer possible to prove whether Osoppo in Friuli had a similar structure, but a comparison of the terrain at both sites, as well as contemporary references to both places as *castra,* make this feasible.[224]

Although Invillino appears to have been abandoned in the seventh century, the settlement center may have continued to exist as a village. Many medieval settlements, both villages and towns, grew up on the sites of Roman *castra*. However, *castra* were not the predecessors, or even the prototypes, of the castle. Equally incorrect is the attempt to interpret the *castrum* in the context of a centrally organized defense system with large numbers of permanent garrisons, along the lines of the *limes*. Rather, a degree of self-defense was probably encouraged by the governing authorities, with the state promoting the construction of fortified inhabited settlements. The *tractus Italiae* may have been nothing more than an administrative system for coordinating preparations in time of need, and for making available military reinforcements.[225]

Continuity and change

In the present state of knowledge, a direct link between the Roman *castrum* and the medieval castle cannot be established. The surprisingly sparse references to defensive structures in the written sources as well as in contemporary literature agree with the evidence from Invillino. The fact that Vegetius speaks of the important fortifications of the large towns and completely ignores the small *castra* no longer seems so surprising.

Examination of the structure of the Roman *castellum*, or camp, makes it clear that it cannot have been the prototype of a castle. The *castrum* was essentially a barracks. It is true that it had a strong military garrison with a large number of trained soldiers in a relatively small area, as is often imagined for the castle. It had a strong surrounding wall with defensive ditches and ramparts.

But there are crucial differences. The *castrum* belonged to the state. It had no permanent inhabitants, still less a lord. The castle, for its part, was not a stopping-off point for troops as was the Roman camp, providing overnight shelter and security, or a barracks, but was rather a place of permanent residence. Furthermore, the individual importance of the lord who exercised his power in such a castle cannot be ignored. As a result, the dimensions of this lord's home were small. It would have been difficult for a medieval castle to have accommodated a garrison as a Roman camp could.

In the few recorded examples north of the Alps of the reuse of Roman defensive structures, it is clear that these came about by chance rather than by design. They show, furthermore, how difficult such reuse was. In the Low Countries, at the time of the Viking threat, the local inhabitants took refuge in the Roman fortifications, which had been abandoned for centuries and had fallen into ruin. Elsewhere, smaller defensive structures were built into the late Roman constructions along the *castella* on the *limes*.

The decay and collapse of Roman fortifications and associated buildings was a fairly slow process, lasting for centuries. The defenses became quarries for building stone. Only fairly large groups of people, working in an organized fashion, could have made use of the often huge ruins themselves.[226] Nowhere can continual use of Roman defensive structures into the Middle Ages be demonstrated.

The *Castellum Pucinum* at Duino

The only place where archaeologists have been able to establish continuity between a Roman *castrum* and a medieval castle is Duino.[227] Archaeological excavations in the area of the burg of the upper castle, covering the area of a single house, appear to confirm the hypothesis that the castle at Duino is the *Castellum Pucinum* referred to by Pliny as situated between the Timavo and the Sinus Targentinus.[228] Miotti's theory that the main tower at Duino is Roman would also appear confirmed. However, here too the situation is not as simple as would appear.

In studies of Duino, both of the castles which exist today have been taken in turn to be the site of the Roman *castellum*. Pichler and Bravar, however, place the *castellum* on a third site, in the area of modern Valcatino, where, until quite recently, remains of walls could be seen and which was traditionally known as the "castle of Attila."[229] According to this theory, in the tenth century the king of Italy, Berengar, transferred to the patriarch the rights over a fortified village, which is referred to as a *castellum*. We do not know, however, whether there was a manor farm on the Roman remains.

Excavations in the area of the new castle at Duino have confirmed the existence of a Roman settlement here as well, though its function and character are not clear. It is therefore possible that there was Roman occupation here as well as around the older lower castle, as has always been supposed.[230]

There are no Roman remains to be found in the old castle. The position of the tower here is typical of castle towers, controlling access to the courtyard behind.[231] In any case, the stonework and vaulting of the tower rule out the theory that it was a Roman lighthouse or guardtower.

The old castle is in every aspect a typically medieval construction. In order to gain maximum advantage of the natural defenses, a site was chosen that Vegetius would have found unsuitable on several counts: no drinking water, inadequate space, difficulty of access (making rapid intervention difficult), and higher ground overlooking it

(making the castle vulnerable to arrows and siege weapons).

While in Roman times all these factors would have ruled out the site as a fortress, they are precisely what made it attractive in the period that saw the appearance of the first castles. The restricted space was adequate for the modest requirements of the time. Bombardment, given the limited military technology available, was not something to be feared. Sufficient water for a short siege could be stored in a cistern. The whole structure was a secure, impregnable residence for the patriarch's administrator.

The splendid main tower of the new upper castle, which rises so impressively behind the walls, has often been considered Roman, particularly on account of the quality of the stonework, which Miotti refused to accept could be medieval. However, such a view derives from the fact that the stonework of other Friuli castles, with the exception of Tricesimo, is mediocre or poor. A fairer comparison would be with the quality of workmanship of the great feudal castles of France and Germany in the Middle Ages.

The tower of Duino Castle

The main tower at Duino is unusually situated in the courtyard, and looks out of place. It does not stand square either to the rest of the building or to the fortifying wall opposite; instead it stands at an angle, sticking out into the courtyard. Even the refacing of the base of the tower,[232] which was carried out at the beginning of the twentieth century, cannot succeed in making the tower look as if it belongs to the ensemble.

But even if the position of the tower is proof that it must be older than the buildings around it, this does not make it Roman. Indeed, towers positioned obliquely in this way are found in a number of medieval castles. Not only do they give an impression of strength in relation to the surrounding walls, but they also reinforce the outer wall at the point where outside the castle there is an open area, thus giving special protection to the courtyard behind it.[233]

Thus the position of the tower is typical of medieval architecture, whereas it cannot be explained on the basis of Roman fortifications. There are also other indications that the tower is medieval.

First of all, the tower is too high. Roman lookout towers were of a fairly fixed height, corresponding to about three floors, less than a third of the height of the Duino tower. It is not possible that the tower was added to at a later date since the stonework is all of the same date.

Second, in neither of the two openings which were made at a later date in order to allow access to the front wall of the castle, does the thickness of the walls show any sign of *opus picatum*,[234] the Roman masonry technique for infilling, which gave walls greater flexibility and hence greater strength.

Third, none of the large stone blocks has the hole typically found in Roman masonry which enabled them to be lifted by a crane.

Fourth, if the tower was originally a Roman watchtower or lighthouse, or the central feature of a small *burgus*, it would not only have been placed square to the sea but would have had much thinner walls as it would not have needed to withstand attack. Instead, the walls vary in thickness between a meter and a half and two meters (five and six-and-a-half feet), and the two thicker sides are on the landward side, the side most exposed to danger in the present arrangement.

Fifth, there are only small windows on the sides facing away from the entrance, while there are none on the sides that in the Middle Ages would have been regarded as crucial. If the tower was originally a lookout tower, or *burgus*, it would have had larger openings on all sides, allowing it to offer secure quarters for a small garrison.

Sixth, the entrance to the tower, which is three meters (ten feet) from the ground, is typical of medieval towers of this kind. The round architrave has been made, in a primitive fashion, with a crankshaft. Inside the tower are features typical of a medieval tower—holes for supports for wooden door frames and hinges, and the particular technique used for the wooden floors.

Finally, the height and impressiveness of the walls demonstrate that the tower, besides its important function as a reinforcement for the outer castle wall, also functioned as a status symbol of a medieval feudal lord, visi-

ble from far away and a sign of his power. Such a construction, which was beyond the means of the average feudal lord, was also a sign of great economic strength.

The Roman tradition at Duino

It is clear from all these features that the tower at Duino cannot be regarded as the Roman nucleus around which the medieval castle grew, although a Roman presence on the site cannot be excluded.[235] It is only in the area of the burg that evidence of Roman settlement is absent. Even under the present outer wall remains of walls have been found that may be Roman, since they reveal the use of *opus picatum*.[236] This means that at Duino it is possible to speak of continuity of occupation, attested to by archaeological investigation and the evidence of structural remains.

Duino is therefore a typical example of continuity of settlement, with a Roman *castellum*, the site and form of which were however irrelevant to the subsequent development of the site. The patriarch received this *castellum*, with associated political and economic privileges, along with many other properties elsewhere. The patriarch may have given Duino to a *ministeriale* to administer for him as early as the tenth century. Such a *ministeriale* would have had a noble court typical of the period, probably in the area of the old *castellum*. This may have been destroyed several times, and changing circumstances may have obliged the *ministeriale* to defend the site. Following the example of other knights, he would have constructed a solid castle, creating an independent power base.

Thus the seat of power would have been moved to the place which at the time seemed the most favorable, that is the cliff overlooking the sea. Over the following centuries, the changes in the way of life, the growing need for displays of power, a more autonomous position of strength, and the need to control the nearby road all made it necessary to build a new castle on a different site.

The choice of new site fitted the changed circumstances. Although it still overlooked the sea, it was invulnerable on three sides, accessible only from one side, almost at sea-level. The site offered the further advantage of dominating the surrounding countryside on all sides. Moreover it was not vulnerable to attack from a higher position as it was not overlooked.

Taking all this into account, what significance do any Roman remains have at Duino? In essence, none at all. Whether or not there was a Roman *castellum* here, the choice of

the particular circumstances that conditioned the choice of site in the Middle Ages. In the case of Duino, the significance of the architectural ensemble of the oblique juxtaposition of the outer wall and the tower has not been sufficiently examined precisely because the tower has always been regarded as Roman, awkwardly integrated into the medieval building.

Ruins of the old castle of Duino, with the new castle in the background.

site for the castle in the early Middle Ages would have been the same, and the medieval castle would have taken this form.

In conclusion, we can say that this continuity of occupation occurred only due to the fact that the topographical situation of the Roman settlement happened to have coincided with the needs of the medieval builder.

The search for Roman remains has little relevance because it does not take account of

The Castle of Duino

Ruins of the old castle of Duino, on a crag by the sea. Only in the tower does a small room, once the chapel sanctuary, survive.

The old castle

There are two castles at Duino: one, still inhabited, has medieval parts that give it a fortified appearance; the other, on a cliff overlooking the sea, is in ruins. This, the earlier castle, occupies a site whose natural features make it extremely well-defended. A steep rocky outcrop is linked to the mainland by nothing more than a narrow and low saddle of land.

It is hard to discern very much of the buildings that once stood here, and the few surviving fragments of the outer wall give only an approximate picture of the original appearance of the castle.

The outer wall is reached by a steep path that leads first downhill then uphill. This wall is protected by two gateways that in turn guard the narrow entrance on to the saddle. From here, a steep staircase leads up to the interior. The entrance is close to the main tower, which performs the classic defensive role as the center of the building.

The western wall of the tower has broken off and fallen into the sea. It would appear that there was a building here, since the attachment of vaulting that may once have belonged to a gate can still be seen. Above the gate there was another vaulted room, which is still recognizable. This must have been the castle chapel.

On the east side of the tower a small Romanesque window survives, with well-preserved traces of frescoes on the inside. As well as revealing some ornamental frames,

From here, more steps lead up to the largest space in the castle, a courtyard that was probably open on the landward side.[238] In the southeast corner, facing the sea, are the ruins of two buildings of so modest a size that they may be later additions, as suggested by Ebhard, who identified this as the site of the owner's living quarters.[239]

A long flight of steps between the two buildings led up to a small area of flat ground, the edge of the cliff on the south. Here the remains of a well were found. Given the nature of the site, this must have been a cistern.[240]

these are decorated with medallions which are about 50 centimeters (20 inches) wide.[237] Above the probable site of the altar, at the springing of the vaulting, protrudes a slab of stone that may have been a lectern.

Chapels are often found in towers or over the gate of a castle. The chapel at Duino, where both conditions are met, was in the ideal position.

Next to the tower was a tiny construction that may have been the gatekeeper's house.

The scantness of the remains elsewhere in the castle, the primitive building techniques found in the walls, and the lack of datable details, make it difficult to say anything more about the rest of the castle. It should also be borne in mind that the rebuilding and restoration of the last two hundred years have further reduced the original parts.[241]

Duino is mentioned in documents from the tenth century onwards. In 921 "Berengar gave the castle to the patriarch Federico,"[242] but it is

The chapel of the old castle, still recognizable from the small Romanesque window (detail left), the vaulting above the sanctuary, fragments of frescoes, and the stone lectern.

not until 1158 that we find reference to a family of *ministeriali* installed by the patriarch, who took the name of Duino.[243] We know nothing about any fortification dating from the Roman period. As we have seen, this was most probably not on the site of either the old or the new castle but in "the area called Valcatino."[244]

A sculpture in the grounds of the castle of Duino. The grounds have many ancient statues and sculptures, probably of local provenance.

It is impossible that the site of the first castle can already have been fortified in Roman times, since it can only have acquired significance as a site in the Middle Ages. At this later date, the limited space available would have been sufficient for the modest demands of the time, there was no threat of attack, and sufficient water could be collected in a cistern. The whole site could well have been an exceptionally secure and impregnable residence for the patriarch's governor.

We do not know at what point the governor moved here, nor even, following Berengar's donation, whether there was a noble residence at Duino. In fact, the earliest records date from the mid twelfth century, the period in which castles built on high places were becoming more common and lords were beginning to abandon their feudal manors.

The change of site

The differences between early medieval and late medieval castles generally became less obvious as a result of constant rebuilding as well as restoration.

At Duino, in contrast, the distinctive characteristics of the older and the newer buildings have been preserved. The building of the new castle not only left intact the form and dimensions of the old one, but the change of site is indicative of the reasons that led to the abandonment of the security of the cliff.

There is no doubt that the old castle was too small for the demands of the nobility of the late Middle Ages. The lack of a convenient access route meant that horses and wheeled vehicles had to stay in a courtyard outside the castle.

Moreover, although the castle enjoyed an excellent view over the sea, it was not in a position to observe what was happening on the landward side, though the important road to Trieste passed close by. For the medieval nobility, always short of money, control of roads was an important source of revenue.[245] Under the pretext of protecting passing merchants, the owner of the castle would demand tolls that, in a period of rapid economic expansion, could amount to considerable sums of money. The patriarch had to keep reminding his vassal at Duino that his duty was to protect the road and allow the merchants to pass, and he had to compel the master of Duino to reduce the tolls he was charging.[246]

The choice of site for a new and larger castle fell on the highest point in the area. This would not only guarantee a view of all the surrounding area, but would also mean the castle was conspicuous from all directions, symbolizing the power of the lords of Duino to all who traveled the road to Trieste.

We do not know when construction of the new castle began. Neither do we know who was responsible for it, and whether it was built for a specific purpose. However, the reason was definitely not the destruction of the old castle, as from 1363, and even in the seventeenth century, this was referred to as *Duinus Vetus* or *Rocca inferiore* (Old Duino, or the Lower Castle), to distinguish it from the new or upper castle.[247]

The new castle

Visitors to Trieste are struck by the imposing construction which dominates Duino. When they reach the village and look for the castle, however, they are surprised to find nothing but a small tower and gate, surmounted by the arms of the della Torre family. Nothing else is to be seen from here. Beyond the gate extends the site of the old burg which, after destruction in the First World War, was turned into gardens.[248] An avenue leads up through the gardens to an imposing wall, which appears even more impressive as a result of the quality of its workmanship and the half-tower which strengthens it in the center.

Behind the wall, dominating the whole castle, stands one of the finest towers of the region. Like the wall, it has battlements. The tower appears to rise directly out of the half-tower curve in the center of the outer wall, although in reality it stands slightly behind

Protected on the seaward side by a sheer cliff, the new castle of Duino, with its splendid tower, is defended on the landward side by a solid shield wall.

Luxuriant vegetation in the gardens at Duino. Because of the steep terrain, the only way to create a garden was on small, typically Mediterranean, terraces.

125

Four-light mullion window in Duino new castle. Though it looks Romanesque, it is probably a 19th-century imitation.

A blocked two-light ogee window in Duino new castle.

it and to the left. The visual impression is designed to persuade anyone approaching of the strength of the castle. Few other castles can boast of such an intriguing façade, or one which is so aesthetically pleasing.

The effect must have been even greater up to a century ago, when the outer wall was still standing near the present moat. The original appearance of the fortified entrance has been described by Bodo Ebhard and Pichler as it was at the time of the First World War:[249]

The first enceinte is formed by a wide moat defended by an antemural. A drawbridge over the moat leads to the first entrance to the fortress. A second wall with battlements follows, with a strong bastion placed at the end towards the west to defend the entrance… But the best defense against the new siege machines was the third bastion to the north, beneath which another deep ditch still contains the dungeons which were used for prisoners.[250]

Today the entrance still consists of a gate in the west wing, under which a broad passage leads into the courtyard after a sharp bend. Unlike the external wall, the courtyard is welcoming and pleasant. Three-storey buildings, their façades pierced by rectangular windows, stand on three sides. The fourth side is taken up by the tower, which protrudes into the courtyard. The courtyard was once a large open area that now is enclosed completely by buildings; these, generally only one room deep, appear to be of relatively recent date.

In the eastern wall there is what appears to be a Romanesque window with four arches, probably post-medieval.[251] The ogee arches of a blocked two-light window in the south wall may be older. The ogivals, which are much weathered, have been carved from a single piece of stone and are in a deliberately archaicizing style.

The architectural history of the castle is uncertain. We have no inscriptions or documents which refer to it. All we have is a plan which was made in 1639 by Giovanni Pieroni, the Hapsburg military engineer, in connection with the planned rebuilding of the castle, which by then was in a state of disrepair. The plan shows a castle that in general is very similar to the present one.[252]

The building history of the castle can be divided into four phases: the original medieval construction, and additions and alterations in the Renaissance, in the seventeenth century, and in the nineteenth and twentieth centuries.

The medieval castle

The medieval part of the castle comprises only a small part of the present building. The adaption of the castle into living accomodation has so masked the medieval core that only detailed architectural analysis can identify the original parts.[253] There is a walled-up Gothic window in the part of the castle overlooking the sea, the least vulnerable side. This would suggest that the oldest part of the castle was here.

The only recognizably medieval part of the castle is the tower. This, with its dressed rectangular blocks of stone and imposing size, is certainly the finest castle tower in Friuli. Miotti thought it Roman precisely because of its size and its unusual position at the corner of the inner courtyard, with no connection to the rest of the buildings.

This odd arrangement is, however, similar to a feature which is found in a number of castles built in southern Germany in the thirteenth century. This is the so-called protecting wall, which in the later Middle

The massive shield wall and the tower behind it make the new castle of Duino the most powerful of all Friuli castles.

FOLLOWING PAGES:
The new castle of Duino, one of the finest buildings on the Adriatic, where, partly thanks to its owners, many celebrated artists and writers have gathered.

Ages was constructed in castles on the model of Duino in order to protect them on the side most vulnerable to attack. Such walls, which were particularly high and already quite strong, were made even stronger by the addition of corner towers. Within the wall there might be the main tower, though this was not always the case. In all the cases which are known to me, the position of the castle made it possible to develop a much more open and welcoming

similar date, despite its medieval appearance, but it is deliberately archaicizing, an ingenious feature to make the tower and wall look like work of the Hohenstaufen period. The lighter, decorative rustication cannot date from the medieval era. In the center of this new fortification there should however be an older wall, dating from the period when the tower was built.[254] This wall, which may have been as high as the present outer wall, was more than one meter (three feet) thick.

As in all castles, the tower door is situated at a height several meters from the ground.

The corner of the shield wall at Duino, with rustication reminiscent of that of the Middle Ages but less solid and more decorative.

style of architecture behind the protection of the outer wall, exactly as can be seen at Duino.

The outer wall that we see today is certainly of a later date, given that its five-meter thick construction reveals the desire to create defenses which would be strong enough to withstand cannonfire. The rustication found on the tower and outer wall is of a

The medieval parts of the castle at Duino are exceptional and without equal in Italy. At the beginning of the twentieth century, Bobo Ebhard noted that the architectural models for Duino have to be sought in the castles built around 1200 in Austria, and, above all, in southern Germany. Given this unusual choice of model, the question of the origins of the design of Duino Castle is intriguing. In

the long and well-documented history of the castle, only Ugo VI could have undertaken to build this castle, since he alone had the financial means to fund such a costly venture.

It is difficult to form any conclusions about what particularly influenced the architectural details, beyond observing that Ugo VI traveled a great deal and would have seen many castles being built. His construction of the castle at Trieste, which he himself paid for, is evidence of his activity as a builder of castles,

century, then the castle of Duino is a relatively late example and cannot have provided models for other castles in the region. Duino is a classic example of how difficult it is to date castles, which is often made worse by lapses in the typology.

The interior of Duino castle, for the most part restored after the damage of the First World War to recreate rooms which are typical of a medieval castle but also of a Baroque palace.

for which he most probably used master builders, experts who offered their services in all the great constructions being undertaken at the time. In the fourteenth century, for example, we find at Tricesimo evidence of an expert engineer whose rather unusual methods caused a sensation.[255]

If, as seems probable, the tower and original outer wall date from the mid fourteenth

The Renaissance

Although Ugo VI left numerous offspring at his death in 1391, by 1395 the Duino family had already died out. The castle passed by marriage to the Walsee family, which, up to its neck in debt, in 1472 sold it to Emperor Frederick III.[256] From this time the castle of Duino was lived in and administered by

Portrait of Mathias Hofer, attributed to Lambert Sustris. In the 16th century, the Hofer family, lords of Duino, rebuilt the castle in the form it retains today.

one would expect of an earlier date: the lack of openings for cannon and the narrowness of the platforms for them are typical of the early period of firearms, not of the years around 1500, when bastions had taken the place of walls.

By 1500, the development of the bastion, which could withstand cannonfire, was well advanced, yet this seems to have had no influence at Duino. This absence is easily explained: the proud Hofer lords of Duino were interested not so much in a castle that could safeguard imperial power as in a traditional castle that could satisfy their desire for a secure seat for their own power and could convey their status.

Changes in castle architecture came about, then, not so much for military reasons as to express power. It is for this reason that Duino preserved its medieval appearance. Only a private individual would have had the idea of decorating the corners of the building with rustication like that found in the Hohenstaufen castles, a style with a long history which, quite apart from any practical value, had served to distinguish the architecture of the feudal castle.

We know that it was the Hofer castellans who were responsible for this restoration, since they paid for most of it, lending money to the emperor. They were thus able to obtain an extension of their mandate, which was scrupulously observed, "until repayment in full is obtained for all the expenses which have been sustained for the new defenses and their maintenance."[259]

The wing with the living accommodation was most probably refurbished at the same time as the rest of the work. The buildings around the courtyard must also date from this time. Thus, for the first time, the castle had the dual functions of defense and accommodation, the characteristic feature of Duino today, though in reality defensive aspects were still clearly subordinated to the castle's principal function as the family seat. The result was that while still respecting certain military requirements, Duino became the splendid residence we see today.

castellans, the most important of whom belonged to the Hofer family.

In 1508, after a siege lasting just a few hours, Duino fell to the Venetians,[257] to revert after only a few months to Hapsburg control following the victory of the League of Cambrai against Venice in 1508. Johannes Hofer, the new castellan, had the task of rebuilding the castle so that it would be strong enough to withstand further attack.[258]

The present outer wall, and the walls in the field in front of the castle, which were recorded by Pichler and Ebhard, probably date from this building campaign after 1508.[257] Here, too, the construction is what

*The beautiful oval staircase
in Duino castle, part of the
17th-century restoration.
It is in the style of Bernini
rather than of Palladio.*

*FOLLOWING PAGES:
The furnishings and furniture
in the castle, now dispersed,
were a mixture of Venetian
and Austrian. Marie Thurn
und Taxis, the patron of
Rainer Maria Rilke, restored
the castle and its interiors
after it suffered damage in
the First World War.*

The seventeenth century

Later modifications can be described fairly briefly. We know what the castle looked like in 1639, thanks to the plan made by the Hapsburg engineer. This stated that the defenses needed strengthening and that the steps were in a poor state of repair.

In 1653, the Thurn family, inheriting by way of the female line, took over the castle from the Hofers. Thanks to the Thurns' wealth, the castle was once again restored but no change was made to the defenses.[260] Any such improvement would not in any case have been in the owners' interests since the decision to avoid a military role meant that Duino would not be involved in war and would thus be safe from destruction. The Thurns were instead more interested in improving the living quarters.

It is to the Thurns that we owe the beautiful oval staircase, always referred to as the "Palladian staircase." The staircase, however, does not appear on the 1639 plan. Although Palladio designed a beautiful oval staircase in Venice, and included many others in his plans, such a formal element became common only in the Roman High Baroque, when Bernini designed one for Palazzo Barberini. The staircase at Duino, the only Baroque element in the castle, must therefore belong to the work carried out after 1639.

The nineteenth and twentieth centuries

More work was carried out in the nineteenth century. Both the last Thurn owner of Duino when it was passed down to a Thurn daughter when the male line ran out and her daughter in turn, who married a prince of the Thurn und Taxis family, were deeply attached to Duino and did much to preserve and embellish it. The pseudomedieval walls and castellations were added to the old castle by this last Thurn owner, who also added the castellations on the entrance wall and tower in the new castle, replacing the turret top on the tower.[261] The layout of the garden also dates from this period. With its terraces, it is a good example of the contemporary taste for eclecticism that was popular in garden design too. This last work was carried out by her

The long gallery, one of the finest rooms in the castle, had a remarkable collection of busts, paintings, and chinoiserie.

137

The external wall, with a classic Erker.

The wellhead in the courtyard.

daughter, the first Thurn und Taxis owner, who after the First World War considerably extended the gardens, taking in the area of the burg.[262]

The restoration carried out as a result of the extensive war damage seems for the most part to have respected the integrity of the castle. The building to the west of the tower over the present entrance, which had been completely destroyed, was reconstructed in a medieval style.

Despite the extensive restoration and rebuilding, today Duino Castle is essentially a sixteenth-century building which retains the essential elements of the medieval plan dating from the mid fourteenth century. Since the medieval castles of Udine and Gorizia have not survived, Duino is the most important castle in Friuli. The castle of Udine was completely rebuilt as early as the sixteenth century, while the castle at Gorizia is a very free restoration of a medieval castle in the spirit of the 1930s. Only the castle of Tricesimo, unfortunately disfigured by inappropriate restoration, can be compared to Duino as a major example of secular architecture in Friuli.

Once again, it would appear that a precondition for the survival of a castle is continuous occupation by a family that has owned it for centuries and is prepared to devote itself

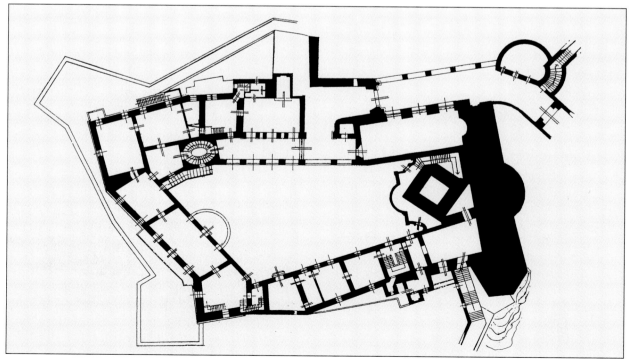

The entrance is decorated
with classical statues which,
together with the luxuriant
Mediterranean vegetation and
the view over the sea, make
the castle seem more like a
delightful villa.

Ground plan of the castle,
showing clearly the strong
shield wall with the tower
obliquely across it.
The courtyard is surrounded
by residential wings just
one room deep.

unstintingly to its conservation. The local authorities in Friuli had the responsibility of ensuring that this splendid and unique castle, almost a thousand years old, should survive for the enjoyment of future generations. Unfortunately, the autonomous region of Friuli has recently fallen short of its responsibilities, allowing the collection of furniture and art treasures—a collection formed over many centuries—to be dispersed. After this serious loss, the current threat is that the castle will be used for administrative offices. This would cause irrevocable damage and mar the appearance of the castle.

Continuity between the Roman world and the Middle Ages

Politics, society, and economy

Although the often proposed hypothesis of continuity between Roman defensive structures and medieval castles is, as we have seen, of no relevance, recent historical work has uncovered an entirely different kind of continuity. Traditionally, the period between late antiquity and the early Middle Ages was always regarded as marking a drastic historical break, politically, socially, and economically.[263] Nowadays, however, historians are beginning to speak in terms of continuity. If we regard the period between late antiquity and early Middle Ages as a time of gradual transformation rather than one of abrupt change, then the origins of castles and of the feudal system also need to be regarded differently.

The Roman origins of feudalism

Two major problems threatened the Roman Empire in the last two centuries of its existence: the growing pressure of nomadic tribes on its border and the increasing inefficiency of the bureaucracy and financial administration. The emperor Diocletian reformed taxation so that it became based on the amount of agricultural land used, which was easy to verify. In order to avoid these taxes and fines, which could be heavy, in the fourth century freemen or entire villages began to hand over their land to rich lords, often members of influential senatorial families, whose connections and private military forces meant that they were little affected by the increasingly onerous taxation.[264] Peasants who handed over their land to such a protector often received it back as a tenant, and had the benefit of the landowner's protection.[265] Later, while tenants were required to work on an agreed area of land, the owner succeeded in gaining the right to tax them, in this way gaining considerable discretionary power over them.[266] The process reveals not only how the possession of land was increasingly becoming the economic and political basis of power, but also how close the bond between peasant and the landowner—and the land itself—already was.

At the same time, the great landowners took on administrative and juridical functions. In particular, the chief functionaries of the Empire concentrated power in their own hands, just as the feudal lords would subsequently do. It is significant that they already had the title of *comes* (count).[267] The *comes civitatis* (count of the state) had wide-ranging executive powers. Within the district he was responsible for, he had control of the army and of the administration of law and taxation.[268] By the time of Constantine, the *comites* already had his place in the hierarchical system of the court.

The same phenomenon was to be found in all the Germanic kingdoms, where the old administrative positions of *comes* and *dux* (leader) now referred to followers of the king or to military leaders.[269] It was only in the Carolingian period that the title of *comes*, which traditionally referred to an administrative position, became an inherited title referring to nobility.

Roman traditions in the age of the barbarian invasions

Late antiquity saw not only the transfer of many state functions into the hands of powerful local lords but also the beginnings of the formation of the medieval nobility. Major senatorial families were able to maintain their position in late antiquity only if they succeeded in holding on to their land. This

Sculpture and decorations of the 8th-century Lombard Tempietto in Cividale, clearly showing the continuation of Roman tradition in the Middle Ages.

was possible only if they were politically astute and if their land was favorably sited.

In southern France, senatorial families had an important role throughout the period of domination of the western Goths, the Burgundians, and the Merovingians. Right from the beginning, their power was based not on imperial patronage but on their own revenue.[270] For them, the links with the Roman world consisted primarily in the preservation of the culture of the elite and of its privileges; as far as they were concerned, the Roman Empire had never ended.[271] In fact, their circumstances even improved as a result of the various problems experienced by central government. Their economic, politi-

cal, and military power continued to grow; it was they, above all, as representatives of Roman culture, who appointed the bishops. In this way they also gained control over municipal power.[272]

The senatorial families of Gaul were certainly not the only ones to be unaffected by the epoch-making events of 476, when the Roman empire in the west came to an end. The Roman army had for a long time included many Germanic soldiers, while emperors now came from all corners of the Empire—and rarely were as educated as Theoderic was to be.[273] As far as the Byzantines were concerned, the Gothic kings were magistrates, equivalent to the highest

Roman functionaries. The king was regarded as a military officer employed by the Romans, the only difference being that hired officers did not need to be appointed by the emperor. The king fought wars on behalf of the imperial government. In a sense he was employed by it, the commander of a barbarian kingdom, without putting into doubt the integrity of the Empire.[274] Under Odoacer and Theoderic, the late Roman state continued seamlessly, without interruption. With the separate provincial administrations, the barbarian kings needed the skilled Roman bureaucracy more that ever.[275] The Roman aristocrats were the possessors of the cultural inheritance of Rome and held the key posts in administration and the Church, as well as being the major landowners. The Germanic leaders, on the other hand, controlled the army and occupied the main political positions, as much as they could do in view of their small numbers.[276] It was only at the end of the transitional period, with the emergence of the medieval system, that the two ruling classes merged into a new, single elite.

More dramatic change came with the Byzantine reconquest, which began with the aim of restoring the Roman Empire. The long wars meant destruction on a large scale, the depopulation of cities, and a further weakening of trade and crafts. Agriculture became increasingly the main feature of the economy.

The Byzantine wars also accelerated the replacement of an army that was controlled by the center with locally recruited militias that provided garrisons for the towns and *castra*. Soldiers lived like dependent peasants in state, church, or private encampments. Their commanders, known as *tribuni* or *duces*, came to be local governors, and civil officials began to disappear.

The seat of government in Byzantium was soon unable to control these regional potentates, whose power became hereditary in the families of the great landowners.[277] They had long had control of local jurisdiction and the collection of taxes, and they continued to play a decisive role in the organization of the local militias, which were made up of peasants who paid tribute, often to them.

In this way, a protofeudal political system of local government emerged out of the Roman imperial administration.[278] These powerful local lords clearly served their own local interests rather than the wider ideal of the Empire. Thus, even before the emergence of a fully-fledged feudal system, its negative sides, which were to remain with it for its entire history, were becoming apparent.

This combination of landownership, office-holding, and political power continued under Longobard rule, when the office of *gastaldi* came to play a decisive role. Originally no more than administrators of the royal estates, they extended their own legitimate public powers so much in relation to those of the *duces* that the most powerful of them succeeded in gaining the title of *comes*. This process continued under the Carolingians. Great landowners, in their role as judges and major office-holders, became *comites*, succeeding in changing this appointment into a claim to nobility which eventually became hereditary.

Land and power

When the Goths invaded Italy, their king Theoderic promised a third of the country to his soldiers as a reward, in this way spurring on his followers by granting them extensive state or imperial lands.[279] A similar phenomenon occurred under the Carolingians, who obtained the loyalty of their vassals by sharing out land among them. This land was at first immense, but when it was all divided up, imperial power fragmented.[280]

The seizure of land by the Goths did not, however, lead to the expropriation of the Roman *latifundia*, or landed estates. The fears of the landowners, to their own surprise, proved unfounded; King Theodahad himself maintained that the Ostrogoth occupation could not be compared to that of the barbarians.[281]

The subsequent Longobard invasion was very different. The power and authority of the king still depended solely on his personal following, which could be obtained only by means of gifts of land, since every Longobard lived off his land.[282] Furthermore, the Longobards were few in number and only a small proportion of the population of Italy.

In Friuli, the first Lombard duchy in Italy, the duke installed there was Gisulf I, nephew of King Alboin, on the condition that "there stay with him the best *farae*, that is, those family groups on whose military skills one could depend, together with herds of strong mares."[283] The new duke divided the land among his followers in such a way that one might speak of an almost total expropriation of the land.

Thus free Longobards, called *Arimanni*, did not remain purely a warrior class but in addition to their land ownership gradually came to take up administrative roles, becoming responsible for law and order and justice, and acquiring privileges.[284] As the Longobards expanded westwards and southwards, the number remaining behind in occupied areas increased, meaning that those who moved on were increasingly dependent on the collaboration of the local population.

The result was that the class of rich landowning Romans did not everywhere disappear. While loyal Longobard soldiers were rewarded with expropriated estates, it was also prudent to gain the support of Roman landowners by allowing them to retain their land.[285]

The great estates

In this period, the relationship between town and country changed dramatically. While it might have been expected that, in view of their way of life, the Germanic conquerors would have preferred the country, they instead exercised their rule from the towns, inheriting and reviving Roman institutions.[286] They lived in Roman buildings and used Roman public buildings in the towns, and never lived in the countryside.[287]

But while the towns survived as political centers, the economic center of gravity moved to the country.[288] After the Byzantine conquest, towns and trade declined dramatically. The edict of Rotari makes no mention of any commercial or manufacturing activity, showing the extent to which these two areas of economic activity, so essential under the Roman Empire, had declined in importance.[289] Towns were now little more than administrative centers with meager populations.[290]

They remained important in terms only of defense, by virtue of the solid walls that protected them and their role as supply bases for the military.

The majority of the Longobard soldiers lived on the land they had received from the duke. From the point of view of our study, the main question is to look at the kinds of buildings and houses they inhabited. The Longobard conquerors lived in large family units in wooden houses that resembled large huts. It is unlikely that in Friuli the Lombards reused Roman villas, since houses divided up into rooms like this did not suit their needs, especially as at first their way of living was too different from that of the Romans.[291] In contrast to northern France, where excavations have revealed a number of examples of the fate of Roman villas after the end of the Roman Empire, there is no such archaeological evidence in Friuli to suggest what happened to villas here. The Franks never lived in the Roman villas, but used them for building stone for their cemeteries.[292]

The typical Longobard rural dwelling before the Longobards became Romanized would have consisted of a courtyard surrounded by walls. Paul the Deacon described the dwellings of even important Longobard lords with the disdainful eye of a Roman, as merely a few huts protected by a palisade.[293] An anecdote from the seventh century tells of a night spent by one Judicael at his house in Penpont. In the morning he was woken by the peasants crowding on to the bridge in order to bring their tributes into the courtyard,[294] which was surrounded by a deep ditch or moat, as would be found later in mottes and fortified farmsteads.

Despite the lack of archaeological evidence, it is likely that as early as late antiquity there were many such nobles' homes protected by palisades, thorn hedges, mounds, and, where the topography allowed, moats, as at Invillino. They must have been made of wood, like the first castles, as otherwise it would be impossible to explain why so little evidence of them survives.

We can say, therefore, that the development of the castle began already in late antiquity. Since it is generally agreed that hilltop castles are a relatively recent phenomenon, we must conclude that noble families,

if it is taken as a generalization… Many villas survived the invasions, wars, and succession of rulers…"[296]

There is not a single Roman villa known in northern Italy that was reused by the Lombards. Nonetheless, it is not possible to say that the villas were systematically destroyed. There are references to villas still existing in occupied territories from the eighth to the tenth century.[297] Documents attest to the fact that great rural estates and their villas frequently ended up being given to the Church, and as a result monasteries

Many of the frescoes at Pompeii depict villas with varied architecture and numerous towers.

even in the eleventh century, lived mainly in dwellings of this kind.[295] The late antique dwelling of a rich lord, whether he was Roman or Germanic, is thus the source of the medieval castle. In them lived the dominant rural class which, in the centuries between antiquity and the end of the Middle Ages, acquired the juridical position that marked out the owner of a medieval castle.

Roman villas under Germanic rule

It is commonly believed that the Roman villa disappeared with the barbarian invasions. According to Azevedo, who has studied specifically the survival of Roman villas, this is wrong: "Nothing could be more mistaken,

were often built on the site of villas.[298]

There are at least three documented cases of Roman villas being reused by new owners: on the Moselle in Germany, at Nenning and Berthelming, by the Merovingians;[299] and in Italy, where the *comites*, Adalbertus and Vuidus—of Germanic origin, to judge from their names—had villas. A certain Geronimo, a subdeacon and owner of a villa, is also mentioned in the sources, but he was evidently a Roman who had retained his property.[300] The number of examples is small not because few villas were reused, but because written documents from this time are quite rare.

The document that tells us of Adalbertus and Vuidus, who administered justice in their villas, shows clearly how continuity between late antiquity and the Middle Ages, from the *villa rustica* to the castle, took place on a a variety of levels.[301] Adalbertus and Vuidus, Germanic conquerors living in a Roman house and holding Roman offices, already possessed the two conditions for territorial power that would be characteristic of the Middle Ages: the administration of justice and ownership of land.

From villa to castle: architectural continuity

Many scholars have studied the survival of Roman defensive structures in medieval castles but to date no evidence has been found to demonstrate continuity between the Roman villa and the castle. The reason for this almost certainly lies in the fact that the image that we generally have of the Roman villa has nothing whatsoever to do with castles. We think of the villa as a spacious complex with green spaces, low and open, the country house of a rich citizen. This image is, however, totally mistaken, because it omits all the essential characteristics of the typical country villa. Like the medieval castle, the villa was also a busy farm, more cattleshed and grain store than palace. It was a small self-sufficient unit, run by a landowner and his family who had long ago abandoned the town for the country. Long before the Germanic invasions, it was defended by a wall and towers.

Crucial for the understanding of the form of these villas is Förtsch's study of Pliny's letters. The two villas Pliny describes, which date from the first century after Christ, had towers.[302] Förtsch provides a wealth of illustrations of such villas in Roman frescoes.

In the Roman villa, the tower did not have a defensive function. On the upper floor it had loggias or dovecotes. As an architectural feature designed to make the seat of a rural lord stand out, the tower is therefore not only a medieval phenomenon.

It is hard to establish when towers acquired a defensive function. The late Roman villas already give an impression of great solidity and are surrounded by towers. At a time of increasing danger in the countryside, when bands of robbers were making property inse-

cure, the walls around villas would have been made higher.

The same is true of the imperial villas, such as the Palace of Diocletian at Spalato, which looked like the classic *castrum*. Similar villas, though more modest in size, have been found in Albania, in the Balkans, in the Moselle region, and in Roman Gaul.[303] The example of Pfalzel, near Treviri, shows that such structures could survive the barbarian invasions.[304] According to Miotti, excavations carried out in 1823 by M. della Torre near Moimacco uncovered a first-century BC villa that had been occupied for centuries and which in the late Roman period acquired four towers.[305]

The transition from the villa or large country house of late antiquity to a defensive

Wall frescoes at Pompeii. The top of the tower of the landowner's villa has curved elements, which prefigure medieval crenellations.

145

construction—and thus, in the final analysis, to the castle—was also encouraged by the fact that by the late Empire peasant settlements organized along military lines had begun to spring up around such villas. In emergencies they could help defend the fortified heart of the domain.[306]

As such complexes had fewer defenses and could guarantee only a modest degree of security, they cannot be called fortifications in the sense that they defended the surrounding area. But it is precisely because of this limited military and defensive role that they resemble castles. It is not surprising then that in France there are cases of the survival of Roman villas as well as of their transformation into castles.[307]

Often it was not a Roman villa that became a castle but an early medieval rural farmstead belonging to a noble. The fact that documents of the tenth century speak less of the *curtes* and more of the *castrum* allows us to date this shift to this period.[308]

The palaces, especially the royal Carolingian palaces, that are always cited as the forerunners of the castle, really had much more in common with the seignorial country house than with the true castle. They reveal how little the great rural dwellings changed in either form or function from the buildings of late antiquity. The shift that led to the emergence of the castle on hilltops, on the other hand, was surprisingly swift and far-reaching. This did not occur until the Middle Ages proper; the castle is a purely medieval phenomenon.

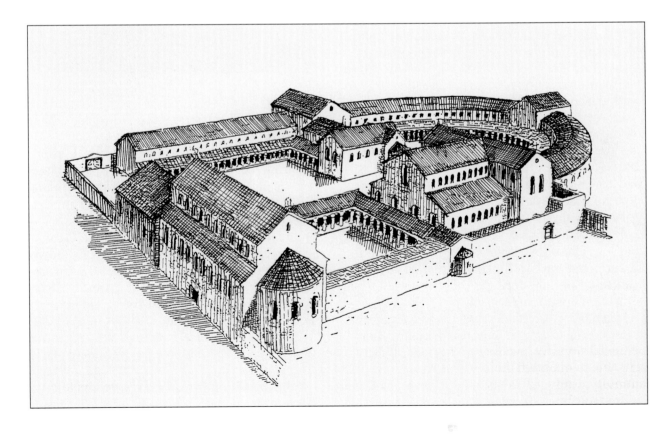

The reconstruction of the royal and imperial court of Ingelheim, an interesting example of Roman tradition surviving in the architecture of power of the early Middle Ages. The complex has more in common with the Roman villa than with the medieval castle.

From Lavariano to Strassoldo

The origins of a noble castle

In the marshy land lying between present-day Palmanova and the Adriatic coast, the raised area within the loop of a river at Strassoldo was an attractive site for a fortified settlement, even though cultivation was not possible in the immediate vicinity. Neither a village nor a seignorial residence could have existed here in late antiquity.

The placenames themselves reveal no trace of Roman origins.[310] The name Strassoldo itself is Germanic, deriving from the combination of *Strasse* (road) and *Au*, in its old meaning of island.[311] In a depopulated area, placenames were derived from features in the landscape, in this case an island near the road. The change in name attested around 1200, from *Strasau* to *Strasolt* (*Strassen-Halt*, "a halt on the road"), reflects the fact that by this time the castle on the island must have been seen chiefly in its role as controlling the road.[312] All this does not permit the first castle on the site to be dated to earlier than the first form of its name.[313]

Unlike the majority of the castles in Friuli, Strassoldo was not a fief belonging to the patriarch. The family was one of the few houses of independent lordships, quite distinct from the great majority of feudal families. While these latter arrived in the region only with the patriarchs, the property rights of families of independent lords and their castles had much older origins.

For this very reason, the longstanding Strassoldo family legend of the investiture of Woldariche by the patriarch of Aquileia in the eleventh century has no basis in truth. The apparently plausible suggestion given by A. Rossetti that the patriarch Poppo reorganized his feudal possessions between Aquileia and present-day Palmanova in the 1030s, freeing all the land that would later belong to Strassoldo, might seem to give support to this oral tradition. However, rather than start, as did Rossetti, from the premise that the patriarch gave these lands to Woldariche, we must remember that the patriarch was not in a position to give the lands away because they did not belong to him.[314]

The case of Strassoldo is interesting not only because the castle was built in a marshy, and therefore secure, area, but also because it

The coat of arms of the counts of Strassoldo, frescoed over one of the fireplaces in the castle. It shows clearly the relationships between the noble families of Friuli.

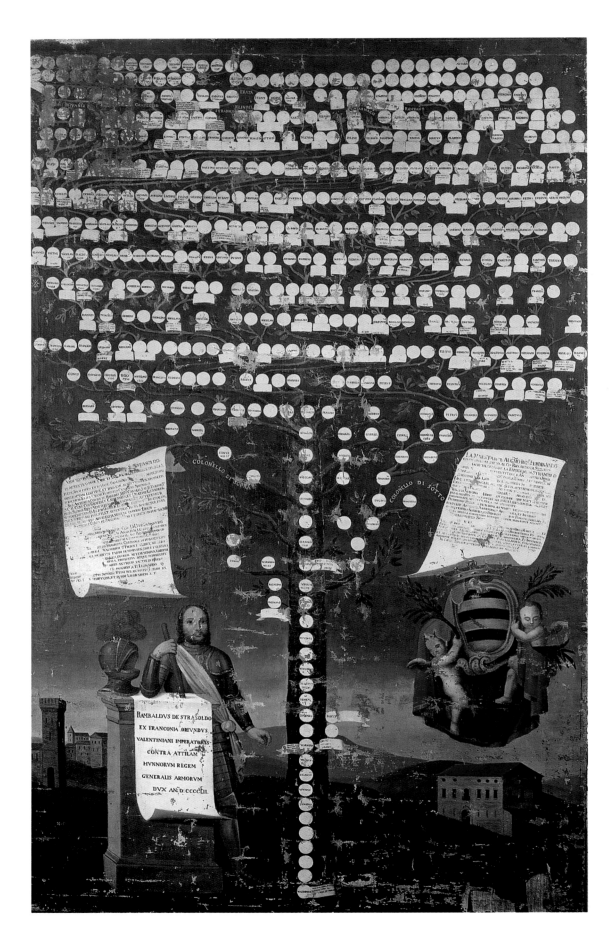

A fine 18th-century family tree in the upper castle at Strassoldo, illustrating the oral tradition according to which the founder of the family was a Roman commander who fought in the army of general Flavius Etius against Attila the Hun.

yields evidence about the origins of the family. Slightly to the west, in the present-day Castions di Strada, was situated a large Roman estate which at the time of the Longobard invasion[315] had been assigned, along with other estates, to a Longobard military leader whose base was present-day Lavariano. Lavariano is a Roman place-name; it may derive from the "villa of Laberius."[316] The residence of the new Longobard lords was probably a typical Longobard rural farmstead, out of which the medieval *cortina* developed.[317]

There is evidence that in 776 the district was in the hands of a Longobard, a certain Walando di Lavariano, who was killed near the river Brenta while fighting in the army of the Friuli duke Rotgano against Charlemagne. His lands were confiscated and given to one of Charlemagne's followers, a certain Paulinus, who is described as educated and who in fact later became patriarch. The land at Lavariano may also have passed to the patriarchs. However, this legal transfer must have been annulled at a later point, otherwise it is not possible to explain how the family could have owned allodial property—that is, property not given in fief by the patriarch—in Strassoldo and elsewhere. It may be an example of the many restitutions of expropriated estates that were made to great landowners by Louis the Pious, successor to Charlemagne.[318]

Only in 1190 does the name Lavariano again appear, with a certain Bernardus de Lavariano. By the following year he has become Bernardus de Straso. In 1210 three brothers, Lodovico, Corrado, and Artuico di Lavariano are recorded, though the following year they are referred to as *de Strasho*.[319] It is evidence of the survival of Longobard law. The change of name reveals a transfer of residence from Lavariano to Strassoldo.

Throughout western Europe in this period, noble castles were being constructed on hilltops and noble families were taking on the names of the new castles, the new symbols of dominion. Castles were built by preference on hilltops and peaks, which meant that the nobles had to have suitable terrain available. The lords of Lavariano had no suitable hilltop sites on their land. The raised land in the river loop in the middle of the marshes, at the heart

of great estates and close to a major road, fulfilled all the criteria for the building of a castle in the early Middle Ages. Even if no documents tell of the construction of the castle of Strassoldo, it can nevertheless be dated to around 1190.[320]

Strassoldo is a good example of how castles originally developed. At a certain point in history, noble castles emerged out of rural seignorial manors. This occurred when the medieval system of dominion, with its system of the blood feud, required that the feudal lord should be protected by stronger walls of a castle.

The clearest indication of the extent to which the castle had become a center and guarantee of power for the resident family, and a symbol of that power, is the families' adoption of placenames as their own family name. Enclosed within the walls of the castle, the lord felt himself to be invulnerable.

An 18th-century painting still in the upper castle of Strassoldo, showing the departure of the children for the Jesuit school.

FOLLOWING PAGES:
The splendid complex of the upper and lower castles at Strassoldo lies in a loop framed by the arms of the river.

The Castle of Strassoldo

Where the plain of Friuli has almost reached sea level and the deep layers of sedimentary rock come to an end, the waters which have soaked into the ground at the foot of the Alps burst out again, to form streams and rivers that flow towards the sea. Between the arms of two such rivers that have emerged into the light of day, lies Strassoldo, perhaps the most picturesque castle in Friuli.

The site on the river, surrounded by extensive marshes and woods, was ideal for the building of a lowland castle, one that was to become the new power center of one of the most important families in the area.

What made the site additionally desirable was its proximity to major roads, such as the Stradalta, which linked Trieste and Venice and passed a few kilometers to the south; and the Via Julia Augusta, which corresponds more or less to the present road leading south to Aquileia and Grado. Many historians have erroneously believed that the position of the castle of Strassoldo was dictated by strategic considerations, and saw it as controlling the crossroads. But Strassoldo's distance from the Stradalta makes this theory implausible. Nor was Strassoldo built, as were the castle of Gradisca and the fortified town of Palmanova, as a bulwark against attack by the Hungarians and the Ottoman Turks.[321] The site was entirely inappropriate for such a purpose, since no one would have passed this way by choice.

The present building retains only a very few medieval parts. Even if in the Middle Ages it suffered little damage, it was badly damaged in the early sixteenth century and then abandoned for more than a hundred years by its owners, who preferred to reside elsewhere.[322] In the seventeenth century the surviving buildings were transformed into the Baroque residences, with their extensive gardens, that we see today.

It is, therefore, extremely difficult to form

The lord's residence of the upper castle, adjoining the old tower, is the most significant evidence of its secular past.

even an approximate picture of the appearance of the medieval castle. Nor is it possible, on the basis of those documents which have been published, to establish what reconstruction work was carried out before 1700. Strassoldo is therefore a rich area for study since the records concerning it in the archives in Venice have not yet been studied.

The fact that the documents mention—in a chronological order that has clearly been altered—various members of the Lavariano family, who have changed their name to

Strassoldo, suggests that by 1190 two different branches of the family had moved to Strassoldo, giving rise to the double castle structure, divided by an arm of the river, which is still visible today. The earliest surviving description of the castle already mentions two structures, each with a tower.[323] In his book on the castle, Marzio di Strassoldo argued plausibly that the castle would have been surrounded by a palisade and that the dwelling would have been on a modest scale and almost wholly in wood.[324]

The upper castle

An inventory of 1322 describes the state of the upper castle. The reason for the compilation of this inventory was the division at this time of the inheritance—a phenomenon typical of Friuli—between five brothers, each of whom was to obtain a share.

The date of construction of the tower, which is large enough to have been inhabited in the Middle Ages, is not known. Until the 19th century it had a fourth floor.

The most unusual feature of the inventory is the mention of a wooden tower (*balfredum de lignamine*).

Wooden defenses around the early medieval castle and its associated houses are to be expected, but the survival of a wooden tower in Italy in the early fourteenth century is surprising. The term *balfredum* is unequivocal evidence that this was no minor tower but the principal tower of the castle, probably even inhabited.

The importance attributed to this ancient feature, which would have dated from the construction of the earliest castle, can be deduced from the fact that the heir who received it was obliged to pay out of his own pocket for substantial restoration of part of the curtain wall. He was required to provide suitable foundations and rebuild the wall to the same height as the original.

Near this central point of the castle were the curtain walls, either one or two towers, and a gate, as well as two smaller entrances. Houses and storerooms are recorded within the boundary wall, though the inventory does not reveal their size or position.

Outside the boundary wall, to the north, was situated the burg, which is still visible today, and then the *porta Cistigna* (gate to Cistigna). The burg had "a dozen houses," stables, and outbuildings. The houses inside the castle enclosure were occupied by the lord and his family.[325] In the burg was the house of the *comune*, whose *loggia* was the center of the administration of "the use of common land, the collection of dues, the demarcation of boundaries, and the upkeep of roads, bridges, and defenses, as was customary throughout Friuli and the eastern Veneto."[326]

Despite the precision of the inventory, it fails to resolve many problems that arise in the context of the present structure. The imposing tower which today closes off the mansion on the left is unanimously described in the literature on the subject as dating from the tenth century, though there is nothing to suggest so early a date.[327] Indeed, the lack of any mention of a tower in the 1322 inventory means that it must be of later construction.

The tower's size and its imposing walls make it a striking piece of architecture. With an area of seven meters by nine (23 feet by

30), this was no ordinary tower, but one which could be lived in. Inside, the tower had no dividing walls, which was not unusual in such a building. The three floors were connected by three simple internal staircases. From the outside, access was by a ladder that could easily be pulled inside.[328] The ground floor of the tower was probably used as a storeroom for provisions that would not be spoiled by cold or damp. Plenty of stones were kept in the tower for dropping from the top should it come under attack.[329]

A tower in the walls, which is mentioned briefly in the 1322 inventory, cannot be the imposing one seen today. While towers in curtain walls were individually assigned to a split inheritance, the main towers, due to their importance, normally remained common property. Only in exceptional circumstances were they assigned to an owner (as was the case, for example, with the wooden *balfredum* at Strassoldo). If

ownership of a wooden tower was worth the high cost of building new walls, it follows that a stone tower must have been exceptionally valuable.

The tower at Strassoldo must therefore have been built after 1322, probably to replace the earlier wooden one.[330] The tower is almost completely built of brick, though the work is of poor quality. However, there is not one wall in the castle with dressed stone in which might be seen some evidence of local stonemasonry skill. Even the oldest walls are crudely built of rough stones, which are placed at random.[331] Since brickwork is found only in later phases of building, the materials used would also suggest that the tower was not built until the end of the fourteenth century.

The ground plan of the castle reveals a sharp corner near the side that always gives access to the interior of the castle. This feature, which is characteristic of bastions,

The 18th-century church in the middle of the upper castle, built on top of an earlier building which was recorded in the 14th century.

would suggest a date from the beginning of the early modern period. Such a date would appear to be confirmed by the powerful barrel vaults in the interior, heavy constructions that have no decorative function. The most likely explanation is that they were used as platforms for small cannon. They would therefore date from around 1500, or a little later. From what can be inferred from the plastering, these vaults are a later addition, and are

efforts to defend Friuli against devastating Hungarian invasions. The implausibility of this theory is demonstrated also by the doubts expressed by respected historians concerning the extent of the danger posed by the Hungarian attacks on Friuli.[333]

Still more puzzling is the problem of the church. Though this large building acquired its present form only in the eighteenth century, a chapel was in existence as early

The complex of lord's residence and church at the heart of the upper castle, a square with central European characteristics that are in part due to the nearness of the old border between Austria and Venice. The marriage of Field Marshall Radetzky to a member of the Strassoldo family took place in this church.

thus another reason to date the tower to the later Middle Ages.[332]

It is not possible, therefore, to date the tower on the basis of the information we have at our disposal. The issues are so complex that a plausible date could be reached only by detailed study. It is curious, however, that none of the many publications on Strassoldo have dealt with this problem. Instead, they have all unthinkingly accepted the assertion that it was built in the tenth century, in the context of the patriarch's

as 1334. This chapel was dedicated to St. Nicholas, the patron saint who protected against flooding, an occurrence that posed a serious threat to Strassoldo.

As a rule, castle chapels are to be found at the entrance to the village or in the lower court of the castle, but they are also found in the gatetower or, occasionally, in the living quarters of the castle. It is never the case that they constitute the center of the whole complex, as the church at Strassoldo does.

It would be necessary therefore to investi-

gate whether the position of the boundary wall has changed and whether the church is on a different site or stands on the foundations of an earlier construction (as is the case with the wooden *balfredum*).[334]

The center of a castle was normally a tower or *palas*, the symbol of the family's power. Churches too could be impressive buildings. The right of appointment to them was certainly an important privilege. At Strassoldo the family possessed two chapels, the earlier of which is now used as the ceme-

tery chapel. All the known family burial places are in the old church outside the castle. The chapel situated inside the walls of the castle became the parish church only in the eighteenth century, on the initiative of the family. Until its extension it was a small and relatively humble building, lacking any particular role. Its position at the center of the complex of the upper castle is therefore most unusual and is hard to interpret. It will remain a puzzle until more is known about the original structure of the complex.

A small raised corridor links the lord's residence with the gallery of the church, where the family attended services.

The lower castle

In 1360 the lower castle was similarly divided up between brothers, as we know from the inventory made at this time. In contrast to the inventory of forty years earlier for the upper castle, the present castle layout can be recognized in this description.

The manner in which the property was divided up is typical of this period in Friuli. The center of the castle, then as now, was a large rectangular building with an area of fourteen meters by seven (46 feet by 23), far bigger than any other tower in the region. The building, which is also called the *domus magna* (big house), surrounded by its own small wall, remained the joint property of all the brothers. Like the tower in the upper castle, this house also had three floors and no dividing walls inside, but had an entrance at ground level.

Expansion of this nucleus must have begun as early as 1366, the date for which we have written evidence of restoration.[335] This was probably carried out on the side that faced the courtyard and which, as it is in brick, not stone, must date from a later period.[336] In 1393 another brick building was added to the side of this. This marks the beginning of extensions that were to continue up to the eighteenth century.

Next to the *domus magna* and its boundary wall was a hamlet, a huddle of small houses and outbuildings including a small kitchen. The lord's household lived here, probably in two or three rows of houses built adjoining each other.[337]

Outside the castle was the so-called Borgo Nuovo (new village), which still today stands out between the two gates. Here there were more houses as well as numerous outbuildings and storerooms. Here too were the artisans who worked wood and iron.[338] Apart from the biggest house here, from this period there survive only the walls on each side of the great gate which led to the village, as well as part of the outer wall. The oldest parts of the outer wall, however, have been incorporated into houses built later, while the stretch of wall which is visible today, with its battlements and a gateway knocked through it for access to the courtyard, are more recent.

The differences between the upper and

The square block of the lord's residence and the beautiful gardens of the lower castle are reminiscent more of the villas of the Veneto than of a medieval castle.

lower castles, as is apparent from the two deeds of subdivision, are indicative of the rapid changes in castle-building in the fourteenth century. The ground plan for the lower castle has no sharp angles since from the outset the solid central construction

important and the lord's house became the center of the castle. If the fortified dwellings reached a height adequate to their importance, they might also take on the function of a central tower, a mark of power that was visible from afar.

Flanking the entrance with its obelisk, the distinctive symbol of feudal residence in Friuli, is the great medieval lord's house, in 1360 already called the domus magna (big house).

comprised the rectangular center of the structure. The internal defensive wall must have been built around it in a regular fashion. The days of the earliest castles, which had been of a somewhat temporary nature, and included many wooden features, were definitely over.

The earliest castles in general retained the character of a stronghold: they were built to an irregular layout, with large empty areas and small houses. Eventually they gave way to ever more solid and imposing architecture. Living accommodation became increasingly

It is no surprise then that apart from the tall *domus magna* no other large tower is mentioned. In any case, such a tower would have remained shared property. Instead, only the small towers on the curtain walls are mentioned as being divided up equally among the brothers.

Destruction and reconstruction after 1500

The first period of prosperity of the castles at Strassoldo dates, then, from the fourteenth century. This coincides with the peak of the family's power in the struggle for control of the area.

The later collapse of the rule of the patriarch in Friuli signified the end of the autonomy of the lords of Strassoldo. For this reason, the family initially put up a strong resistance to the new Venetian overlords. We do not know whether this oppostion resulted in damage to the castle. The only evidence of building activity at Strassoldo in the fifteenth century is the construction of two new stone bridges in 1492.[339]

The years around 1500 saw the last attempt to exploit the defensive functions of Strassoldo. The castle was included in the efforts to defend eastern Friuli against raids by the Ottoman Turks. After an inspection by the Venetian *provveditore* (supervisor) Pietro Marcello and *condottiere* (military general) Bartolomeo d'Alviano, the castle walls were built higher and were given new battlements.[340] This increased the castle's defensive capabilities, but it may also have been the cause of the serious damage that occurred at Strassoldo in the war between Venice and the League of Cambrai from 1509 to 1513.[341]

The war damage of these years coincided with a general economic crisis brought about by war, epidemics, and bad weather. A marked fall in the population meant that many houses in the village of Strassoldo were empty. A decrease in the area of land worked meant less revenue, making it impossible to think of rebuilding where structures had been destroyed. In any case, the military and political importance of the castle could not have been restored.

The various branches of the family went to live in Udine or in their other residences in the country. A description from 1587 tells us that the upper castle was at least habitable, even if it was not luxurious enough to merit the description *palazzo*, but the lower castle was probably abandoned and empty by this time.

The construction of the town of Palmanova in the late sixteenth century could not have resulted in the loss of Strassoldo's military importance, since this was already no longer.

All the same, the prospect was not received with enthusiasm at Strassoldo: "That fortress—which I am convinced the Lord God does not want—will be the ruin of this whole country. In my opinion, it will be a new Venetian colony." With Palmanova, just a short distance from Strassoldo, Venice strengthened its political presence in the area. The government of Venice had shown almost no interest in Strassoldo, and this move fed fears of a substantial loss of power by the family. The extent to which the Strassoldo

The architectural details of the lower castle reveal a strong Venetian influence, despite its proximity to the Austrian border.

The church dedicated to St. Mark, built in the 16th century as the chapel of the lower castle and extended and embellished in the 18th century.

family's fears were well-founded is confirmed by the advice of the Venetian *provveditore* Alvise Priuli regarding the future of the castle:

> The castle of Strassoldo has been owned by lords from the Strassoldo family … If the decision is not taken to demolish it, it should be taken over by Venice in case it falls into the control of anyone hostile to us. The castle could all too easily fall into Hapsburg control since the Strassoldo family has often rendered personal service at the Hapsburg court. The Hapsburgs would be interested in the castle

because the site, surrounded by water, is easily defended and it would be easy to block the arrival of reinforcements.[342]

Venice, the Serenissima, occupied with establishing peace and the normalization of relations with the lords of Friuli, did not act on this advice, but attempted instead to win over the Strassoldo family. Moreover, the foundation of Palmanova, rather than bring about the decline of Strassoldo, brought it considerable economic advantage, since building material for the new town was transported by river almost to Strassoldo itself, where it was unloaded and stored. A large

number of workmen was also required, all of whom needed lodgings and meals. All this brought considerable revenue to the lords of the castle and the surrounding area.[343] The official Venetian decree for the foundation and construction of Palmanova was in fact signed at the upper castle of Strassoldo, "in my room with the stone staircase," as Ettore di Strassoldo wrote.

This stage of the building history of Strassoldo began with the construction of the chapel of St. Mark, though it was in a entirely different form from what we see today. It was situated at the entrance to the courtyard,

the usual site of castle chapels, adjoining the outside wall of the old *domus magna* (big house). Building would have begun in 1575, but the chapel is not recorded in documents until 1587, the year in which all the owners at Strassoldo listed their territorial possessions for the magistracy in Venice of the *Provveditore ai Feudi* (magistracy for feudal possessions).

For some reason this inventory does not include the chapel, an omission of relatively little significance. However, the description of the old *domus magna* does create diffficulties. The first uncertainty is the problem of to

The moat, once used for defense, is now a picturesque feature of the gardens.

FOLLOWING PAGES:
Behind the medieval domus magna, the 18th-century buildings form a beautiful ensemble, one which has elements of both castle and villa.

what extent the *domus magna* had been extended before the damage of the early sixteenth century. Important, but inconclusive, evidence for this is provided by the fragments of geometrically patterned frescoes which can be seen on the façade of the present building and the back of the *domus magna*, masking the rebuilding and extensions carried out subsequently. An examination of the decoration would suggest that the great square building at the center of the complex is late medieval, while the *domus magna* would already have virtually doubled in size by 1500.

Ruling out this theory, however, is the fact that we know that around 1587 the state of conservation of the castle was so poor that major restoration work was necessary. The plasterwork on the façade must have been redone at this time. In the 1587 description cited previously the building is described as *Torazzo, già palazzo comune* (the big tower, formerly a shared dwelling) and as *torre discoperta* (tower open to the sky) and *casa grande* (big house). These terms would imply that the building had retained its original character and had not been transformed into a large private dwelling by additions of the same height, which would have made it look less of a tower.

The rebuilding of the lower castle which took place at this time was made more difficult by the existence of a tower that apparently stood in the courtyard in front of the old house. The main proof of its existence is an eighteenth-century picture.[344] Both castles appear in the picture in a distorted form since the painter was obviously interested only in showing the extension to the upper castle. In the picture the lower castle looks like a cluster of simple cottages, though the old *domus magna*, with the adjacent sixteenth-century chapel, can be picked out.

The largest building visible in the painting is the tower with battlements, which has a tree growing out of it, an indication of the poor condition the building was in. We do not know whether the owner of the newly restored upper castle wanted to make fun of the owners of the lower castle or whether the detail is merely a reflection of the carelessness of a distinctly untalented artist.

In any case, the tower is definitely not

medieval. Moreover, given that the main building was in the form of a tower, it is unlikely that there would be another tower on the scale of the old *domus magna*.[345] It is also out of the question that a building of such importance would not have been mentioned in a fourteenth-century deed dividing up property, in which it would have been listed

he had it embellished with a medievalizing drawbridge and battlements.

Despite the many questions that arise when attempts are made to reconstruct the appearance of the castle of Strassoldo in the sixteenth century, a plausible explanation of all the apparent contradictions in the sources is that after 1587 it became obvious

Austrian and central European influence is obvious in the furnishings of the rooms in the upper castle, and particularly notable in the splendid maiolica stove.

as an integral part of the innermost area of the castle, which was to remain common property. The fact that this tower is not mentioned in the 1587 description of Strassoldo likewise means that it did not exist then either.[346]

There is a similar case at the castle of Tricesimo, where an imposing tower was built opposite the main building as late as around 1600. Its square shape evidently did not satisfy the owner, who wanted a castle, so

that a drastic rebuilding of the medieval *domus magna* and also its associated buildings was necessary.

During this building campaign, a square house was built. From the outside this looked like a Venetian villa and therefore was no longer the outward representation of the feudal lord and his rights. To avoid this, and to demonstrate the long medieval tradition at Strassoldo and the family's ancient claim to

power just at the time that Palmanova was due to be built, deliberately anachronistic medieval elements were included in the restoration and reconstruction, in order for the building to continue to have the appearance of a castle.

Thus a tower, which serves no purpose whatsoever, was built opposite the solid square house, and the exterior of the new mansion was frescoed with geometric designs in the style of several centuries earlier. The ogee windows in the gables, which can be seen from far away but are too large to be attic windows, probably date from the same period.[347] In the course of this work, around 1600, the original entrance was constructed at the corner of the mansion. Like the nearby wall with battlements, it served no defensive function.

The striking obelisk at the entrance was a popular symbol of power from the late sixteenth century onwards. Formerly, only the Venetian government had had the right to have an obelisk, but the Friuli nobility claimed the right to use it to decorate their own buildings. Usually twin obelisks were placed at the entrance or gate of castles in the area. In constrast, the picturesque placing at Strassoldo is unique.

From castle to mansion

The upper castle, with its eighteenth-century mansion, does not allow for a reconstruction of its appearance in 1600. Here too, we have a description of the property, written in 1587, but the picture it gives is far too vague to be helpful. At least four branches of the family had their own houses within the area, but none of these buildings is specified or can be identified with the buildings which exist today. All that can be said for sure is that the room in which the decree for the construction of Palmanova was signed was in a part of the large manor house that was called the chancery.[348]

The main building of the upper castle gained its present appearance only in the eighteenth century. Essentially, it is a typical Friuli landowner's residence, with a width of just one or two rooms and thus only a very modest number of rooms. It is probable that

as early as the Middle Ages the accommodation for the lord and his family was on this site, built adjoining the meter-thick boundary wall, as is the present house. This wall no longer had a defensive function, however, because large windows that open on to the gardens stretching down to the river were knocked through it.

Inside this building, the internal walls seem relatively new, suggesting that it must

The close link between the counts of Strassoldo and the ruling Hapsburg dynasty is apparent from the numerous Hapsburg portraits.

The charming old kitchen in the upper castle. Even the larder for smoking meats survives.

be regarded as essentially a new building. At the center of the building is a stone staircase that leads to a large hall used for formal events. Decorated with simple fresco ornamentation, it extends up to the tower. The other half of the building is divided into three rooms whose eighteenth-century ceilings and furnishings are reminiscent of fine Baroque central European castles rather than of Friuli.

It is not clear whether the small wing which is built at right angles to the main building was constructed on top of an older building or whether it is part of a changed layout, with a new arrangement of the courtyard as well as a new relationship between the chapel and the principal façade of the mansion.[349]

Last, an elegant bridge, a narrow walkway supported on late Baroque arches, connects the mansion house with the chapel, closing off the courtyard at the side.[350] This bridge gave direct access to the family gallery in the chapel. This had a tiny tower with steps and an outside corridor lit by arrow-slit windows and was decorated in the same manner as the castles.

The large buildings at the back of the chapel were built from the remains of older buildings and stand on the site of the ancient curtain wall of the castle.[351]

Despite all the reconstructions and rebuildings, visitors to Strassoldo can still sense some of the atmosphere of the old castle, with its high walls and arches. This is especially the case in the courtyard behind the chapel, where the walls and slit-windows of the tower, standing obliquely to the other buildings, have so ancient a feel to them that it would be all too tempting to concede that the tower really must be tenth-century.

In the lower castle, the most important and most interesting part is the complex of buildings with medieval origins. In the eighteenth century, however, a mansion was built here surrounded by gardens. Apart from a few

irregularities in its façade, it looks exactly like contemporary Venetian villas. The pseudomedieval tower vanished and the old *domus magna* with its extensions gained its present appearance.

To the east, the extension was continued southwards so as to create a greater sense of perspective. In the center of the building was a simple but broad staircase. This led to the first floor where there is a wide corridor with large windows giving on to the rear courtyard, and which ends in the women's gallery in the chapel. An ingenious and beautiful architectural solution in its simplicity and its economical use of space, today it is one of the

The kitchen in the lower castle shows how little the everyday lives of the feudal lords of Friuli differed from those of farmers.

Mills were a source of revenue for the lords of the castle, and there were as many as three at Strassoldo, where they were used to grind rice.

most striking features of the castle. It was probably constructed in its present form around 1728, the year of an inscription that records the restoration of the chapel. The restructuring of the façade and of the fine internal hall must date from that year too, being associated with the women's gallery in the chapel.[352] The whole complex was thus the culmination of a long building history.

The gardens

The gardens are also of exceptional beauty. Created in the course of the reclamation of the marshes, the use of water as the dominant feature in the gardens is ingenious. In the middle of the gardens is an area which has been laid out so as to show off the remains of the original castle, rather like a Baroque *parterre*. This dramatic device goes beyond the usual Baroque concept of an enclosed garden; it is linked by an axis to the surrounding area and to the living accommodation.

These gardens are a classic example of the late Baroque art of gardening, one in which formal elements were placed in a completely new relationship with nature. The gardens of Strassoldo mark the beginning in Friuli of the landscaped garden.

Conclusion

In the eighteenth century the Strassoldo family dwelling returned, in essence, to its origins of almost a thousand years earlier. The medieval castle was once again a seignorial residence, with a minimum of defenses, the center of a large estate, and a sign of the power of the owner. Unlike many castles that are still occupied and preserved today, there is little to be seen that is medieval in the present architecture at Strassoldo. While elsewhere nobles who had lost their importance retained their medieval castles in their original form in order to recall the glorious past of their noble families in the Middle Ages, and while newly rich families sought to give an aristocratic, medieval air to their houses, with towers and crenellations, laying claim to an ancient family history, the counts of Strassoldo could allow themselves to

dismantle the crumbling and superfluous towers. The towers were no longer necessary to bear witness to the family's noble origins since in the nineteenth century its members still occupied important offices in the Hapsburg administration.

The importance of the castle of Strassoldo, the seat of an influential family that continues to maintain the whole castle complex as well as its splendid gardens in impeccable condition, is still recognized today.

The gardens of the lower castle, among the most interesting in Friuli. Like the rest of the complex, they are immaculately maintained.

THE DEVELOPMENT OF THE CASTLE

Until recently, the development of castles and their forms was neglected. There are two reasons for this. First, castles have been regarded purely in terms of their defensive role, not as an architectural form was typical of the Middle Ages and which developed specifically in that period. Second, the end of the popularity of castles continues to be associated with the spread of gunpowder and firearms. Any development of castles after the fifteenth century is regarded as impossible.

For some time now, however, the idea that castles have their origin in antiquity has been rejected. There are many studies of the emergence of castles in the Middle Ages, though unfortunately the general reader is not as a rule aware of them.

As far as the development of castles in the early modern period is concerned, however, much work remains to be done, since as a rule studies of the subject have ended with the late Middle Ages.[353] Only U. Albrecht, who has worked on the development of the château in France, and Schütte, who has studied apparently defensive elements in the architecture of castles of the seventeenth and eighteenth centuries, have looked at the castle beyond the medieval period, demonstrating that the castle does not end with the end of the Middle Ages. This, an important subject, will be the subject of a second volume on castles in Friuli.

The beginnings of the feudal castle

While in Roman times and the early Middle Ages, the words castle, *castellum*, and *castrum* were used to refer to strongholds and fortified villages, large landowners and those who held power locally lived in the countryside in large dwellings with little in the way of fortifications. These dwellings differed from the classic Roman villa mainly in the primitive standard of living and in the low cultural level of their inhabitants. Artistic activity, or any kind of sophisticated furnishing, was unthinkable.

The true feudal castle came into being only when landowners took on juridical and military duties as well as their administrative

role, when the person who held power at a local level decided to fortify his residence or move it to a place with natural defenses. This process is given the name *incastellamento*. Documents published by Aldo Settia reveal how *incastellamento*, or the transformation of seignorial residences into castles, reached its peak when there was no longer any need to fortify settlements.

Detailed examination of individual cases would clarify whether castles were the

The motte and bailey, an early form of the medieval castle, is known not only from archaeology but also from five representations in the famous Bayeux tapestry.

successors of the *cortina* or other primitive fortifications for the protection of the local population. Until now, however, it has not been clear whether fortified villages lost their importance because of the building of castles, or whether the coming of more secure times made the traditional *castellum* unnecessary.

An answer to this question would contribute to explaining the role and function of the feudal castle, particularly with regard to its military role.

The motte and bailey castle

Fortified towers built on a mound, normally called a motte, are an early form of the castle.[354] The etymology of the word *motte* remains obscure, although efforts have been made to discover its roots in the hope of thus discovering the origins of the architectural form. Nowadays it is assumed that the word has its origins in the Gallic-Frankish spoken language since it does not derive from Latin,

and motte and bailey castles are to be found above all in northern France.[355]

The earliest evidence for the motte and bailey castle is in the Bayeux Tapestry. In the tapestry, which tells the story of the Norman conquest of England, motte and bailey castles are depicted in five scenes. Though at first sight, these scenes seem quite abstract and fragmentary, closer examination reveals detail and precision. These depictions, together with the few surviving written records and an increasing body of archaeological evidence, make it possible to form a reasonably clear image of the motte and bailey castle and its origins.[356]

The foundation of a motte and bailey castle is a mound of earth which was surrounded by a ditch and a rampart. Earth from the ditch was used for the rampart, which was covered with turf and might be reinforced at the side with a palisade.[357] It is a structure which can be built quickly. Sources from the time of the Norman invasion of England refer to a building which was completed in a few days. Wace's epic poem on the kings of Normandy recounts how the parts in timber were transported on ships, making it possible to build a motte and bailey castle in the course of a single day.[358]

The motte and bailey castle made it possible to render an area of foreign territory secure in a very short time and this is what gave it particular importance in any military conquest. The need for speed made necessary such minimalist constructions, which could subsequently be expanded and raised.[359] In some cases natural mounds were used, in other cases artificially created high ground such as prehistoric barrows.[360]

In contrast to early defenses, the major innovation of the motte and bailey was that it was the permanent home of a family.[361] A good example of this is a description from 1117:

> In Flanders a certain Arnold built a timber dwelling on the motte of Ardres. It was finer than all the others in the area. On the ground floor was a storeroom and larder, on the first floor the lord's chambers, including his own bedroom with an heated room, and accommodation for the servants. In the next room slept his sons and daughters and the watchmen.

Hinz supposes that there was also a open area at the top of the castle from which the enemy could be fought.[362]

It is difficult to distinguish between tower and dwelling-house. As with the *domus magna* at Strassoldo, a building might fulfill both functions. It is not surprising that the building at the center of the motte was often called a house.[363] As a rule, these buildings were made from timber, as is clear from archaeological remains and written records, including the Bayeux Tapestry.

Because of the risk of fire, the kitchen was in a separate building. Only in stone towers was it part of the main building.[364]

Wood was preferred for building for three reasons: construction was faster, there were fewer problems with the foundations on less firm ground, and buildings could be erected even where there was no stone to be had.

Wooden castles

Up to the fourteenth century, not only motte and bailey castles but also many elements in other types of castle were constructed out of wood.[365] From the point of view of defense, wood presented virtually no problems. Even in seventeenth-century Ireland, the motte and bailey with a palisade at Drogheda was still able to offer effective protection to its occupants.[366]

In Friuli, a document of 1322, in which the division of the castle of Strassoldo among five brothers is set out, gives great importance to a wooden tower (*balfredum de lignamine*). The word *balfredum* indicates that this was the principal tower, probably still inhabited.[367] Evidently, the importance and value of this tower, whose origins must go back to the earliest period of the history of castles, was so great that its new owner made for repairing part of the castle wall.[368]

Unfortunately, little evidence from this early period survives and it is difficult to establish whether similar cases existed. Nonetheless, it is surprising to find south of the Alps an example of an inhabited wooden tower at so late a date, particularly in the main castle of an independent feudal family. Where the castles of the minor nobility were concerned which made up the vast majority of castles and were much smaller and more modest it is clear that even long after the twelfth century they were constructed chiefly in timber.[369]

An early fourteenth-century fresco in the Palazzo Pubblico in Siena shows how widespread building in timber was. Represented in the fresco, with great attention to detail, is

building. Since it is obviously inconceivable that the artist should have had any interest in diminishing the importance of the castle, the image is irrefutable evidence that timber was still a common building material in the fourteenth century.

Apart from the importance of the castle itself, the use of wood here is all the more

a castle that had been acquired by the city, one so important that it merited being depicted in the principal civic place, the splendid rooms of the Palazzo Pubblico. Yet even this castle has timber defenses, both around the village and around the central

striking because of the geographical position of the castle, in central Italy. Clearly the use of timber for construction was not unique to remote northern forests where wood was available from clearances, as historians have assumed.[370] Wood must therefore be regarded

This image of a castle in the Sala del Mappamondo or del Consiglio in the Palazzo Pubblico in Siena shows clearly that in the 14th century the external defenses were still made of wood.

as the most common material for the construction of the medieval castle. As late as the sixteenth century, most of the castles depicted in Dürer's engravings still have wooden palisades protecting the area around the castle.

The transition from building in wood to building in stone took place over centuries.[371] In Friuli, the role played by wooden constructions can be clarified only by archaeological investigation. It is probable that beneath many stone curtain walls lie the remains of earlier wood palisades. This is the case at the Ala Nievo (Nievo Wing) at the castle of Colloredo, where buried timber trunks may be the remains of the original wooden boundary wall, as suggested by their position.[372]

All the examples cited, from the *balfredum* at Strassoldo to the remains of early defenses, suggest that a degree of caution is necessary when seeking to date stone walls. Rather than try to identify them—as is usually the case—with the first written evidence of the existence of a castle, we need to remember that the earliest medieval castles were such simple buildings that it is no longer possible to discover their original form.

The burg in the motte and bailey

Wood continued to be used for much longer in the villages or burgs that were an integral part of the motte and bailey castle. The burg functioned as both seignorial village and a fortified stronghold for the local peasants. It would be made up of a few modest buildings and, perhaps, some artisans' workshops.[373] In the written sources the burg is called *suburbium* and the whole complex *castrum cum suburbio*, even when it is a question of only a very small castle.[374]

The relationship of the burg and the motte and bailey castle varied according to the site. They might both be independent entities, or the burg might be spread out around the motte in concentric circles of ditches and ramparts, making the motte the center of the structure.

The example of Husterknupp castle, well-known for the meticulously recorded archaeological excavations carried out there, is evidence that a motte might develop even from a seignorial dwelling. It is, in addition, an example of how different the relationship between castle and burg was in earlier times from the reversed relationship in the late Middle Ages.

Aldo Settia has noted how in written sources the words *motte* and *castrum/castellum* are used interchangeably. While tenth- and eleventh-century sources still refer to noble dwellings near fortified villages, later the term motte seems to come to indicate an outpost. In some cases, the term motte may simply refer to an abandoned castle.[375]

This change in meaning, a significant one, is proof not only of the evolution of the term *castrum*, from fortified village to aristocratic castle, but reveals too the role of the motte as the original form of the aristocratic castle. In

sources from Friuli, however, the term *motte* appears to refer to a mound on which more recent castles are to be found.

The origins of the motte

In the nineteenth century, given the consensus that all castles had their origins in Roman fortifications, it was presumed that the motte was similarly derived from a Roman model and that it represented the survival of the Roman *burgus*. It is true that the only representation of a *burgus*, on Trajan's column, is somewhat reminiscent of the motte.[376]

Another theory maintains that the tower where the governor or custodian of the castle lived developed out of the *principium* of the Roman camp, the center of the fortified structure. However, since it has been demonstrated that the *principium* was neither a tower nor dwelling but a basilica, the place where the standards and arms were kept and where the roll was called, such a derivation is improbable.[377]

Even though there are cases of mottes that were built on top of Roman remains,[378] recent studies have proved that these were not constructed in the early Middle Ages. The earliest definite examples date from the eleventh century, though there are a few written sources which attest to the existence of mottes in earlier times.[379]

The main objection to a Roman origin for the motte, however—apart from the obviously non-Latin etymology of the word—is

the long period of time which elapsed between the last Roman *burgi* and the earliest mottes. Indeed, these medieval attempts to hark back to antiquity themselves reveal how profound was the break in architectural tradition. Moreover, attempts to see the origins of the motte in late antiquity or the early Middle Ages do not take into account the particular characteristics of this form of castle. Motte and bailey castles are the earliest examples of the fortified residences of noble families and, as such, they presuppose the existence of the feudal system.

H. Hinz argues that the motte and bailey castle must have developed in France and elsewhere in western Europe, where the feudal system developed early, and the great plains could be controlled by an artificial mound, while only timber and earth were available in large quantities as building materials.[380] The steady clearance of the wild areas and cultivation to the east made it essential to have a form of defense which could be built quickly.

The motte and bailey castle in Italy

The earliest evidence for a motte in Italy is a document of 881 that describes the foundation of a chapel on an enclosed artificial mound.[381] Shortly afterwards comes a description of the motte belonging to the bishop of Modena (bishop 869–98):

> While the whole area was oppressed by a miserable rabble and the most horrific plunder of goods of every kind, Leodoino,

bishop of the holy church in Modena, built a mound (*tumulus*) and gave it these gates, earthworks, and palisades. Inside he hid arms, not against the most revered rulers, but with the wish to defend the homes of the citizens themselves.[382]

The concentration of motte and bailey castles in northern France, England, and parts of Germany has led them to be regarded as a typically northern European form of architecture and it is presumed that there were few in Italy. Settia, however, records a whole series of Italian examples. More than thirty place-

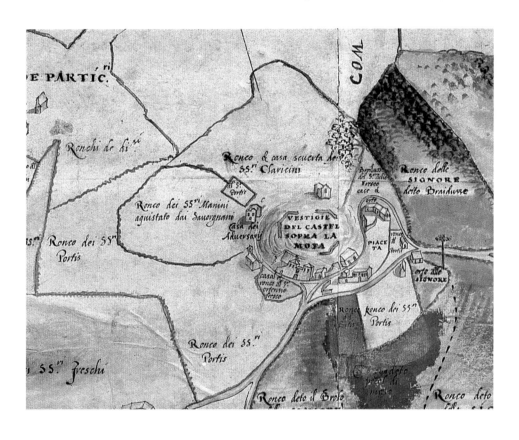

A 16th-century land survey map of the Buttrio family property, showing the importance of the motte as an early form of feudal castle in Friuli.

names include the name *motta*. Of these, twenty are in the north of Italy and twelve in the south. There are none, however, in central Italy. Motta di Livenza, documented from the end of the twelfth century, is the earliest attested placename.[383]

I would argue, however, that the *tumulus* built by the bishop of Modena was an isolated case. It is not possible to determine with certainty whether in Italy the period between the tenth and twelfth centuries saw the phenomenon of motte and bailey castle building in the same way as occurred in France.[384]

In the thirteenth century we find references to motte and bailey castles in Italy. Frederick II, for example, forbade the monastery of San Zeno in Verona to build one: towers might be built only "a terra naturaliter sita" (where the terrain is naturally higher).[385] At the motte in Modena, wooden towers are described by the term *bitifredum*, while wooden palisades and drawbridges are mentioned: "facere unam bonam mottam cum palancato e pontibus levatoriis ab utroque latere pontis de navexellis" (a strong motte to be made with a palisade and drawbridges on each side).[386]

Even if the motte and bailey can be regarded as an early example of an aristocratic castle, because of their simple structure Settia regarded many Italian mottes as nothing more than fortified farmsteads. In any case, such structures clearly show how modest early castles were and how primitive the life of even important aristocratic families was as late as the thirteenth century.

The motte in Friuli

The strong influence of the Germanic feudal system on Friuli and its castles makes it probable that the region had comparatively more mottes than elsewhere in Italy.[388] Mottes are mentioned only four times in sources in Friuli, always in connection with castles. In all these cases, all that is to be seen today is an obviously artificial mound, with no evidence of what kind of buildings were once found there. The lack of archaeological investigation adds to the difficulty of assessing this topographical evidence.

At Brazzacco two mottes are mentioned, in both cases in connection with a *castellum*. In 1349 Nicolò di Brazzacco sold "his third share of the [upper] castle and motte to Francesco di Colloredo."[389] Just three years later, there is a reference to the "castle and the motte of lower Brazzacco" on the occasion of the investiture of ancient feudal rights on "Tomaso di Brazzà."[390] A glance around the immediate vicinity of the two medieval castles today reveals that a few 100 meters away (some 300 yards) is an artificial mound which might be an ancient motte.[391]

The close association in both sources between motte and castle would suggest that originally the motte was on the site of the present castle. The site of the upper castle at Brazzacco Superiore supports such an interpretation: the castle mound, as it stands today, cannot have been formed naturally.[392] However, the archaeological excavation in the castle courtyard ended before it was possible to clarify whether there was a motte built on pre-existing high ground or whether the one-meter (three-feet) thick layer was formed only of rubble and rubbish from the castle.[393]

Gramogliano

The best documented example of a castle built on a motte is the residence of the lords of Gramogliano, described in a deed of 1323: "in castro sive turri de Gramogliano et Motta sive colle eius castri cum terris cultis et incultis" (the *castrum* or tower of Gramogliano and the *motta*, or hill of this *castrum*, with all its lands, both cultivated and uncultivated). It would seem then that this is a castle which could also be described as a tower. Additionally, there is a motte which is also described as "the hill of this *castrum*." The castle therefore stands on the motte. In this context, the word *motte* must mean "hill." But since the castle on the hill is primarily a tower, it is the complex as a whole which appears to be a classic motte.[394]

The first source referring to the castle dates from 1292, when "the brothers of Gramogliano sold by right of legal fief to Giovanni di Zuccola the tower of Gramogliano."[395] Nothing is known of the shape of this tower or of its position on a hill, perhaps because—as in almost all cases—the original deed is known only through a summary in a later register. The text of the only record concerning Gramogliano that I have been able to consult in its entirety only once uses the word *motta*, which would certainly have been omitted in the scribe's shorthand and abbreviations in the later summary.[396] It is for such reasons that archival material is difficult to use.

In 1298 the ruling family at Gramogliano requested, and obtained, permission to build a new tower surrounded by a moat, informing the patriarch that they had built "a magnificent tower."[397] Here too I would be inclined to consider this building a motte and bailey castle; indeed a tower that could be considered a tower house is later mentioned. It is not possible, however, to establish if this tower was in timber or whether the source described it as *balfredum* or similar. The fact that Gramogliano has no medieval walls whatsoever suggests that the castle was built of wood and should therefore be defined as a motte because of its shape and position.

The ancient castle of Gramogliano, near the village of Corno di Rosazzo, stands on raised ground and is surrounded by cypresses and vineyards, in the middle of some of the finest countryside in Friuli.

The Castle of Gramogliano

In 1323, as we have seen, the castle of Gramogliano was described as "castro sive turri de Gramogliano et Motta sive colle eius castri" (the *castrum* or tower of Gramogliano and the *motta*, or hill of this *castrum*). It is clear that this was a classic example of a fortified tower. We can still see today an inhabited tower built on an artificial hill.

There is a reference to the tower as early as 1292, when the Gramogliano brothers sold it.[398] This tower cannot have been particularly important since in 1298 the Gramogliano family was already building another one with

The chapel of St. Leonard, referred to in the Middle Ages as the seignorial chapel of the lords of Gramogliano.

OPPOSITE:
The slender round tower, like many others built to adorn rural aristocratic residences in the early modern era, and the only feature which today suggests a castle.

a ditch around it, informing the patriarch that they had built "a magnificent tower."[399]

In 1321 Francesco di Manzano referred to a sale of "houses and towers" at Gramogliano, but the plural seems to have been a mistake since there is nothing to suggest that there was ever more than one inhabited tower.[400] In 1323 the above-mentioned sale of the fortified tower on the motte took place, and in 1353 damage to it is recorded.[401] In 1376 a chapel is mentioned for the first time, when a certain "Urle, or Votrico of Gramogliano, citizen of Gorizia" left to the "church of San Lorenzo in Gramogliano a silver chalice."[402]

A chapel of San Lorenzo still exists today, though it is not in the area of the old castle but opposite it, halfway up the steep rise.[403] In its present form the charming building may date from the sixteenth century, which can scarcely be regarded as medieval.

This is the case also with the building which is now called the "castle of Gramogliano." It is sited in the middle of slopes of vineyards on top of a small, obviously artificial mound with a flat rectangular top, far too big, at more than a 100 meters (330 feet) long, to be a medieval motte. In the middle is a picturesque stone house with a round corner tower but no evidence of medieval construction.[404] The corner tower, whose wall is 60 centimeters (almost two feet) thick, is certainly not medieval; it recalls many other small towers in the surrounding area.[405]

Miotti suggested that the original castle was a rectangular building with four corner towers, but there is no evidence for this reconstruction. No walls survive to support his suggestion, and the surface of the raised area is too large even for a medium-sized aristocratic castle.

A castle belonging to minor feudal family such as the lords of Gramogliano would have been small. For this reason,

the image the written sources suggest—an inhabited tower, surrounded by ditches and, at most, a turf and wooden enclosure—is without any doubt preferable to Miotti's somewhat fanciful reconstruction. The castle we see today, therefore, has nothing to do with the original construction, details of which could be brought to light only by archaeologists.[406]

The role of the motte

At Buttrio it is possible to study the way in which the castle developed out of the motte. In a sixteenth-century plan describing the

The castle of Buttrio in a late medieval drawing. The few architectural details shown here are confirmed in the surviving records.

division of the property of the former lords, the castle is indicated as the *castellum sopra la Motta* (castle on the motte). The medieval ruins were dismantled by the last owner and all that can now be seen at the site is an artificial mound whose diameter of about 25 meters (82 feet) corresponds to the size of mottes elsewhere.

Thus there arose a medieval castle on the motte. This was described in 1347 as "surrounded by a strong wall of massive work with a large gateway and a tall square stone tower with a pointed top." A drawing which according to Miotti dates from the first half of the fifteenth century also records the castle as looking like this.[407]

In the drawing, however, the principal tower is not situated, as in the classic motte and bailey castle, in the center, surrounded by the outer wall. Instead, the drawing shows a large, apparently inhabited, building in this place. Such an occupied tower is typical of a motte and bailey castle.

The present castle buildings, which date from a much later period, are not on the motte itself but at the foot of the mound. They were probably erected on the area of the former lower village, as archaeological excavation has shown was the case at other castles.

As the motte and bailey castle gradually became a stone castle, it maintained its original form. Thus the plan of the castle was determined by the line of the outer wall on the hill. The result was a typical medieval castle with tower. This type of stone castle, which is called a tower castle, came into existence even before the building of mottes reached its peak.

This castle too was formed by a narrow outer wall with an inhabited tower in the middle. However, it was no longer built on top of a mound. Conspicuous in the center was the novel element, the lord's residence. The whole structure was markedly smaller than earlier fortified complexes.[408] The noble castle is a compact, tall architectural form which seeks to stand out. It thus has nothing but its name in common with the castle-refuge of earlier times, which had been protected by palisades behind ramparts and ditches.

A description by a Zurich preacher reveals the extent to which in the twelfth century castles with towers had become the dominant architectural form: "We use the word castle to describe a tower surrounded by a wall, where both elements give protection to each other."[409] The importance of the tower castle is underlined by the case of the Schlössl near Klingenmünster, where the tower, built of dressed square blocks between 1030 and 1050, was given an outer wall only in the years around 1100.[410] Evidently it was only later that it was thought necessary to fortify noble dwellings. The fortified manor was the starting point of this process.

The difference between the motte and bailey castle and the first stone castles is the absence of the motte, or mound. The earliest tower castles are almost all located on plains or lowland. They represent an important part of the evolution towards castles built on raised ground. As Hinz describes it, the motte was a response to the diffusion of the tower castle. Since there were neither time, materials, nor the workforce available to erect a stone structure, a motte would be built, which could provide the same protection in a much shorter time.[411]

Castle types

None of the attempts made to classify castles in a precise typology has yet produced useful results. Because of adaptations to changing circumstances, variations in castles developed which are so individual that it is more or less impossible to think in terms of homogenous types.

In the fifth volume of Miotti's work, Giorgia Nicoletti-König attempted to set out a typological classification of castles, examining the structure and site of the *palas* (tower), external wall, and chapel. However, she makes no distinction between castles, abbeys, and towns. She also defines the keep variously as tower, *palas*, and the center of the castle, resulting in confusion. Moreover, she describes castles in terms of their appearance today, with the result that nineteenth- and twentieth-century alterations are treated on the same level with original medieval features.[412]

Maurizio Grattoni proposes a more coherent classification in the publication of

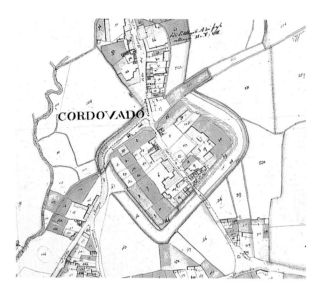

Two main types of castle can be discerned in Friuli, as elsewhere in Europe. The first is castles on a rectangular plan, as at Cordovado (left), often regarded as influenced by the Roman castrum. The second, with a circular plan, can be seen clearly in the plan of Spilimbergo (below).

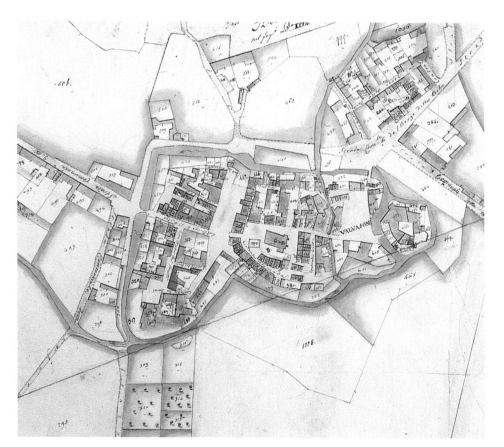

FOLLOWING PAGES:
The castle di Valvasone with its two rings of defensive walls. The walls of the later buildings were built alternately against the inner and the outer circle.

the Consorzio per la Salvaguardia dei Castelli Storici del Friuli-Venezia Giulia (Commission for the Conservation of Historic Castles in Friuli-Venezia Giulia). He distinguishes abbeys and *cortine/cente* from the medieval castle per se. However, not only does he describe structures in the outmoded terms of the nineteenth century,[413] but he also describes the typical growth of a large castle over the centuries without analyzing its different architectural forms.

It is true that Grattoni attempts to classify aristocratic residences, distinguishing fortified dwellings from castles. However, the attempt is doomed to fail, because a fortified dwelling as he defines it, as a burg and an area within the castle, "the *domus magna*, the lord's residence, with thick walls and a large central tower, protected by two circles of walls," is not differentiated in any way from a castle built on the plain.[414]

It is equally hard to classify castles accord-ing to their function. Different functions required different solutions, which changed with the passing of time. Today, for example, it is impossible to assess the defensive role of a twelfth-century castle compared to its function as a dwelling or as a place to entertain important guests, since there is no evidence in the sources and castle ruins from this period are difficult to evaluate.

Another potential distinction could be made between castles which belonged to rulers and those which belonged to feudal nobles. In Friuli, however, there is the problem that the ruler, the patriarch, did not live and govern only in his most important castles, such as those of Udine and Tricesimo, but also enjoyed the right of access to his vassals' castles and might often go to live there, often even for extended periods. There is archival evidence that the patriarch often stayed in the castles of Fagagna and Soffumbergo, while a *palatium patriar-*

The castle of Zoppola, the finest example of a castle on a rectangular plan in the region and the only one to adopt Italian models.

cale (patriarchal palace) at Maniago is recorded in a seventeenth-century drawing.[415] Yet it is no longer possible to see what, if anything, distinguished these three castles architecturally from others that were owned by *ministeriales*.

There are also splendid and large castles in which the patriarch stayed only rarely, precisely because the owner had increased his own power at the expense of the patriarch himself. The castles of Gorizia and Duino, for example, have the characteristics of princely castles for reasons particular to them.

In short, the imposing castles of Spilimbergo, Porcia, Zoppola, and Colloredo show how at a later period the dominance of certain families encouraged them to build what today are magnificent castles. It is irrelevant whether the aristocrats were imperial counts, belonging, because of their origins, to the free feudal classes, or were mere *ministeriales*. In the late Middle Ages and subse-quently, growing family wealth was the main reason for the building of large castles. Such cases, however, are of no importance for the purpose of classification, and it is best to avoid all attempts at classification, since they impose unacceptable simplifications on a complex situation.

Despite all these reservations, two essentially different types of castles can be identified. They merit special attention in Friuli since it is here, as has been said, that the two types exist side by side: castles with a polygonal or round ground plan and castles with a square or rectangular ground plan, sometimes almost a perfect square. The existence of both types has long been the subject of debate in the history of the subject and has always been linked to the question of the origins of the two very different models.

In Friuli, however, the subject has never received the attention it deserves from scholars, even though it is precisely here, where both forms, unusually, co-exist, that there lies the possibility of casting light on the still unresolved problems. In the following pages I will discuss the two types of castle in Friuli and suggest some possible answers to these unresolved problems.

Round and polygonal castles

While elsewhere in Italy almost only square castles are to be found, the majority of those in Friuli have a round, oval, or polygonal plan. These castles, with their simple curtain wall following the slope, a dwelling built adjoining the curtain wall, and, often, a free-standing tower in the middle of the courtyard, closely resembled the motte and bailey castle and the tower castle. Their similar appearance implies that they represent an early form of castle.

The castle of Brazzacco

The castle of Brazzacco is a typical example of a well-preserved medieval castle. As it was never converted into a dwelling house, and has been constantly repaired and maintained, it is an excellent example of the aristocratic castle of the early Middle Ages.[416]

The complex is formed essentially by an outer wall more than a meter (three feet)

thick whose polygonal course has been adapted to the contour of the slope. This wall is interrupted only at the point where today a building in the form of a tower overlooks the rest of the castle.[417]

It is not possible to say much about the buildings inside the small outer wall, which measures about 15 meters by 30 (50 feet by 100). The building known as the *casa del Capitano* (the Captain's house) in its present form dates back only to the sixteenth, or even the seventeenth, century. It was probably built on the ruins of a longer building, the end of which today seems to rise in the form of a tower, giving a picturesque impression, though it is not possible to say with certainty that there was originally a tower anywhere in the castle.

It is precisely the simplicity of its structure which allows the castle of Brazzacco to offer a true picture of a noble castle. Today a narrow track still leads up to the mound, perhaps an artificial one. At the foot of the hill was the lower courtyard, enclosed by a palisade, where the chapel is to be found today. Horse-drawn vehicles would have had to stop here because the road up to the castle was narrow and the gate so small that no wheeled traffic could enter the castle. Such difficult access would have been unthinkable in bigger and grander castles, where large quantities of food and firewood were required. At smaller noble castles, where an obscure *ministeriale* family would have needed food only for themselves, a common sight would have been the lord of the castle and his family carrying their day-to-day requirements up and down the track.

Within the outer wall there was room only for a house, a small storeroom, and, at the most, a small stable. Even without any animals, the upper courtyard of the castle would have been cramped. The castle was probably built in the twelfth century as the seat of a *ministeriale* of the patriarch, to protect him as necessary, assure his survival, and guarantee the exercise of his responsibilities within the domain.[418] A tower—of which there is in any case no evidence—would not have been necessary. Such a symbol of power would probably have been beyond the means of the modest lords of the castle, which was continually being subdivided among numerous relatives.

The plan of Brazzacco castle, showing the castle's original shape. The external wall was modified at the entrance in order to create a tower.

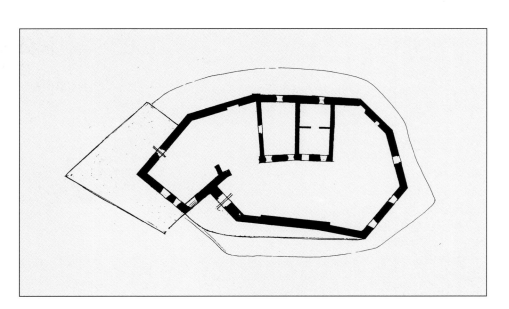

The Castle of Brazzacco

In the middle of the dense chain of castles to the northwest of Udine, in the valley east of Moruzzo, is the small castle of Brazzacco Superiore.[419] More than any other castle, it gives a good impression of the original form and scale of a knightly castle.

The castle stands on a high mound, almost certainly artificial.[420] It comprises an outer wall little more than a meter (three feet) thick, ending in the west in an elevated construction of a tower. Here, protected by the tower, is the picturesque entrance to the castle, with a small round arch supported by dressed stone and a narrow passage inaccessible to wheeled traffic. Inside the wall is a two-storey dwelling known as the *casa del Capitano*, the house of the captain, formerly the site of the chancery. Examination of its structure reveals that this house dates only from the sixteenth century, or even the seventeenth, although it was probably built on the foundations of an earlier building.

Dating castles is always problematic. The name Brazzacco is recorded for the first time in a document of 1186 naming a certain Federico di Brazago (from Brazzacco), suggesting that there was already a castle at Brazzacco.[421] An association of the castle with a certain Braitan, recorded in 983, is impossible as there was no castle on the site that early, as archaeological excavation has confirmed.[422]

As usual, there are few written sources and to date no record of any building work at the castle has been found. However, we know of damage to the castle during the well-known *giovedì grasso* revolt of the last Thursday of Carnival, since the leader of this revolt was the lord of Brazzacco.[423]

The record of his trial in 1525 gives information on the condition of the castle and tells us of a tower long since demolished, whose foundations had been five paces wide:[424] "In dicto castro Brazachis superioris alias fuit una turris loco fortiliciis cuius apparet sola fundamenta et vestigia nec ut hominum memoria …

quis forma vel si fuerit habitata" (at the said castle of Brazzacco Superiore there was a tower in a strong place. Only the foundations and some ruins survive … No one can remember … its form or if it was inhabited). In the same document it is recorded that this tower was "diruta jam annis ducentis" (in ruins for two centuries).[425] Clearly the idea of a tower was merely local tradition, an attempt to make sense of the surviving ruins; it does not prove the existence of a tower, particularly as the area was so small.

The document records the existence of houses in the castle in the sixteenth century, one of which belonged to Ettore di Brazzà: "unam domum in dicto castro restauratam alias primo loco fabricatam a … tempore non est hominum memoria" (a house in the said castle which has been restored on the original site. No one can remember when it was built). Another house had a staircase whose gutter "cadebant super fundamenta dictae turris" (spouted on to the foundations of the said tower). The gate to the castle was at this time closed "cum clavis et penulo seu catenatio" (with a key … or a chain) or, as another witness indicated, "cum legno in traversum posito ab intus" (with a wooden bar across the inside).

Despite this description, only a tentative reconstruction of the medieval castle is possible. The lower burg was below the mound, near the present chapel. It was protected only by a flimsy wall or even by a palisade. Today the narrow track ends in a few stone steps at the doorway, which is situated in the only place where there is a bend in the outer wall, formed by the tower.

The tower, however, is not medieval and cannot be the oldest part of the castle, as Miotti assumed.[426] Not only are its walls thin but it also has no rear wall. It is not possible that a rear wall once existed and has been destroyed since there are no irregularities in the side walls of the tower or in what remains of the foundations. The tower building must therefore belong to the dwelling whose form can still be seen clearly today, and to which the "casa del Capitano" belonged.[427]

It is hard to know whether there were houses adjoining the southeastern part of the outer wall. There are many window openings

The newest part of the wall and the most sophisticated, built of large dressed blocks of stone.

A tower whose date is unknown, more ornamental than defensive, near the narrow track leading to the castle.

OPPOSITE:
A view through the medieval doorway of the castle of Brazzacco down to the complex of the modern villa, with the road flanked by 17th-century barns.

The casa del Capitano (house of the captain), the part of the castle with the longest history of occupation, evidence of the importance of the castle as the political and administrative center of the fief until the 18th century.

PRECEDING PAGES:
The new house built at the beginning of the 20th century on the site of the 17th-century villa that had burned down. As the villa had once been, the new house continued to be the focus of the whole complex.

and stone abutments but overall these give the impression of a later reconstruction which aimed at the picturesque.

In its present form, the castle has numerous additions and extensions which have left their mark in the outer wall. The most conspicuous part of the wall, by the entrance, is built of dressed stone, giving an impression of age and massiveness. Yet this is the newest part, where stone was added to an older wall which had been destroyed.[428] This suggests that this front area, where the entrance to castles was customarily found, had been broken down and the walls destroyed, perhaps in the *giovedì grasso* rebellion.

The reconstruction of the wall and entrance sought above all to create a striking visual impression. The circuit of the outer wall was moved inwards by about two meters

(six feet), emphasizing the presence of the house, which was given the appearance of a tower. In contrast to the actual situation in the Middle Ages, a new castle without a tower was unthinkable, as towers had become a mark of feudal nobility. The quality of the stonework in this newer part can be seen in other examples from this time, such as the new wall at Villalta between the castle and the town, which was built by using forced labor of the peasants as a punishment for their rebellion.

The reconstruction made for a picturesque, but no longer useable, castle. The effect was calculated with a view to the impression it would make on visitors. The same is true of the façade, behind which there is virtually nothing to be seen. The idea of a dramatic and effective façade developed in the seven-

teenth century, when a central axis was created, as can be seen in many aristocratic palaces.[429]

Rather than adapt the castle to suit its new way of life, the family at Brazzacco moved to a new dwelling which was extended and refurbished several times over the centuries, leaving the castle to symbolize the family's privileges. The castle became the showpiece of a growing complex of buildings—an excellent example of the rediscovery of castles as symbolizing history and lineage.

In the seventeenth century or even the eighteenth, the pseudo-tower may have been given a plinth such as those of bastions, and this would have increased the impact of the whole structure on anyone passing.

During the later restoration of the area and its transformation into landscaped gardens,

the ruins of the castle were thus used for other purposes. Following contemporary fashion, these ruins, now lacking any military, political, or economic function, were used above all as a picturesque background. The main wall was once again rebuilt, and a large window with a pointed arch was created in the tower.

The whole complex, which has been well maintained by its owners, is today a noteworthy work of art, one in which, despite all the changes, we can see a medieval castle in a good state of conservation.

This early 19th-century watercolor shows that successive rebuilding in the Romantic era did not change the overall appearance of the castle.

Other round castles

Brazzacco is certainly the best-preserved example of a castle of almost circular ground plan in Friuli, but the region has other examples of castles of this type. One is the castle of Toppo, recorded as early as 1188, whose well-constructed outer wall is one of the best examples of fortification. The entire complex is now owned by the state since the last Toppo-Wassermann owner left the family estates and castle to the city of Udine.

Unfortunately the castle has been neglected by its new owners. Apart from strengthening the wall with reinforced concrete—entirely inappropriate from a conservation point of view—the castle is being allowed to collapse and is becoming so overgrown that it is impossible to have an idea of the whole. The great outer wall, almost circular, is still visible. Inside, within a tiny area, is a house and a tower. Of the second circle of walls there is now no trace.

Even the chapel, next to a still recognizable door, is in a terrible state of conservation.

The castle of Colloredo was also built to a polygonal or round plan. The innermost building inside the curtain wall has been called a so-called keep, a misleading name as it was built later. Originally there was probably the standard internal courtyard enclosed by a wall, with a house and perhaps a tower.[430] The present huge castle, below the old medieval fourteenth-century nucleus, should be regarded as a later extension which was carried out when the family split into a number of branches, each of which wanted its own house within the walls.[431]

Of the present complex, all that can be regarded as definitely medieval is what lies inside the old nucleus of the castle, that is, the "keep" and also the outer wall, which was destroyed by the 1976 earthquake. This important complex is therefore an example of a castle of the modern epoch, whose description and history cannot be a subject for this volume.

Although the castle of Toppo is in ruins, its imposing appearance and the quality of workmanship in the walls make it one of the finest castles in the province of Pordenone.

OPPOSITE:
The castle of Colloredo.
The disastrous earthquake of 1976 destroyed the oldest parts of the building and nothing survives that can be dated with certainty to the Middle Ages.

OPPOSITE:
The entrance tower, restored after the 1976 earthquake.

The plan shows how the castle of Colloredo was made up of a ring of buildings around a narrow courtyard, an arrangement typical of Friuli castles.

BELOW:
A splendid view of the castle of Colloredo, the largest in the area. Despite the excellent condition of the complex on the left side, its ruinous state at the other end makes an authentic reconstruction impossible.

Allegato V

COLLOREDO DI MONT 'ALBANO

Another well-preserved castle built on an almost elliptical plan is Fontanabona. Here, on a small hill a few kilometers north of Udine, is a building dating from 1800 and incorporated into the castle. Its garden in the form of a courtyard is fully enclosed by a small wall, built partly over the ancient outer wall. The house north of the central complex and the small chapel are of the late medieval period.[432] Where the present main building stands was once a small house with a loggia, which in turn was built where the old stables were found.[433]

Fontanabona, mentioned for the first time in 1192,[434] is a typical example of a small Friuli noble castle. An outer wall following the shape of the hill, two small houses, and a chapel, together made up the castle. At the center was a round tower. Only the foundations of this tower—an unusual feature in Friuli—remain, since the tower became dangerous and was demolished in the nine-

Fontanabona, an example of a castle with a circular plan. The main central building dates from 1800.

teenth century. As usual in Friuli, it was built in the courtyard, isolated from and facing the other houses.

The castle of Gorizia

The castle of Goriza is a particularly good example of a castle built to an almost circular plan. A building of great antiquity—it was probably begun as early as the eleventh century—today it is one of the best-known castles in Friuli as a result of the 1930s restoration which created a fairy-tale castle, fully satisfying visitors' expectations.

Unfortunately, visitors are largely unaware that, as in many other similar cases, the reconstruction was determined by the prevailing mood of the age, and not by historical accuracy.

The results of the restoration can no longer therefore be regarded as authentic medieval architecture. Given that the parts which retain most of their original character are the sixteenth- and early seventeenth-century fortifications, the castle should really be considered in comparison with other fortresses in Friuli.

Since we do not know the appearance of the original medieval castle, and since the changes of the 1920s and 1930s have not been examined, it is difficult to give a true picture of the present form of the castle. The site of the original entrance, for example, is a vexed question.

The entrance arch under the so-called Palazzo dei Conti is undoubtedly relatively

The original "Salcano" entrance to Gorizia castle. The entrance is now on the opposite side of the castle.

recent. The gate leading into the interior of the castle, with its huge lion of St. Mark, installed in the Fascist period, also appears to be modern.[435] The original access must have been above the Salcano gate which, high up and accessible only by a drawbridge, offered maximum security. The question of the position of the access to the center of the castle remains open. The curve of the curtain wall in the area of the Salcano gate, which was apparently discovered after the First World War, cannot be medieval. It is unlikely to have been an entrance since it could not be defended from the side and is more likely to

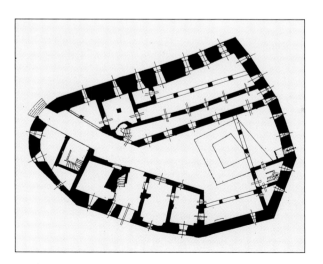

Of the three rings of walls at Gorizia castle, only the inner wall can be considered medieval.

FOLLOWING PAGES:
The imposing walls of Gorizia castle, built in the 16th century when the Hapsburg emperor and archduke sought to protect the lands they had inherited from the counts of Gorizia against Venice's expansionist policy.

A view of a courtyard in Gorizia castle. During the major restoration of the 1930s, the foundations of the old central tower were discovered.

be a bastion from the early modern period.

The conventional definition of this part of the castle as a Venetian tower does however seem acceptable, provided that it is a construction erected during the thirteen months in which Venice controlled Gorizia in the early sixteenth century.

In the light of these difficulties, the structure at Gorizia has to be assessed with reference to the medieval form of the castle.

sharp angles were found on the side exposed to attack, as indeed this would have been if the entrance was on this side. The Salcano gate is located, instead, on the other side of the tower.[437]

The question of the position of the *palas* similarly shows how problematic the analysis of a medieval castle can be. The building that today passes for the Palazzo dei Conti certainly has some attractive two-light

The apparent authenticity of rooms like this dining room satisfies visitors' expectations but does not reflect the world of the Middle Ages. The room would have been too small for the counts of Gorizia and their court and household, yet too luxurious as servants' quarters.

There is an almost-circular wall, interrupted almost at 90 degrees by the Palazzo degli Stati Provinciali, a fifteenth-century addition to the castle.[436]

The most conspicuous central point of the castle was an imposing tower, the huge foundations of which have been excavated in the courtyard. On its south side, this tower has an oddly sharp angle which cannot be explained by the vagaries of medieval construction. Normally, such

Romanesque mullion windows, but hardly any of these are medieval.

Moreover, the thinness of the outside walls of this building reveals that in this part, which was particularly badly damaged, later reconstruction has removed any evidence of the original appearance of the building.

The position of the building, in the immediate vicinity of the tower, makes it even more unlikely that the earliest residence was to be found here. It was most probably in a corner of the courtyard, opposite the tower and thus right on the route to the Salcano gate in the Venetian tower.

In the Middle Ages the castle of Gorizia must have looked quite different from its present appearance. It would have been much closer to the typical Friuli combination of an outer wall and central tower, rather than the present one of medieval castle, additions and restoration over the centuries, reconstruction after the First World War, and transformation during the Fascist regime of the 1930s.

Arcano: a classic noble castle

No other castle in Friuli demonstrates a near-circular plan in a form as pure and unchanged as that of the castle of Arcano. The inner wall surrounds a spacious courtyard on a plan similar to that at Fontanabona, with buildings on three sides. This nucleus has a much larger second circuit of walls around it, with a chapel and outbuildings in the gap between the two walls.

Even though substantial parts of the present walls were built or rebuilt only in recent times, the castle of Arcano today still has its early medieval structure. In the middle of the long residential block the medieval *palas* can be seen, adjoining the outer wall.[438]

The tower, which had already been demolished by the beginning of the seventeenth century, may have been facing the *palas*. In 1559 Valvason Maniago wrote that the castle had "a strong tower in the middle," but around 1630 a writer observed that the tower was "now destroyed, razed to the ground."[439] The site of the tower is still unclear. Archaeological excavation would be necessary to determine what stood on the site of the present courtyard. Maurizio Grattoni assumes that the house between the loggia and the entrance is built on the site of the tower. This would be the most logical place, opposite the *palas* and close to the entrance it had to guard.[440]

It was not unusual to rebuild on the foundations of an older building, but the explicit "razed to the ground" means that the old walls cannot have been used.[441] The tower would have been, as in similar cases, in the immediate vicinity of a wall which originally

stood here, as is clear from the difference in ground level still evident today.

The present form of the main building no longer corresponds entirely to how it was in the Middle Ages, when, in contrast, the courtyard occupied the whole area of the present entrance and the tower. Such reconstructions often resulted from damage and destruction. Arcano was besieged at least three times and was occupied twice, and is known to have suffered serious damage during the notorious *giovedì grasso* (Carnival Thursday) rebellion, as well as, perhaps, at other times.[442] There is an old, perhaps medieval, addition at the front of the present dwelling, where the circular layout is interrupted by a protruding rectangular building, as can be found in many castles, in particular at Villalta.

Even if in the Middle Ages the *palas* was markedly smaller, it represented an important example of medieval architecture in Friuli. Along with the outer wall and the tower (which is frequently mentioned in the sources and which was large enough to be lived in),[443] it meant that Arcano was a noble castle which might even be considered as a castle for the patriarch.

As in cases elsewhere, the ambitious architecture at Arcano can be explained by the circumstances of its builder. As early as 1208, Leonardo di Tricano was "appointed podestà (chief official) of Pirano for his meritorious deeds, and in 1225 he was elected marquis of Istria and castellan of Castel Venere." In return for Leonardo's services and his loyalty to the patriarch, around this time the family was also given the important title of *marescalchi e confalonieri* of the patriarch of Aquileia.[444] This high status would most likely account for the outward appearance of the castle.

Since the family is only first referred to with the name of the castle at the end of the twelfth century, and the family's period of greatest prosperity was over by 1265, the building we have briefly reconstructed must have been built in this period.

Despite the absence of a tower and the constant restoration and reconstruction, the castle of Arcano is a richer example than usual of a noble castle of the Middle Ages.

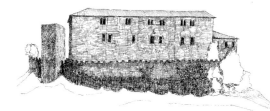

The Castle of Arcano

The hills between San Daniele and Fagagna, still mostly unspoilt, form one of the most beautiful parts of Friuli. In the middle of this area is the hamlet of Arcano Superiore, with panoramic views in all directions.

The view of the castle is particularly evocative. The castle stands on a small mound just below the village; it looks as if it had been built here for aesthetic reasons, since the choice of site cannot have been based on defensive considerations. As with so many other castles, it is odd that higher ground was not chosen. Vegetius would certainly have advised against building a castle on this site. Its position can be understood only if we remember that the castle had limited military importance, whereas its function as the central point of the estate had far greater significance. It is likely that the main properties of the lord of Arcano lay in the valley toward San Daniele, from where the castle is particularly conspicuous. When choosing a site for a castle, it was not seeing that was important, but being seen. What mattered most was to be seen by others as powerful.

The castle of Arcano was probably built in the late twelfth century. The name is recorded for the first time when a certain Ropretto called himself *di Tricano*, although in 1161 his father had been recorded as "Leonardo di Corno." Corno is the name of the small river in the valley below the castle. There must

The rebuilding of walls and crenellations in almost every century of its history does not detract from the medieval appearance of the castle of Arcano.

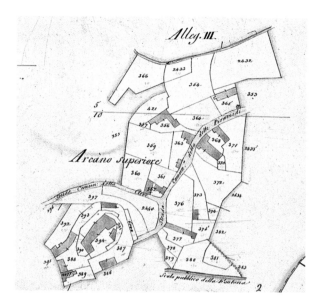

LEFT:
Coat of arms of the lords of Arcano, called Tricani because of the three dogs in the central shield.

RIGHT:
Plan of the castle of Arcano in the early 19th-century, as it appears on the Napoleonic land survey.

have been another castle on high ground near the river, where there is still a small chapel today. A Roman villa has been excavated nearby, indicating that the place had been a seignorial seat for a long time.[445] The transfer from this estate, which was later called the lower castle, to the new castle on high ground is marked by a change of name. Ropretto called himself and his castle Tricano, taking the name from the three dogs on his shield,

Documents in the family archive record that there used to be peasant houses in the gap between the two circuits of walls.

FOLLOWING PAGES:
The castle from the San Daniele side. The large main building has a row of two-light windows in Romanesque style.

while his brother Bertoldo, who stayed on the family estate, kept the name Corno. We do not know what happened to Bertoldo's descendants or when the seignorial seat referred to as Arcano Inferiore (Lower Arcano) vanished, though it is still recorded in the Napoleonic land register.

The present castle is surrounded by three rings of walls. A small door with a wall in front of it forms a picturesque entrance. All these walls are post-medieval. The tower is too weak and the wall too small to be medieval defensive architecture.[446] The slender tower on the road to San Daniele must be sixteenth-century as it is visible in old drawings. That its function was not defensive is clear from the thinness of the walls and the site chosen, picturesque but quite inadequate from the practical point of view.

In the absence of archaeological excava-

tions, we do not know if the medieval village corresponded to the space between the outer and inner walls. The surviving documents reveal that the space was once occupied by a number of small houses or hovels, but now only the chapel, with its surrounding outbuildings, remains to suggest how the village might have looked.[447]

The houses where the peasants and the lord's household lived were separated from the internal part of the castle by a high wall. Today this wall still runs along the steep slope of the hill, so that from the castle terrace it looks like a low parapet though on the other side it is five meters (16 feet) high. All the walls have recently built simple battlements which do, however, give a medieval air to the whole complex.

A late seventeenth-century list of restoration work carried out already includes numer-

ous references to the restoration of battle-ments. This would suggest that for the owners, even in the seventeenth and eigh-teenth centuries, it was important that the building should look like a castle. Evidently it is not just in the nineteenth century or today that pseudo medieval walls were built. Such continuing interest preserved the castle from ruin, but unfortunately makes it more difficult to date. Only the walls of the *palas*, in parts two meters (six feet) thick, are undoubtedly of medieval origin.

From a distance, the main building, with its two-light Romanesque mullion windows on the top floor, seems to have been built all at the same time. When examined close up, however, it can be seen that there are four quite different parts, which must have been built at different times.

The earliest part has stonework of a unified and particularly solid type right up to the roof. This construction, about 12 meters (40 feet) long, must be the original medieval dwelling of the castle. Its windows are of a later date and the original opening of an *Erker* latrine is walled up.[448]

The next section to have been built is the first sector of the block. With medieval walling, this sticks out at a right angle from the almost circular outer wall. It was proba-bly a house built in the course of the numer-ous divisions of property between heirs. The wall between these two houses is of a much later date, from a period in which the occu-pied area was enlarged in order to include all the buildings in a single wing.[449]

The dating of the Romanesque two-light windows on the top floor is problematic. It is because of them that, despite all the differ-ences in stonework and the joins between

The palas of Arcano. Despite its unified appearance and the row of regular two-light windows, closer examination reveals four distinct building phases.

sections of building, the *palas* as a whole is considered late Romanesque.[450] In theory, it is possible that an original window has been repeated the length of the building in order to make for a unified effect and to suggest great age. Indeed, if the windows are examined closely, it can be seen that part of the mullion is made out of cement and the ogee arches have been carved recently out of a soft sedimentary stone. Only one window, with a stone frame, looks earlier, but this is to be found in the newest part of the building. The windows must therefore be regarded as a nineteenth-century addition.

From the inside it is obvious that none of these windows is original, because this whole floor, which from the outside looks like living accommodation, is taken up by one huge loft. Even in the Middle Ages this space cannot have had any important function since the typical medieval stone windowseats are absent on the short wall, which is certainly of medieval construction.[451]

In front of the large *palas* is a sunny internal courtyard reached by a wide ramp lined by obelisks. Obelisks, fashionable in Venice as a mark of the highest position in the government, were quickly taken up by proud Friuli aristocrats and became indispensable in castles in the region. At Arcano they serve

The large courtyard of the castle, enclosed on three sides. Only the side least conspicuous from the outside was left open in order to admit light to the houses.

Detail of an 18th-century portrait, which shows that the layout of the castle has changed very little.

to mark the entry to the way up to the village and castle on the road from Fagagna to San Daniele, since at this point the castle is hidden from view behind the hill.

In the seventeenth century, the entrance to the courtyard was widened and improved, leaving little that is medieval.[452] The rear of the outer wall with its battlements is clearly more recent.

Nowadays the *palas* contains a charming series of smallish reception rooms, decorated with cheerful scenes of aristocratic life from the eighteenth century. The themes and style of these pictures are of fashionable aristo-

The interior of the castle, evidence of the care and dedication of the many generations who have lived there.

cratic residences of the period, vast gardens with villas in them. It is extraordinary that during this very time the ancient castle was being so well maintained and was even being extended according to medieval traditions.

The careful conservation of the castle of Arcano in the past shows clearly how mistaken it is to think that the demise of castles coincided with the early modern period. The castle walls reveal, instead, that after the castle's original construction in the twelfth century, it was added to and preserved in every period. Prompt rebuilding followed any destruction. The present walls were built over the course of many centuries and it is impossible to date them.

Until recent times, the castle was, as it had always been, the living symbol of a once important family. It is thanks to the unflagging interest in this building that Friuli has a castle conserved in such an exemplary fashion.

221

Square and rectangular castles

While most castles in Friuli are built on a circular plan, or nearly so, elsewhere in Italy castles were generally built to a square or rectangular plan. In a study of castles in Lombardy we read that "the square plan was not unique to the Lombardy area but was widely used, as is well known, throughout northern Italy and elsewhere."[453] The round castles of Friuli are therefore unique in Italy, though they are the norm in South Tyrol, Austria, Germany, and elsewhere in northern and central Europe.

Square and rectangular castles, in contrast, are found not only in Italy but also in those areas of western Europe that were most influenced by the Roman world, that is, in southern France and Spain. In the nineteenth century, the idea arose that this pattern of distribution suggested that the rectangular ground plan was derived from the Roman *castrum*. It is still the case today that castles built on a rectangular plan are often presumed to derive from the *castrum*:

> Southern Europe—Italy, France, and Spain—remained faithful to the Roman practice of building military encampments according to a set plan. Where the topography allowed, these remained within precise boundaries. The ideal was the *castrum*. In northern Europe, on the other hand, the choice of ground plan appears to have been random. Here the ground plan of castles depended entirely on the local topography.[454]

However, as we saw earlier, there is unlikely to be any direct connection between the layout of castles and Roman *castra*. There is no known example of the Roman model determining the layout of a medieval castle.

It was because of this difficulty that in 1930 Carl Schuchard interpreted the different types of castles as "expressions of national identity" in his *Die Burg im Wandel der Weltgeschichte* (The Castle in the Course of History). Though the date of publication is indicative of the ideological background to this theory, the basic tenet of the book still deserves consideration—that is, that the explanation for the square plan may be found in the Latinate culture of the countries of the Roman Empire, even independently of the direct tradition of the *castrum*.

Castles with square ground plans are not in fact to be found only in Italy, France, and Spain. From the fourteenth century they were the dominant model throughout Europe. The change from the round form to square, which is particularly striking in Friuli, needs to be examined to see if it is to be interpreted as a reflection of a historical development. In other words, are castles built with rectangular plans really more recent?

In this connection, Friuli provides an exceptionally valuable field of research for scholars of castles seeking to establish the reasons for the preference for different structural forms. The dividing line between the two types of castles lies in western Friuli. The castles of Porcia and Zoppola are not typical of the region.

The *castrum*-type castle

The wide difffusion of rectangular or square-plan castles in those Latinized countries where Roman culture was at its strongest and lasted longer than elsewhere would seem a persuasive argument for those looking for continuity between Roman and medieval fortifications.[455] The idea that square-plan castles derive directly from the Roman *castrum* must, however, be rejected for several reasons.

First, the assumption that the basic plan of the medieval castle derives from the Roman *castrum* presupposes that the latter existed in order to be copied. Not one example of the widely accepted form of *castrum*, that is, either a temporary wooden building or a permanent stone barracks, has been discovered anywhere in Friuli. Until an example is found, we are in no position to know whether buildings erected subsequently draw on them.

It is clear from the Roman writer Vegetius that the Roman *castrum* did not necessarily adopt the classic rectangular form. If anything, the rectangular form was a model to be followed only if the particular topography made it appropriate. Excluding the towns and fortified settlements, the few examples known of Roman defensive works in northeast Italy that are referred to as *castra* adopt quite different forms. They are not encampments, but rather primitive fortified refuges. Such structures can be regarded as precedents of the *cortine* but not of square castles of the so-called *castrum* type.

Third, the only known examples of the *castrum* type of medieval castle, which for their size and the quality of their stonework surpass all other types of Italian castles, are situated in those very areas where the Roman *castrum* was unknown. The only castles in which Roman walls have clearly been reused, on the Rhine and the Danube and in the Low Countries and England, do not follow the *castrum* model at all. They are in general too large, being big enough to have accommodated large settlements in the early Middle Ages.

Even if we accept the idea that there were *castra*-type castles in Italy, this does not explain why it should be the case that in Friuli, a border region vulnerable to invasion, such castles are absent, or exist only in the west. Roman *castra* would have had to have been destroyed so utterly in eastern Friuli that the memory of their form was lost for ever, while nothing of the sort occurred to the west of Spilimbergo and Valvasone. The idea is preposterous.

It would be preferable, then, to attempt to explain the origins of the form of the *castrum*-type of castle without reference to Roman architectural traditions. These castles relate more to an ideal of Roman military architecture than to actual buildings. At most, the tradition of these types of buildings may have been passed on indirectly. Between the last Roman *castra* and the earliest *castrum*-type castles, there is a gap of several centuries. If we want to argue that Roman tradition lies behind the *castrum* type of medieval castle, the only architectural model available is the functional and juridical precursor of the castle, the Roman villa, or country estate.

Rather than there being an architectural continuity between Roman encampments and medieval castles, it may be the case that there was a process of *incastellamento* (the development of castle features) in seignorial residences in Italy, parallel to the process that was taking place in the north, where small seignorial centers were becoming motte and bailey castles and, finally, stone castles. The aristocratic Roman estates that took over from the villa were probably roughly rectangular structures, designed and built in accordance with Roman architectural tradition. However, it has not been possible to find enough archaeologically documented examples of such continuity—a continuity which might seem suggested by common sense—since there are so few examples of medieval castles where the foundations of a Roman villa have been found.

It is clear, nonetheless, that the flexible rectangular layout derives in Italy, in each case, from Roman tradition. The influence of Roman architecture can be seen in the layout of monasteries, just as in many ground plans of early medieval buildings or royal courts north of the Alps. The possibility remains, therefore, that in Italy a sense of a more distinct and sophisticated form survived compared with what one might expect to the north, which had been far less influenced by the Roman world. Essentially, I would argue that an orderly square ground plan reveals a higher cultural level than the somewhat arbitrary castle plans which are found north of the Alps and in Friuli. The development of castles in Germany, which over time reveals increasing interest in the overall form, to which first individual parts are subordinated and then the whole structure, represents such a process.[456] The culmination of the process, the classic square castle with four corner towers, will survive as long as the civilization of the west survives.

There are innumerable instances of the persistence of the Roman inheritance in many areas of life in medieval Italy. It is strange, then, that so fundamental a skill as the design of large buildings is not evident in seignorial residences when it is be be found in the monasteries, whose abbots belonged to the same families that built the neighboring castles. From this point of view, we need to consider whether the northern European round castles can be explained by the fact that those who constructed them came from northern Europe and chose familiar models for their new dwellings.

The rectangular-plan castles of the thirteenth and fourteenth centuries, above all the celebrated castles of Frederick II in Puglia, are considered by some historians to be based on Islamic buildings, which would have been known through the crusades. This would suggest that Roman traditions were preserved better in Asia Minor and North Africa, through the influence of the eastern Roman Empire with its capital in Constantinople.

The castles of southern Europe that recall Roman *castra* can be seen in the context of the influence of the crusades and fourteenth-century castles in Europe only if we accept the theory that they were built later than those of northern Europe. According to such a theory, the reason for the absence of round castles in southern Europe would be because the vogue for building noble castles reached these countries only much later, when it had been evolving in northern Europe for centuries.

But it is not possible to prove that noble castles did not already have a rectangular form in the twelfth, even the eleventh, century. All the same, I have not found a single convincing example in the literature on the subject, and Friuli offers a good opportunity to examine its rectangular-plan castles in regard to this problem.

Some rectangular-plan castles

Castles with rectangular ground plans are only occasionally found in the eastern part of Friuli. In every case, however, the archival evidence proves that they were built in a later period. The focus of the complex is always a square *palas*, as at Tricesimo and the lower castle at Strassoldo.

In the west of Friuli, on the other hand, is the castle of Zoppola, a square complex with four wings, which is typical of castles elsewhere in Italy. It has no equal in Friuli and historians disagree about its date of construction.[457] The other castles in the west of Friuli—Santo Stino di Livenza, Torre di Pordenone, and, above all, Porcia—are similarly great rectangular blocks, but without an internal courtyard. In this chapter we will examine whether the reason for this layout was that those responsible for their construction were heirs to Latin culture, or because the castles are situated in the western part of the region, or, finally, simply because they were built later.

The archduke's castle at Zoppola

A little to the west of the castles of Spilimbergo is the ancient dominion of Zoppola, which was originally Austrian. A certain Alpuino di Zaupola is mentioned as early as 1103,[458] but the castle is recorded only after 1360, a surprisingly late date.[459] Up to this time, the feudal lord must have lived in a seignorial dwelling which, unlike the village and the dominion, was his private property. The unusual name of the lord supports this, as it is not derived from the name of a castle, as is the case with the majority of the families in the region. The village itself must have belonged, like Pordenone, to the dukes of Austria.

Only in the later Middle Ages, in the period in which the blood feud and abuses increased, did the duke of Austria decide to build a castle at Zoppola, which in 1360 he gave in fief to the lords of Zoppola. This castle, built to a rectangular layout, may have consisted only of a strong outer wall, with small houses and outbuildings inside. It must have occupied the southern half of the present castle area and probably did not have a tower.

In 1405, the patriarch Antonio Panciera, from a wealthy patrician family in Portogruaro, managed to purchase the castle for his family and in 1411 he had it drastically restored. It was at this time that the residential buildings in particular must have been improved, as is indicated by the fact that a tower was built in the northeast corner of the old complex.

Only in a third phase, perhaps at the beginning of the sixteenth century, did the castle reach its present dimensions. The area of the castle doubled in size, the height of the walls was increased, and the tower became the central feature of an imposing front about 50 meters (165 feet) wide. The patrons who had this substantial work carried out were the descendants of Panciera's nephews. The forms they chose corresponded in every way to those of buildings being erected at the time by ruling families elsewhere in Italy, that is,

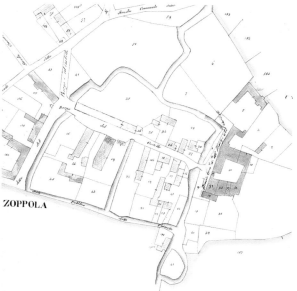

The castle of Zoppola, a classic Italian castle built to a rectangular plan. The four wings of the palace enclose a central courtyard.

ZOPPOLA

The early 19th-century Napoleonic survey plan of the castle of Zoppola. In front of the castle is a burg enclosed by a low wall and a stream.

rulers in Lombardy and even the Medici around Florence.

The kinds of buildings being built were on an urban scale, large structures with spacious living accommodation, splendidly decorated, and so tall as to make them extremely expensive to build. The focal point of these castle-like buildings, in the country as well as in the town, was always a high tower whose exterior was embellished with ostentatious military forms. For this reason, what appear to be parapet walks are in reality storerooms, while rows of small windows are placed to look like battlements.

Buildings such as this, which resembled castles, were built by the Medici at Cafaggiolo, Trebbio, Careggi, and Petraia. At the beginning of the sixteenth century, Pope Julius II built such constructions in Rome and Bologna as seats for administrative bodies.

Vertical elements were provided at the corners to increase the overall impression of a castle,[460] a feature apparent at Zoppola in the southeastern corner.

In Friuli, scholars have been unanimous in dating the castle of Zoppola to the eleventh century; it is held that it was built as a defense against the Hungarians. But in fact it is a typical Italian castle of the late Middle Ages and the early modern era.

The rectangular layout of the castle is an example of how castle construction changed after the fourteenth century. Though the basic form of the castle determined the changes that followed, the later castle bore very little resemblance to the original. On the site of a relatively simple late medieval castle, with an outer wall and a few houses within it, was erected a large building embellished with defensive towers and parapet walks, that displayed the power of the occupants.

What is the connection, if any, between such a castle and the Roman *castrum*? The new castle complex at Zoppola was built in this form because an essentially urban family, with Italian origins and traditions, wanted to create a grand, powerful, and expressive building, on the lines of those seen everywhere in Italy. The same forms are found both in the urban castles of the aspiring lordly families, and in the Palazzi del Comune, the seats of government in republican Florence and Siena, symbols of the city's liberty. Such buildings were also constructed by families who wanted to give a feudal appearance to their villas in the countryside, such as the Medici, and as in fact happened at Zoppola.

Bearing in mind how arbitrary the meaning of architectural forms can be, it is not surprising if the typology of Medici villas is the same independently of whether buildings were totally new or developed out of the conversion or extension of a medieval castle. In any case, buildings were erected whose forms cannot be explained in terms of a defensive function. Rather, they are in every way an expression of the particular cultural and political circumstances in Italy, in which urban power moved to the countryside and was exercised by urban patricians from palaces with an urban air. From castles, the new elite essentially adopted only the structures of dominion over the countryside and some cultural elements associated with a particular way of life: the idealized court and chivalric culture that lies at the heart of the literature and art of this time.

The form of this *castrum*-type castle can therefore be explained first by its much later origins and, second, by its particular patronage, and thus by contemporary urban culture, that had nothing in common with the chivalric culture still flourishing north of the Alps. The dominant urban patrician class, at this time extending their power over the whole of Italy, stood in stark contrast to most feudal lords in Friuli, who were beginning to perceive the danger that the enormous wealth of this newly emerging social class everywhere posed to their power and to themselves as a class.

While the bricks of the frieze give the impression of a parapet walk, the balconies and their beautiful door frames are typical of a town palace.

The Castle of Zoppola

Of all the castles in Friuli, the castle of Zoppola is the one which corresponds most closely to the idea of the typical Italian castle. It is a tall building, on a uniform rectangular plan which is slightly irregular only on the northern side, with an equally rectangular internal courtyard.

The castle, which still today is the center of a large complex, may have been originally surrounded by three circuits of walls. No

Gothic windows, probably originating in late fifteenth century.

In front of the castle building, one crosses a fine stone bridge to reach the long narrow space from which the façade, the most striking of all Friuli castles, rises. Almost 50 meters (165 feet) long and exceptionally high, the rough surface of unplastered simple brickwork contributes to the overall effect. Three-quarters of the way up, a graceful

Beyond the moat is the imposing long façade of the castle, a great aristocratic palace.

The interior of the castle, with its courtyard, recalls many 15th- and 16th-century palaces in Lombardy, Emilia Romagna, and central Italy.

trace of these survives, however.[461] Outside, a stream flows past the castle, with a small bridge which leads to the entrance. The modest walls, on the scale of garden walls, show no sign of medieval work.[462]

Below the castle stretches about 300 meters (330 yards) of gently falling land with farmhouses and well-preserved, picturesque barns. Two of the latter structures have small

cornice of round window arches closes the broad surface, on which simple rectangular windows are placed at irregular intervals.

Under the roof a further series of rectangular windows forms a line which creates the visual effect of battlements rising up from the frieze below. This way of closing off the wall under the roof is a recurring motif of sixteenth-century aristocratic architecture.

common in Tuscany and Lombardy. In Friuli it is found, for example, at Cassacco.

Originally the façade was plastered and frescoed, as can be seen from surviving fragments at the join with the roof. The decoration was probably typical of the period,

The effect of the façade was even more impressive before the 1976 earthquake. The tower, which is now entirely incorporated into the complex, was much higher, rising several meters above the main block and ending at the top with large rectangular open-

mainly rich and elaborate ornament, examples of which survive in the courtyard. Of the original wall decoration, there remains only a round cornice with typical Renaissance decoration and the balconies with their fine iron railings. Of the stone modillions, only the northernmost ones are sixteenth-century. Two others, with a traditional medieval lion motif, cannot be easily dated.

ings that looked like battlements protruding from a frieze. The roof was pointed. We do not know to what extent the tower was original or resulted from the restoration carried out in the nineteenth century. A drawing of the castle represents it, if vaguely, as already having such a tower, suggesting that the tower must date from before 1800.[463]

A similar architectural element on the

frescoed. Substantial restoration is also recorded in 1411, as well as partial reconstruction after the damage of 1511.

On the basis of these unfortunately few points of reference, the history of the castle can be divided into three phases. In the fourteenth century, the first castle was built. This was powerful for its time, with solid outer walls, on a more or less rectangular plan. The castle must have been commissioned by the duke of Austria who, once it was built, gave the feudal domain of Zoppola in fief to his administrator, together with the castle, which was still recorded as his property in 1388.

The scale of the castle, even assuming that it occupied only half the present area, would have been far beyond the means of private patrons such as the lords of Zoppola, mere *ministeriales* from the lower nobility. Lacking property, they would never have been in a position to pay for such a building out of their own pockets.

The castle of Zoppola was therefore not built as a typical seignorial Friuli castle. Its main purpose was to provide the duke of Austria with a guarantee of security over his estates to the east of Pordenone through an impressive demonstration of his determination to show his control of the area.

I have been unable to establish why the duke of Austria should have then lost both the castle and the dominion. Whatever the reason, the castle finished up in the hands of the patriarch Panciera, who handed it over to his brothers as a family property. This urban family, which had acquired wealth through trading and industry, was already living in Portogruaro in the early fourteenth century, enjoying high status as regards wealth and social standing.[474]

When Antonio Panciera became patriarch in 1402, his family certainly benefited financially. It is not therefore surprising if just three years later a purchase agreement was drawn up and substantial reconstruction began. We do not know, however, what this work involved. The phrasing in the source excludes the possibility that it was an enlargement. It is possible that Antonio Panciera built the tower, although the evidence of the joins in the stonework suggests that the tower cannot have been erected at the same time as the extension of the façade.[475]

OPPOSITE:
Axonometric cross-section of the so-called patriarch's study in the castle of Zoppola.

The 16th-century ceiling of the study, with the patriarchal coat of arms in the center.

Small rooms were created from the principal wall, which is almost two meters (six feet) thick. One such room, shown here, is traditionally known as the patriarch's study.

The decoration on the façade must have been executed sometime after the destruction of the *giovedì grasso* rebellion. The frieze adds weight to the theory that the enlargement of the castle was indeed undertaken during the course of the same work. The result was a large, typically urban, castle, which, like many others of the time, was overlooked by a tower that was impressive and decorative but, from the point of view of defense, entirely superfluous.

Thanks to the recent work carried out self-lessly and with dedication by the Panciera family, the castle of Zoppola can be regarded as one of the most beautiful and impressive castles of Friuli. Its architecture, unique in this region, gives it a special place.

The castle of the counts of Porcia

The castle of the counts of Porcia, in the village of the same name, is similarly on a rectangular plan but is quite different. The counts of Porcia were once the most important family in the region. Both the family and the castle, their seat, have ancient origins. The origin of the family name is Latin, while the earliest written sources record the family's status as members of the free nobility, in full possession of their estates and castles. They are the only family to have been confirmed by all the patriarchs with the highest form of investiture—standard and sword—attesting to an ancient origin both of the family itself and its namesake seat.

Showing marked political skill, the family succeeded in keeping its power and property from late antiquity right through the restless times of the late Middle Ages. A family story claims that its origins date back not only to Cato the Elder, but even as far back as the kings of Troy.

Archaeological excavations would be needed to find out whether the foundations of a late Roman seignorial court or one of the early Middle Ages are to be found underneath the walls of the present castle. This might account for the rectangular complex of the present castle. However, here too, there is no need to look for a Roman *castrum*.

Setting aside such speculations, the castle of Porcia is typical of numerous Italian castles that were converted into dwellings or mansions. At the heart of the structure stands a massive tower, whose age is obvious. Roman origins have been claimed for this tower since the sixteenth century,[476] but in view of its size it is clearly a remarkable medieval tower house. Its walls, three meters (10 feet) thick, enclose rooms of almost 30 square meters (322 square feet), which today are elegant halls, decorated with stucco. The joins in the stonework in the wall on the upper floor show that the tower has retained its original height.[477]

The second distinct phase in the process that led to the emergence of the present-day structure was the extension to the solid square central building, an enlargement that can be clearly seen in the ground plan and is confirmed by the joins in the stonework on the exterior. The larger buildings added on the right and the left are definitely post-medieval and require no further attention.

In 1178 the *castro porczile* is mentioned for the first time, in a deed. However, it is not known in which rooms the contract was signed, nor can this be understood from the present building. Only the tower, because of the thickness of its walls, though without any other evidence, can be identified as medieval, but it is not clear what the rest of the complex was like. In and around the castle and the present house there is nothing to suggest where the fortified nucleus of the complex, surrounded by walls, would have been.

It is uncertain whether the *castro porczile* of 1178 referred to a castle as we would now understand it. Everything points to this *castrum* having been no more than a fortified and inhabited center in the old sense of the word, just as Girolamo di Porcia described it as late as 1567: a castle surrounded by walls, with a belltower like that found in St. Mark's in Venice. "Large, with fine living accommodation, a good water supply, and respectable, well established houses. There are several doctors and notaries, fine counts' houses and two fine towers."

This rich variety of different elements would have been found in the area of the medieval center of the village which is still visible today, that is, from the parish church beyond the castle up to the northern gate. This complex must have been surrounded by eight towers, most of which were identified by Forniz.[478]

Rather than attempting to reconstruct around the present tower a stronghold for whose existence there is no evidence, it would be preferable to seek to reconstruct the medieval castle on the basis of entirely different premises. The counts of Porcia, respected and powerful, were lords of huge estates, farmsteads, non-fortified villages, and other *castri* and *castelli*, of which the most important was without doubt Prata, which unfortunately we know nothing about because it was destroyed by Venice.

The castle of Porcia, on the other hand, could be distinguished from the villas of the area because of three characteristics: it was surrounded by walls and was therefore strong and secure; it was the seat and center of a medieval dominion, and thus had a vote in the Friuli parliament; and it was the residence not of some mere *ministeriale* of the patriarch but of the foremost and most esteemed family of the region. From this castle, the counts of Porcia conducted a vigorous expansionist policy that was not particularly effective, since they were not afraid of coming repeatedly into conflict with the city of Treviso.[479]

There is nothing to suggest that a classic seignorial medieval castle was built in order to become the basis of such political aspirations. The reality is that in the thirteenth century the owners, who were also the political and economic lords, lived in a small settlement which had not yet reached the size of a town and was surrounded by walls and towers. We need to imagine their residence as a tower house of extraordinary dimensions, which inside provided more than enough space for its inhabitants. Normally the tower houses of this period, whether in towns or in small seignorial castles, were much smaller.

At the end of the Middle Ages, therefore, the tower of Porcia was still regarded as an entirely satisfactory residence for a family of important rank. Furthermore, it was surrounded by walls which were protected by numerous inhabitants who, in view of their trades, enjoyed a modestly comfortable way of life at least up to the sixteenth century. The imposing tower of the lords would have thus been surrounded by small houses, and the route of the road still indicates today how this stronghold, this family tower in the countryside, was the central point of the whole area.

Only when the need for more space arose, with a new emphasis on a more luxurious style of living, did it become necessary to increase the accommodation available. The old tower was enlarged and became a solid square building, though its remarkable height meant that it continued to mark out the castle as a lordly residence.

There was now no need whatsoever to have defensive walls immediately around the central nucleus. Castle and dominion could function perfectly well without them. If our conjectures are correct, the reason the castle eventually came to have a rectangular plan is that the later enlargements of the small medieval nucleus did not take into account the original circle of the walls. The exten-

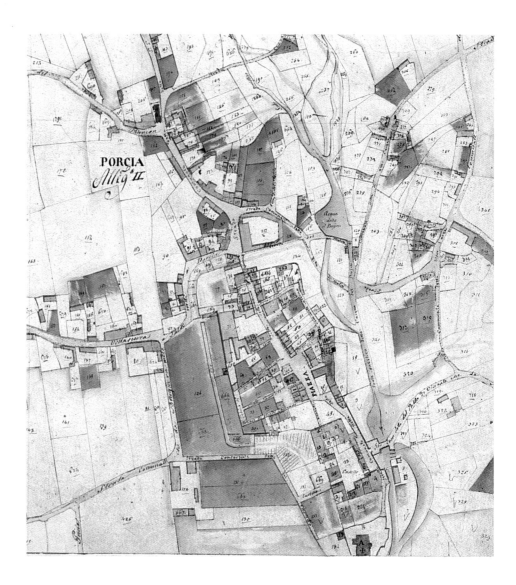

sions were thus carried out with the same freedom of building as had occurred in the palaces of aristocratic families in the towns of the late Middle Ages.

This map from the Napoleonic land survey shows that even in the 19th century Porcia still had the appearance of a fortified village, that is, a castle in the early sense of the word.

The Castle of Porcia

At Porcia, west of Pordenone, one of the oldest and most important castles of the region is to be found. The entire complex is now on the edge of the village because the construction of several streets has considerably interfered with the entire context of which it was formerly part.

In contrast to other castles in Friuli, at Porcia the castle consisted of much more than the buildings which are still to be seen around the ancient central tower. The old *castellum* was much larger, as was recorded by

This 19th-century watercolor shows the 17th-century Venetian-style palace as it once was, next to the tower. The top two floors were removed after an earthquake in the 19th century.

Girolamo di Porcia in the sixteenth century:
Porzia, a castle with an outer wall … has [a bell tower] built on the model of that of St. Mark's in Venice. It can be ascended on horseback. The castle is large, with living accommodation, is reasonably well supplied with water, and has respectable, well established houses. There are several doctors and notaries, fine counts' houses and two fine towers.[480]
The inner part, the part which is today defined as the castle, is situated on a small

rise at the southern end of the village, though there is no evidence visible now of any wall separating the castle from the village.[481] The central point is formed by an imposing brick tower.[482]

On the left, a tall building has been added, with similar walls of considerable thickness and a tower at the rear. Originally the façade was plastered and frescoed so that it resembled stonework.

To the right of the tower is part of a once imposing building, in Istrian limestone. Originally it had five floors and was the same height as the tower. Subsequent demolition of the top two floors because of weak foundations has made the tower stand out more, but the majestic effect of the façade has been lost because the proportions have been altered.

In the early twentieth century, another wing was added on the eastern side. Inside was built a grandiose staircase, following the taste of the time. This wing ends on the courtyard side with a majestic loggia, from where there is a fine view over the riverbanks below the castle.

On the edge of this area is a spacious courtyard where, over time, houses have been added in an unsystematic way, and which connects with the present wine store that occupies the first two floors of a sixteenth-century building damaged in a fire.

Behind the wine store, but isolated and with no direct connection either with the castle or the village, is the neo-Gothic parish church, with a fine sixteenth-century bell tower. Girolamo di Porcia recounted with pride that inside the tower was a ramp which could be ascended on horseback. Originally the bell tower was inside the outer wall but it is unlikely to have had any defensive role even if, according to tradition, a secret passage led from the well, about three meters (ten feet) down, to the castle, perhaps emerging in the tower, where there was a similar well.[483]

Near the entrance tower, the houses retain the characteristic features of a medieval castle burg.

Ground plan, showing the different phases of construction of the castle of Porcia. In the middle is the medieval tower, surrounded by the late medieval rectangular complex and later additions. The great Baroque palace is on the right.

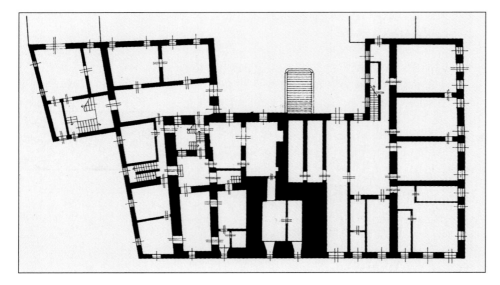

The present village is on the opposite side of the castle. This was formerly surrounded by an outer wall and protected by several towers. Only the imposing gate tower remains on the northern side. From here the main road, flanked by arcades, led to the tower of the castle. This is the only place where it is possible to gain an idea of the original structure.

Halfway along the road, on the right, behind an open area, is a large building with Venetian arched windows, which was built by a member of the family around 1600. The elongated windows accentuate the Mannerist features of the façade of this too tall building, whose walls are, however, plain and white.

242

The road ends in a small piazza where there is a fine house which must date from the sixteenth century. This, the seat of the *Comune* (local council), has an arcaded loggia on the ground floor. In the same period was built the charming church which was the chapel of the castle but is now separated from it by a road.

Finally, opposite is to be found an unusual building, painted white, whose façade must formerly have closed off the courtyard of the castle in a striking way. A charming stucco frieze of crowned dancing figures seems to be a self-deprecating and ironic reference to the legend that the counts of Porcia were descended from the kings of Troy.[484]

The history of the castle of Porcia has still
to be clarified. In 1178 a castro porczile is
mentioned for the first time as the place
where a contract had been drawn up.[485] But
not even Antonio Forniz, an indefatigable
scholar of the medieval history of the village
and castle, was able to find out much more.
Although there are repeated references to a

castellum, there is no information in the
sources about its form. Even Miotti has
found no information about the attacks by
the Ottoman Turks and the damage the castle
suffered over the course of time.[486]

The first description of the castle, by
Girolamo di Porcia, dates from 1567, when
the castle comprised two majestic towers

245

In the first years of the 20th century, the old residential wing of the tower was greatly enlarged and was enriched by this splendid staircase in Venetian Renaissance style.

("belli palazzi dei conti," fine counts' residences), as well as other fine houses for the residents of the village. In addition, Miotti cites "un cronista del tempo" (a contemporary chronicler), unfortunately without indicating his name, who apparently referred to many such residences.

Besides the Baroque building in Istrian stone that Forniz rightly attributes to Tommaso and Francesco Contin, which was probably built at the beginning of the seventeenth century[487] for 50,000 ducats,[488] this chronicler recorded another residence "which had paintings by Pordenone and high walls and ceilings with fine gilding, quite apart from the comforts which the eye can see."

The chronicler claims that this earlier residence, where Emperor Charles V stayed in 1532, was worth at least 30,000 ducats, in part because of its precious furnishings. He listed some of the rooms: "a large hall, the guest room, the dark room, the room with the wardrobes and diamonds decorated with the family coats of arms with golden fleur-de-lys on an azure field."[489]

Apart from these two houses, there was a third called *vescovado* (the bishop's house), which still exists in part today. Forniz has written a study of this house and its paintings.[490] It is unlikely that the second of the houses named can be the building still seen in the village today, because its architecture cannot be of so early a date. There may have

been a building on the side of the present unplastered wing, a theory that is supported by family tradition. The huge bell tower, whose size is now disproportionate for its location, was perhaps built as a symbol of aristocratic power in the space between the church and the present castle.

The little historical information that we have refers to a castle dating back to the Middle Ages, but the structure we see today is the result of building works carried out much later. We should not therefore be surprised if the castle seems no longer to preserve a medieval character anywhere, with the exception of the tower.

The Porcia family coat of arms: an azure field with six gold fleurs-de-lys and head of gold.

The double entrance to the palace, dating from the Renaissance.

Minor castles of the counts of Porcia

Of particular interest to the whole question of the classification of castles is a comparison between the castle of Porcia and two others of rectangular form found in western Friuli, at Santo Stino di Livenza and at Torre di

We might ask if this common ground plan is mere coincidence. Is the reason for the common rectangular form of the castles of western Friuli that they followed a specific idea of their patrons? At Torre di Pordenone, this question is complicated by the fact that in the sixteenth century, according to Girolamo di Porcia, the castle was still only a tower: "A castle comprising a single tower where the residence

An 18th-century fresco depicting the castle of Torre di Pordenone, showing the original building, before the demolition in the 1920s of the arcades and the round tower.

Pordenone. Both these castles are complex buildings to which a tower has been added on two sides, making a clearly defined block. The castle of Santo Stino is referred to for the first time in 1186, shortly after the first reference to the castle of Porcia.[491] The first mention of Torre di Pordenone occurs only in 1259.[492]

The ground plans of the two castles place them with the group of castles owned by the Prata branch of the Porcia family, and it would be interesting to know if the castle of Prata was also of the same form.

of the lord is to be found, and the *villa*, which previously belonged to the patriarchs."[493]

However, knowing the present complex, it seems unlikely that prior to 1560 only the fortified nucleus of the tower should have existed, with much thicker walls. It is probable, therefore, that Girolamo di Porcia, in saying that the castle consisted solely of the tower, meant that there was no village and that the seignorial residence, a tower house, was surrounded by a rectangular circuit of strong walls.

The castle of Torre

Hidden away and largely forgotten, at Torre di Pordenone there is a small castle which shares the sad fate of so many buildings that have become lifeless ruins. And yet this intriguing building merits close attention.

The last owner, Giuseppe di Ragogna, devoted himself to the history of his castle with the enthusiasm of a dilettante of the old school. He dated the tower—indisputably the oldest part of the complex—as follows:

From the third floor upwards [the castle] is built in brick and dates from the Roman era… If these buildings more than two thousand years old are constructed of such material, then a building of stone blocks placed one on top of the other without mortar must be attributed to the Minoan civilization, whose stonework used regular dressed and carefully placed blocks. Such a provenance is supported by other archaeological finds at the site which come from Aegean culture or, at the very least, from its direct influence.[494]

This claim demonstrates a total ignorance of medieval architecture, as well as a striking zest for the implausible romantic fantasy that was typical of the era.

The center of the little castle, the imposing tower which gave its name to the place, is a typical medieval tower house. Over an area of more than ten square meters (110 square feet) were built walls which are two and half meters (eight feet) thick. These walls were swiftly rebuilt after destruction, without much attention to style. We know that on 12 April 1402, the city of Pordenone took vengeance on the arrogance of the owner, Giovannino di Ragogna, burning down the castle with all the family inside. The sources reveal how the town council of Pordenone, which had for some time wanted to appropriate the castle, restored it, "nuper ruinate et combuste" (recently damaged and burned down), in great haste.[495]

To help date the original structure, we have only the base, whose impressive stonework of dressed blocks is badly eroded. On the right corner of the base, where the first extension to the tower is joined on, some better preserved blocks reveal typical medieval rustication which would make it possible to date the tower to the twelfth or thirteenth century.[496] The earliest source referring to the castle dates from 1259, when Guecello II of Prata gave the castle to the patriarch as a sign of reconciliation.

The size of the castle and the rustication, typical of Hohenstaufen castles in Germany, suggest that the tower was built in the early thirteenth century. Sources that can be used to reconstruct the history of the castle are, however, scarce. We know only of a complaint in 1317 by the patriarch Gastone della Torre of Avignon against the count of Gorizia, who had occupied the castle illegally and strengthened its defenses.[497]

The huge tower is still obvious in the center of the ground plan. To one side, where

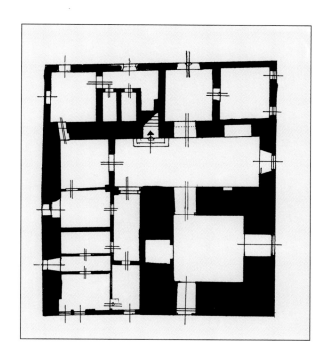

Ground plan showing how a castle with a rigidly rectangular plan developed around the large tower with its imposing walls.

there was once a little courtyard with a charming eighteenth-century loggia with four arches, and where the castle once ended with a semicircular fortified tower, today there is an ugly building dating from the 1920s.[498] The present plan, therefore, can be used for a reconstruction of the architectural history of the castle only on the other two sides of the tower. The first phase of enlargement can be seen in the outer wall, a uniform rectangle. The thickness of the wall, a meter and a half (five feet), testifies to its medieval origin. Since all the other walls are noticeably less thick, corresponding to the modern norm of

Aerial photograph of the castle of Torre di Pordenone, revealing its classic square form, surrounded by forest.

about 60 centimeters (two feet), the reinforcement of the castle carried out in 1317 should be recognized in this wall. Originally there were probably no other buildings and the tower would have stood in a courtyard measuring four or six meters (thirteen or twenty feet) wide.

On the side that was destroyed because of the new building, the foundations of the wall indicate a less regular plan. The archaeological excavations that brought to light the base of the semicircular tower (the whole tower can be seen in an early twentieth-century photograph) suggest that the tower probably marked the limit of the rectangular outer wall. From here another wall began, on an irregular line, belonging to another phase of the building work.[499] The window apertures recognizable in the early photograph of the castle prove that the tower must have been added at the beginning of the early modern period and is not medieval.

In the fourteenth century, even the narrow area next to the courtyard was transformed into a house. The loss of the typical appearance of a castle as a consequence of the opening-up of the windows in the early modern period was compensated for by a parapet walk with swallow-tailed crenellations, a picturesque and elegant completion of the tower. The small arches protruding from the sloping terracotta ledges make it possible to date this fairly securely to the sixteenth century. Since Girolamo di Porcia described the building as a tower in the 1560s, this extension was probably built only at the end of the century.

From the same period may date the enlargement of a door which from the outside seems extremely solid but which, because of the thinness of the walls, could have had only a symbolic function, to display power. The dwellings to the left and right of the original door and in the widest part of the internal courtyard were built in a later phase. In this way the castle acquired its present appearance of a mansion.

Rectangular-plan castles: a possible explanation

The question posed is whether the castle of Porcia and the smaller castles of Santo Stino and Torre can help us find an answer to the problem of the predominance in Romance-language countries of rectangular-plan castles, often referred to as the *castrum* type. A direct derivation from Roman encampments is impossible. In contrast to the castle of Zoppola, the castle of Porcia does not have even a rectangular outer wall, the basic element of the *castrum*.

The reason why castles that are very different from one another still have a rectangular plan may derive from the fact that we are in the presence of an architectural tradition not of northern European origin but belonging to countries with a Roman tradition. It is an urban, civic tradition, which must have led to the development of forms completely different from those used by families who lived under the *lex longobarda* (Longobard law) in the minor seignorial castles in the eastern part of the region. In cases such as Porcia, it is quite impossible that there would have been a main tower built of wood, as at Strassoldo, even though here too the village enclosure will not initially have been in stone.

If the castles in the western part of the region have a rectangular plan, this is due above all to the fact that the currently visible forms emerged relatively late. In earlier times, a feudal residence or tower house was sufficient. The rectangular plans of the castles of Friuli should be linked to similar structures in the rest of Europe which became widespread beginning in the late thirteenth century.

The Friuli examples thus suggest a somewhat surprising explanation of the clear predominance of the so-called *castrum* type in Romance-language countries. In these countries, real feudal castles began to be built much later than in the lands north of the Alps, in South Tyrol and in eastern Friuli. In the Romanized area, with its established urban culture, the need for a more ostentatious style (appropriate to the nobility and the counts belonging to the free nobility) seems the building of classic feudal castles only much later—much later, in any case, than in the feudal society of northern Europe, where the simple tower house has already become inadequate by the twelfth century.

This phenomenon confirms once again, the relative lack of military importance of the noble castle as it was not needed for the security of the region. The defensive role became important only when other lords had similar buildings in the immediate vicinity.

Princely architecture of the Middle Ages

History and archaeology give the impression that in the Middle Ages secular buildings were of a very modest size. In general, larger castles started to appear from the fourteenth century onwards, when the living accommodation was enlarged in response to new needs, akin to the situation in the towns.

The rapid development of castles in this period is thus to be attributed only in part to improved economic conditions and to greater disposable income among the nobility. The growing demand for a higher standard of living resulted in expenditure on a scale that many feudal lords could not sustain. Archival sources reveal information about the debts incurred by the aristocracy and mortgages on castles that many families were obliged to quit or to sell. In this way, urban patrician families came into the possession of castles and were in a position to construct, enlarge, or improve them with the financial means they had available, as, for example, occurred at Gronumbergo.[500]

The major constructions of the period are the seignorial castles which, thanks to the wealth of their princely patrons, became enormous buildings, particularly when they were the preferred residence of their owners.

With the destruction of the old castle of Udine in the sixteenth century, the most important medieval princely residence in the region has been lost. To have an idea of what this building may have looked like, we have to examine the less important castles of the patriarch, especially that of Tricesimo.

The castle of Tricesimo

The castle of Valentinis at Tricesimo is exceptional for a number of reasons. To start with, the heart of the old castle is still a square construction in Venetian Baroque style which, however, if looked at more closely, reveals a medieval *palas*. Thus, here we have a castle that is much older than its external appearance would suggest.

The medieval *palas* has walls more than a meter and a half (five feet) thick, which rise on a square plan with sides of almost 20 meters (65 feet). The exterior, on the unplastered sides, has three two-light windows which were later walled up and which, from their Gothic form, must be fourteenth-century.[501] So few windows would have been insufficient to light such a large building; originally there must have been an internal courtyard, meaning that the present layout and the roof are the result of subsequent alterations.[502]

The castle was thus made up of a strong outer wall against which small internal buildings were built, as can be seen in drawings of other castles.[503] From the outside, the effect would have been that of a compact regular block, visible from far away. A courtyard was then added on the eastern side, forming with the *palas* a complex that is entirely atypical for Friuli.

However, there is also a shielding wall. This may make Tricesimo the only example in Italy, apart from Duino, of a type of castle that is typical of southern Germany. The wall had the task of protecting the castle on its most vulnerable side, facing the plain, where there is now a rather ugly church. Although the wall and its towers no longer correspond to the medieval form, and are obviously a post-medieval reconstruction, the historical sources prove that the concept is faithful to the original.

The castle must have been built in the early fourteenth century. Work carried out on two separate occasions is recorded: Raimondo della Torre, the most enthusiastic builder of castles under the patriarchs, acquired the old building in 1295, and in 1332 one of his successors had a *magister [master] Dominicus Marangonus* come to Tricesimo from Padova in order to be present during the construction of defensive works.

The *palas* was perhaps begun by Raimondo della Torre, while the courtyard with its shield wall was probably built at the suggestion of Domenico Maragono, which may be the reason for its unusual form. The reconstruction of the original form of the *palas* is the key to the interpretation of its historical function and site. Like several other late medieval *palas*, Tricesimo tends towards a regular square plan, a grand and impressive architectural form.

A similar example can be found in the *palas* of Verres in Val d'Aosta, built by the count of Challant in 1390, where the square *palas* has a courtyard which is no larger than any of the eight rooms in the building enclosing it.[504] Similar structures are also to be found in northern Europe, where castles surrounded by moats tended increasingly to have regular plans. Examples include the castle of Rheden near Graudenz[505] and the famous castle of Moyland near Kleve, where a square building encloses a spacious courtyard on three sides. The archetype of this type of castle built on a geometrical plan is the octagonal Castel del Monte in Puglia, built around 1240 by Emperor Frederick II, a building with three floors enclosing a courtyard, itself octagonal.

All these constructions show how in the early Middle Ages buildings were marked by the rationality and ability to plan that are generally regarded as distinctive hallmark of the Renaissance, inasmuch as they are the expression of a scientific and mathematical way of thinking that is essentially modern.

The present *palas* at Tricesimo is thus one of the most important examples of fourteenth-century secular architecture. Within Friuli, it was an extraordinary achievement for its form and size, which immediately identified it as a patriarchal castle.

The beginning of construction in the early fourteenth century coincided with the final phase of consolidation of the patriarchal overlordship. The *palas* of Tricesimo was no longer required for the security of the region, but rather to bear witness to the patriarch's claim to dominion. It was built on a conspicuous hill north of Udine, in the center of a region that has a wealth of castles even though there was no practical need for them.

From the defensive point of view, the cubic form was inconvenient and the quantity of dressed stone would have been better used to strengthen the outer walls. The castle cannot even have been intended as a patriarchal residence or as a hunting lodge, since the proximity of Udine made such an expensive second home superfluous. It is not even certain whether or not there were larger rooms in the interior.

The function of the *palas* or, more precisely, the high outer wall, is mainly

symbolic. It is one of the earliest examples that reveal how the form of the castle was determined by the fact that it was a symbol in stone of dominion and power. In the late Middle Ages, image, from the patron's point of view, began to become more important than effective defensive capacity.

Thus as far as the history of Friuli castles is concerned, the value of the castle of Tricesimo is twofold: it is a fine example of fourteenth-century princely architecture, and it marks the gradual change in the significance of the castle, towards symbolizing its defensive strength. From defensive architecture, the castle became the architecture of dominion, a development whose roots go far back in the Middle Ages.

The palace of the Valentinis castle at Tricesimo. Although its appearance suggests a Venetian villa, the building is nevertheless the original 14th-century palas.

The Castle of Tricesimo

It is not just today that the road from Udine to Tarvisio is a particularly important link over the Alps. Already in antiquity, the Via Julia Augusta linked Aquileia, the great trading place of the northeastern part of the Roman Empire, with the province of Noricum.

Shortly before the point at which this road leaves the plain, at the thirtieth milestone, the Romans founded a colony, or at least an encampment, a *statium*. North of the site is a high hill on which was built one of the most remarkable castles of the region, the central point of a group of smaller fortifications.

The present castle, as is often the case, is the result of building activities that were carried out over the centuries. Already before the building of the *palas* in the late Middle Ages and the first enclosed front courtyard, a castle complex with buildings and a village existed here. Up to the present, no evidence has been found to confirm that the original buildings were built over Roman remains.[506]

A view of the castle of Tricesimo, an important example of a patriarchal castle.

The existence of the castle is attested only from 1253, when it is described as belonging to "the most noble family of Tricesimo," which also exercised authority over several villages.[507] In later documents, this family is no longer mentioned.

The castle must soon have been divided between several heirs because over the following years the patriarch Raimondo della Torre managed to buy all the shares of the estate.[508] It is clear that the patriarch was keen to have Tricesimo for his family, but after his death this led to disagreements.

In 1305 Raimondo's successor, Ottobono Razzi, besieged the castle in order to acquire it definitively for the patriarchate.[509] A distinction was made between feudal lordship over the castle and over its villages: whereas a captain administered

Tricesimo, a steward represented the patriarch's rights in the castle.[510] The steward was also responsible for the maintenance and defense of the castle.[511]

A document from 1332 recounts that the steward, Tommasutto di Pertenstain, was obliged by the patriarch to correct the fortifications of Tricesimo within one year. What is unusual is the fact that the steward was ordered to carry out these works in accordance with the instructions of a *magister Dominicus Marangonus* of Padua and to listen to the advice of the deacon of Rivosa, who had the right to a feudal residence in the village.

The unusual intervention of an architect or military engineer is worthy of note and underlines the special attention which was given to the castle. The steward had to cover the costs of the improved defenses, the renovation work, and even the extensions (*fortificare, reparare, et construere*), for which he was assigned a piece of woodland with the right to cut down trees for timber as necessary.

The lost castle

We do not know what the castle looked like in these years. However, it must have comprised an enclosed village with towers and the castle proper. Miotti, who saw the remains of the walls of the ancient ruin, is of the opinion that the original structure of the castle was situated where the rather dull postwar church stands today. This could be supported by a drawing by Domenico Paghini of about 1840, which shows some sizable medieval ruins behind the square mansion.[512]

Moreover, Miotti interprets the feudal right of residence granted to the above-mentioned deacon of Rivosa as the responsibility to build the existing mansion. As the deacon had to build his house within the burg, the present heart of the castle must have belonged to the burg. Thus the early medieval castle was perhaps situated further to the east.

Neither of these arguments is particularly convincing. First, the drawing by Paghini must have been executed from a viewpoint on the other side of the hill, certainly from the plain below. It depicts the ruins of the present burg very clearly and has probably used artis-

After centuries of
deterioration, in the 20th
century the outside wall of the
castle was rebuilt, respecting
the original medieval form.

tic license to make it bigger. The burg would certainly have been in need of restoration at this time.[513]

In the second place, Miotti's interpretation of the document cannot be sustained. The document is a classic investiture to a feudal right of residence, not an appointment as steward.[514] The court official was permitted only to build a house next to the northern wall of the burg, not a stronghold, as Miotti, referring to the abbreviated version of the document cited by F. di Manzano, supposed.[515] In the document it is stated explicitly that this house had to be built with a "muro forti versus fossatum dicti burgi", that is, against a strong wall built towards the moat protecting the burg.

Such investitures had great advantages for the patriarch: the new inhabitant made a contribution to the fortifications of the burg with a stretch of strong wall, in exchange gaining the right to live there.

The house must have been relatively modest, because the patriarch granted his official only "tres passus terre" (three paces of ground), corresponding more or less to five meters (16 feet), in other words, less than a quarter of the area of the present building.[516] Thus the castle still stands where it always did, and the square building also marks the center of the medieval complex.

Building history

The irregular castle, with its wings and towers, may still correspond to the form the castle had in the early Middle Ages, despite the considerable changes resulting from the reconstruction in 1900 and in recent years.[517] A very detailed drawing of the castle executed in 1647[518] shows that at least the eighteenth- and nineteenth-century reconstructions gave due consideration to the preceding structures.[519]

The real center of the castle complex is behind the burg, separated from it by a huge moat and accessible only by a narrow bridge. It is made up of a great square building, in front of which is a rectangular courtyard, about five meters (16 feet) higher than the surrounding land and entirely enclosed by straight walls. On the side of the entrance opposite the *palas* the wall is strengthened by two round corner towers. The heart of the old structure is still well preserved, even if the towers are in the style of the nineteenth century, when they were radically reconstructed.

The first phase of building must be placed

Ground plan of the castle, revealing a regular and precise form which has nothing to do with the building interventions of previous centuries.

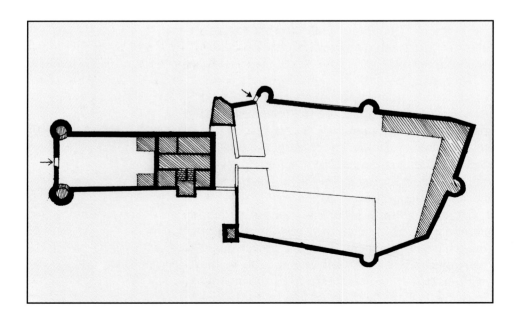

around 1300 since two documents from this time give us information on the works in progress.[520] The patriarch Pagano della Torre enforced peace in Friuli between 1318 and 1332 with his skillful policies, while his successor Bertrando di San Genesio (1334–50) consolidated power and re-established law and order in Friuli. Both patriarchs pursued their objectives of securing their own power base by enlarging and reinforcing the existing castles against the continued threat from the count of Gorizia.[521] This is the historical background to the construction of the castle of Tricesimo; it was built to a form and scale symbolic of the power of a great feudal lord.

The fourteenth-century castle

No other castle in Friuli has so clear a plan as Tricesimo. Above the village, rising on the area of a long rectangle, is a unit made up of a *palas* and a front courtyard. The courtyard elegantly continues the lines of the palazzo, together with which it was designed. It is remarkable not only for the clear concept of the plan, in which the courtyard is joined to the plateau of the castle, the weakest part, by a strong wall flanked by two towers. This concept, unusual in Italy,[522] corresponds to the form of shield wall that was particularly common in southern Germany and in Austria in the thirteenth and fourteenth centuries, of which there is a magnificent example at Duino. The exposed side is protected by a strong wall that assures full security.

Even if today the walls of Tricesimo do not reveal their ancient strength, the concept is still obvious. In the 1647 drawing, the front wall is clearly higher than the side of the piazza and reveals a thickness that is quite out of the ordinary.

The center of the whole structure is a Venetian-style building that rises behind the courtyard. The decoration of the seventeenth-century façade is in harmony with the square form, indicating that the building should be regarded as the Venetian villa of the Valentinis counts.

The scale of this country residence does not surprise visitors, accustomed to the enthusiasm of the Baroque period for large

The fine Gothic two-light window allows us to date the palas to the early 14th century.

and splendid palaces. In the seventeenth century, and even more so in the eighteenth, such buildings were realized with great effect, even when their owners were short of cash, through the use of increasingly economical materials and, in particular, through building ever thinner walls.

However, it is precisely in this regard that the visitor is surprised, as the external walls of the mansion are enormously thick, about a meter and a half (five feet), and therefore cannot be from the seventeenth- or eighteenth-century. The windows revealed in the most recent restoration work confirm that the great square building is a late medieval structure without equal in the region for scale and impression of strength.

Despite its many transformations, especially in the sixteenth and seventeenth centuries, the essential part of the old structure has been preserved and is sufficient to give us an idea of its original appearance. The mansion consists of three floors and is perfectly square, with sides of about 20 meters (65 feet).

On the ground floor and first floor, the external walls have a thickness of one and a half meters (five feet) and can be considered

medieval. The internal walls have the usual 70 centimeters (two feet) thickness of the modern period. The present plan, which corresponds to Venetian town palaces, is thus of a later period.

In the course of the most recent restoration of the outside wall, apart from many early Renaissance arched windows distributed irregularly on three sides of the *palas*, three two-light Gothic windows came to light. Of these, two are on the side looking towards the village while one is on the side of the staircase looking north. These three windows, as confirmed by their appearance, must have belonged to the old fourteenth-century *palas*.

The sole irregularity in the external wall occurs on the second floor: while the north wall has the same thickness as the floor below, the south one is only about 70 centimeters (two feet) thick. It must be assumed therefore that this wall is of a later date.

Other architectural details also show that the *palas* of the late Middle Ages was of a quite different form up to 1500. The external walls must have been practically without windows. Apart from the three two-light Gothic windows, no other apertures have been found that could date from the fourteenth century.

The problem arises, therefore, of how the palace was illuminated inside, seeing that the square body of the construction enclosed what must have been a considerable surface area.[523] An internal courtyard has to be presumed, around which the houses of the steward and the rooms for the patriarch would have been grouped. Perhaps the south side of the building was lower, to allow more light into the internal courtyard from this side. The roofs must have sloped toward the interior on one side only to favor the light and to ensure that from the outside the building would appear compact and large.

The medieval construction must therefore have been a square structure, surrounded by walls and on different levels, with external walls which had almost no windows.

A view of the square palas which forms, together with the courtyard protected by a wall and towers, a strikingly harmonious whole.

From castle to villa

After the Venetian conquest of Friuli, both the village and the castle were governed by a captain appointed by the Venetian government. He had the task of collecting taxes and administering justice.[524] We know nothing about the inhabitants of the castle in the fifteenth century. Ownership is documented again only from the beginning of the sixteenth century,[525] when in 1504 the castle was bought by the Prampero family.[526] However, they sold it in turn to Sebastiano di Montegnacco on 2 March 1531.[527] Records of expenses at this time testify to the fact that in

At the end of the 16th century, the castle was altered. The palas took on the appearance of a Venetian palace but the exterior remained typically medieval, with towers and battlements, as can be clearly seen in this detail of a 16th-century fresco in the castle chapel.

these years the *palas* was transformed into the palace of today.[528] On the exterior, the second floor on the southern side was completed and the roof built. Arched windows were also inserted which would provide adequate light for the interior of the building. The arrangement of the windows most likely already corresponded, at least on the main façade, to the typical Venetian palazzo: a depiction of the castle in the chapel in a fresco from the second half of the sixteenth century already

shows a three-part central window, flanked at some distance by one or two other arched windows.[529]

The inside of the building had perhaps already reached its present form in this first phase. The original courtyard was eliminated and new roofs and rafters were added. From this time, the arrangement of the rooms corresponds to that of a Venetian palazzo: a long continuous central hall flanked on right and left by pairs of opposite rooms.

A surprising feature is that the axis of the central hall does not coincide with the central axis of the building; the rooms on the right are bigger than those on the left. Miotti thought that this unusual feature could be explained by the re-use of earlier walls, but none of the internal walls is of a greater thickness or reveals any irregularity.[530]

On the other hand, it is true that in the fifteenth century no preference was yet generally given to symmetrical construction. The Villa Corner dall'Aglio, created as a completely new building around 1490, has a similar plan. Even in those considered up-to-date and architecturally grand buildings, the medieval lack of concern in ordering the windows had not yet given way to the rigid regularity of later façades.[531]

Recreations of the medieval castle by the Montegnacco family

In the ground plan as on the exterior, the Prampero family castle was transformed into a very early example of a Venetian villa. Inside, however, the heavy vaulting on the ground floor does not seem appropriate to the new urban forms. But many discrepancies in the single spans of the vaults indicate that these were inserted in a later period. The position of the windows was evidently kept in mind, leading to strangely distorted forms, particularly in the corners of the rooms on the right.

Vaulted ceilings are a non-Venetian, non-urban element. In Friuli they are to be found only in the eastern part of the region. In Austria and Slovenia, such forms are frequently encountered not only in castles but also in patrician palaces, which almost always have vaulted entrances.[532]

It was with these vaults that the ground floor at Tricesimo regained the appearance of a castle, corresponding to the way it looked in other phases of its history. The fresco in the chapel, for example, shows us that the façade formerly terminated under the roof with many small rectangular windows, giving the impression of battlements, an architectural motif popular in the fifteenth and sixteenth centuries, when owners wanted to give their new houses the appearance of a castle.

The same motif can be found in the towers of Cassacco, built in the same years by the Montegnacco family. It is no coincidence that the castle of Cassacco appears in the fresco next to Tricesimo. The present moat at Tricesimo and the picturesque gate after the drawbridge, which must have been constructed at this time, have precise formal echoes at Cassacco. Obviously these features were not created for defensive reasons, but in order to form, together with the nearby well, an entrance for the family residence that was striking, aristocratic, and, at the same time, warlike and feudal.

The culminating point of these works was a building of whose existence we know only from two documents of 1647, when the Valentinis family bought the castle with all its feudal rights.

The chapel frescoes are evidence of the high cultural level of the 16th-century patron, a member of the Montegnacco family.

In the middle of the narrow upper courtyard there was at this time an imposing tower,
at least as tall as the house.[533] It occupied
about half the area of the courtyard and was
topped with picturesque crenellations. It
seems that the lower part, at least, served as a
prison,[534] but a tower such as this was obviously not built simply for this purpose.
Instead, it should be interpreted as an attempt
to create a visible and clear sign of the feudal
origins and power of the family.

In this way, at the end of the sixteenth
century, from the patriarchal castle turned
Venetian villa, a castle rose again, following
a trend that in the late sixteenth century had
not only spread through Friuli and the Veneto
but also all across Europe—a nostalgia for
the feudal age, a nostalgia felt not only by
citizens of Venice. The king of France similarly had his hunting castle of Fontainebleau
surrounded with deep moats full of water and
had drawbridges installed.[535]

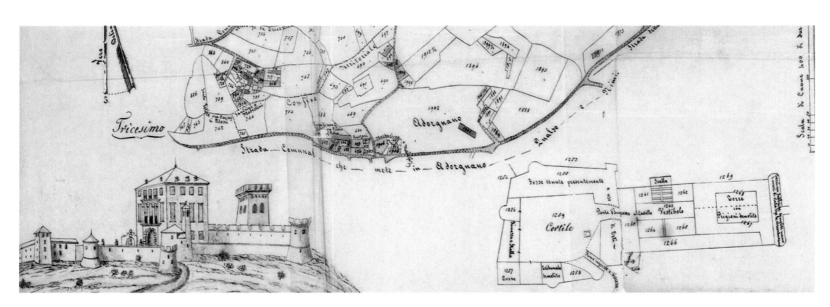

Seventeenth-century transformations

At the beginning of the seventeenth century, the castle of Tricesimo was bought for 4,800 ducats by the Valentinis family. Twenty years later, Nicolò and Coriolano Valentinis obtained in addition their investiture as feudal lords of Tricesimo and of thirteen other villages. As a result, they reinstalled a *capitano* (captain) in the castle.[536]

A document of 2 September 1625 records that the Montegnacco family could no longer maintain Tricesimo and that the building was in a poor state.[537] The restoration undertaken by the Valentinis family around 1647 is summed up by an inscription placed over the portal: *Ab informi... formavit* (formed out of the formless).

This work marked the transformation of the medieval castle into a Venetian palace, a transformation the owner also wished to express on the exterior. The façade was arranged in an up-to-date, urban way, with the insertion of the present rectangular windows. The center of the façade was given emphasis by three large arched Venetian-style windows. The façade ends with a cornice which, however, does not extend the entire width. Perhaps in this way it was intended to accentuate the central part of the façade, but the interruption at the sides is so brusque that it gives the impression of something unfinished and unconvincing.[538]

The new Baroque forms of the main façade could not harmonize with the lack of symmetry of the windows, which had been appropriate to the original building. The portal and the three-light windows were therefore aligned with the central axis of the main façade, which, however, does not correspond to the central axis of the hall. The three-light windows on the right are blind and the doorway is in the corner of the hall. However, this discordance goes almost unnoticed on entering the building, since the doorway on the other side remains in the middle.[539]

The most important step in the transformation of the medieval building was, however, the elimination of the strange tower that blocked the view of the house. As members of the urban patriciate, the Valentinis family had no interest in medieval defensive work, whether it was old or a sixteenth-century

imitation. Thus they had the walls, as well as the towers of the burg and of the front wall, torn down.

Only in the nineteenth century was there a rebirth of passionate interest in the elements that were considered characteristic of medieval castles. With typical neo-Gothic romanticism, the painter and restorer Uberto Valentinis had the outer wall, the front wall with its crenellations and the two corner towers rebuilt, thus restoring to the *palas* its imposing cornice in medieval castle style, even though it was all in fact carried out in the taste of the period.

The inscription above the windows describes the activity of Nicolò Valentinis, who "ab informi... formavit" (formed out of the formless), removing pseudo-medieval elements from the castle and giving it its present appearance of a Venetian palace.

Aerial view of Udine castle, dominating the city from the hill.

OPPOSITE:
The 16th-century ramp leading to the medieval church of Santa Maria in Castello, with its beautiful Renaissance façade.

The patriarchal palace at Udine

The most important castle in Friuli is probably that of Udine, where from the thirteenth century the patriarchs resided ever more frequently. The rapid growth in the number of people in a princely household, above all of the many clerks needed for the administration being created in that very period, made it increasingly difficult to move the court from one place to another, as had been customary in the early Middle Ages. Conferring the function of capital city on Udine was therefore the outcome of a gradual historical process which cannot be rigidly dated.

Before the earthquake of 1511, on the castle hill there were two palaces beside each other. The earlier one may have been on the site of the present sixteenth-century building, while the more recent one was probably built in the middle of the level land on top of the hill.[540] This castle, attributed by Buora to Raimondo della Torre as part of his *cupido aedificandi* (passion for building),[541] is first attested to in a reference to a *palatium novum vel grande* (new or great palace) in 1289. The building was created almost at the same time as the one at Tricesimo, and it would be truly fascinating to know what it looked like.

Two surviving images suggest that the castle of Udine was similarly a square, imposing dwelling. The fifteenth-century seal of the council of Udine shows a building with three outer walls and a square dwelling with many windows and crenellations, flanked by two towers of different heights.[542] While the lower wall on the seal is certainly the city wall, behind which must have been houses, above this can be recognized the castle hill, flanked by the towers of the castle itself. One of these may be the bell tower of the church of Santa Maria in Castello. However, the building above is a square construction with no roof but with crenellations. We cannot deduce the existence of an internal court from this because such images did not necessarily record exact appearances.

More reliable is a fifteenth-century drawing on the frontispiece of the *Tesauro de' Documenti de la Veneranda Fraterna di Sant Maria di Castello*, a collection of documents concerning the confraternity of the church of Santa Maria di Castello. This represents the Virgin, founder of the church, holding in her left hand the model of a castle that must be Udine. The image is extraordinarily similar to the present appearance of Tricesimo: a square building with the roof culminating in a small lantern, and surrounded by crenellated walls with corner towers and two taller towers.

Emperor Maximinus besieging Aquileia, a fresco by Pomponio Amalteo in the hall of the Salone del Parlamento in Udine castle.

OPPOSITE LEFT:
Fragments of fresco from a cycle depicting episodes in the history of the war of Troy, from one of the public loggias in the city, now in the picture gallery in Udine castle. The frescoes were presumed lost when the medieval buildings on the site were demolished in the 15th century in order to build the new loggia del Lionello. The Trojan theme was a favorite subject for the decoration of public buildings in the 13th and 14th centuries by patrons who wished to give a noble gloss to their own origins.

OPPOSITE RIGHT:
A document associated with the confraternity of the church of Santa Maria in Castello, depicting the Virgin holding a model of Udine castle, which is similar in form to the castle of Tricesimo.

Santa Maria in Castello, the oldest church in Udine. The original 6th-century church, rebuilt in the 8th century and enlarged in the 12th and 13th centuries, still preserves its Romanesque interior.

The bell tower of Santa Maria in Castello, dating from 1515, has become a symbol of Friuli.

TOP RIGHT:
A late 16th-century depiction of Udine castle, showing the great palace and the bell tower.

OPPOSITE:
Udine castle, the most important example in the region of Roman Mannerist architecture.

While the crenellated wall can be interpreted as a symbol of the castle, the large building can be recognized as a representation of the patriarchal palace, at that time the seat of the Venetian governor. The palace is represented with a regular articulation of the façade and a wide central balcony. Tricesimo, therefore, was obviously not the only large square castle belonging to the patriarch.

Aristocratic palaces

A number of minor buildings belonging to the local nobility were influenced by the great models of Tricesimo and, possibly, Udine. The rectangular-form castles of western Friuli, which can be classified as belonging to the *castrum* type, already reveal a volume that is geometrically clear and compact. In the three most striking cases—Zoppola, Porcia, and Torre—it is arguable that these are castles of the late Middle Ages whose rectangular form is in agreement with the fashion of the time, rather than being the expression of an older and still surviving Roman tradition.

The beginning of this tendency towards a rectangular plan has been discussed at length. It is difficult to decide whether it derived from the influence of the buildings seen during the Crusades or whether it represents

an independent process of development within the architecture of the period.

The model of seignorial buildings with their great volume may have played an important role. Among these must be included the castle of the archduke of Austria at Zoppola. What can be observed in the whole of Europe around 1300 is true also of Friuli. Similar structures are to be found even in the castles of the lower nobility in the eastern part of the region. The most impressive example of such constructions is the castle of Gronumbergo near Cividale.

The castle of Gronumbergo

Clearly visible from afar, on a hill to the north of Cividale, the rectangular architectural block dominates the entry to the valley of Natisone. As in other cases, the castle was not built on the top of the hill but about halfway up. This certainly weakened the potential for defense, but it made for a better visual effect.

Because of the shape of the site, it was not possible to build a perfectly square construction at Gronumbergo. The plan is almost rectangular but the outer wall follows the slope of the hill. There is still today, on the hillside, an enormous wall that is particularly strong and well built, and which, in the same way as a shield wall, could defend the castle on its weak side. The weakness of the uphill side was perhaps the reason why the wall was kept as thin as possible and the long body of the construction was not built parallel with the slope. Instead, a block was created that protruded from the hill. The effort involved to create the greatest visual effect for a castle is always an essential element to consider when examining the building.

The entrance to the castle was on the valley side. The ruins of the ancient doorway arch are still recognizable. Here it was protected in the best way, since it could be reached only after passing in front of the whole long side of the castle. Furthermore, the steep terrain

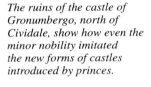

The ruins of the castle of Gronumbergo, north of Cividale, show how even the minor nobility imitated the new forms of castles introduced by princes.

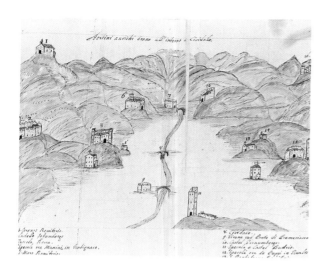

meant it was impossible to use battering rams to break down the gate.

Behind there was a small, narrow courtyard, forming the center of the castle. The foundations can still be seen today. We do not know how high the buildings surrounding it were, but the window openings indicate that they must have been of at least two floors. The front side of the courtyard was occupied, perhaps, by the most imposing building, which backed on to the outer wall and may therefore have been the *palas*.

In the narrow courtyard there was no space for large outbuildings for farm use. It is not even likely that these would have been in the vicinity. It is probable, therefore, that there was a farm in the valley below, possibly in the village of Purgessimo, from where the road still leads up to the castle.

A castle was recorded here for the first time in 1267, in connection with a certain Jacobo di Gronumbergo, or Grünberg.[543] In 1277 it was the property of the noble family De Portis of Cividale, who completely restored the castle in 1304. Unlike a minor noble family who would have been barely able to pay for the walls visible today, the De Portis, the leading aristocratic family in Cividale, had sufficient financial means to build a relatively costly castle.

As early as 1308 the castle was again destroyed by Enrico di Prampero. Rebuilding followed. The walls were strengthened and later, between 1380 and 1386, other reconstructions were carried out.[544] The castle of Gronumbergo must have

achieved its final form in those years, because after that time no further major work was carried out. It has not been occupied since 1854 and is now in ruins.[545]

The castle probably began as the fortified country house of a urban family who, not satisfied with being the most powerful family in Cividale, by building and enlarging the castle sought to take part in Friuli politics and acquire regional importance. The castle was a means to this end: it gave very limited protection from military action—a danger that anyone wanting to enter the circle of lords of castles and the aristocracy was exposed to but it was an impressive sign of the claims made by this powerful family, though with what degree of success we do not know.

From castle to palace

The foundation of the castle of Tricesimo was an important historical event for Friuli. Its powerful construction marked the rise of the typical castle that we are familiar with. It was at this time that the small buildings of the early Middle Ages, partly built from timber, and with only a few cramped and dark rooms, began to become large structures, able to satisfy more demanding needs.

Apart from the increase in size, a formal evolution in castles took place which is rarely given the attention it deserves. In the thirteenth century, on the basis of structures that were originally improvised and simple, with limited possibilities and built to satisfy immediate requirements, palaces with artistic pretensions began to emerge in which, in both the plans and the overall effect, the sophisticated religious architecture of the period is easily recognizable.

The improved quality of construction is apparent in all the details, even in the stonework, which in the thirteenth and fourteenth centuries saw a particularly harmonious period. Enormous blocks of stone were dressed according to the wishes of the patron, but we also find very finely executed stonework with small stones which have been thinned, flattened, and joined with careful regularity. In Friuli many amateur historians attributed such extraordinarily fine stonework

271

to the Romans because they did not believe the Middle Ages capable of it.

In parallel development to the activities of arts and crafts, changes in the functions of the castle also occurred, as is evident at Tricesimo. While initially defense may have been the central element, the flaunting of power now became increasingly important. In essence, already in the twelfth century, but then more clearly in the fourteenth, a new form of seignorial architecture came into being, which was to lead directly to the modern castle.

In a period that saw the process of formation of dominion end in Friuli, and the increasingly clear definition of territory, the importance of the castle as a center of the exercise of power increased steadily. Even for the smaller feudal lords the situation was defined in the same way as it was for the patriarch and his administration of the territory. The importance of the castle increasingly concentrated on its juridical function, because the lord of the castle was the holder of ancient political, economic, and military privileges. The region was divided into dominions with castles at the center, and only those who held the castles could participate in power. In this way the castle preserved for centuries its function as a symbol of power, even when its walls no longer had any military importance.

Cormons and Monfalcone

Castles and territorial power

The fight for control of the castles of Monfalcone and Cormons occupies a central place in the history of the long struggle between the patriarchs and the counts of Gorizia. Monfalcone was particularly important for the patriarch because the narrow territory offered the only way into Istria, the rich and fertile land that in the early Middle Ages was still part of its dominion. The proximity of the castle of Duino, with its insolent lords, who challenged the patriarch and always took the side of the count of Gorizia, was perhaps the reason why the patriarch was particularly concerned with the security of Monfalcone.

The high hill of Cormons, on the other hand, was the natural key for the widening of the count of Gorizia's power towards the west and, therefore, into the territory of the patriarch. The struggles for its possession were unremitting until in 1260 the patriarch signed an agreement that is recorded in the sources. Count Mainardo di Gorizia was granted the fief of Cormons. In return he promised not to disturb "the market and the *muda* of Monfalcone" and to give up all claims to *castro e loco montisfalconis* (the castle and village of Monfalcone).[546]

The *castrum* which had been recorded in all the preceding documents both at Cormons and at Monfalcone must have been a fortified military camp. If this is true of Monfalcone,[547] it must also be true of Cormons, since we know that from 628 onwards the patriarchal residence was for more than a hundred years in a *castrum* which certainly could not be on the hill.[548]

In both places there are now castles whose form has created a great deal of confusion among scholars.[549] No one has been able to explain their origin; everyone stresses their pre-Roman antiquity in order to account for their most unusual form.

Only Belluno managed to progress beyond such positions as these, identifying the structure of the castle of Monfalcone with the bleakness and agricultural poverty of the surrounding region.[550]

Both castles, despite the obvious differences, particularly regarding their size, have the same structure: a body of great regularity on a circular plan, with no windows and no adjoining constructions.[551] There are no other buildings around to mar the clarity of the shape of the structure, surrounded only by a large outer wall situated a good distance away. Monfalcone is the more impressive, with its wall in a perfect circle and the tower at the center. This unusual regularity indicates that the castle and the outer wall were contemporary. In the present structure no parts date back to earlier defenses, though excavations have shown evidence of prehistoric settlements.

No one has so far been in a position to date the walls. Historians have stressed the ancient tradition of defensive works and the fact that very different cultures may have re-

The castle of Monfalcone, a good example of how imposing forms have been preserved despite transformation, destruction, and reconstruction from the 16th century to today.

used the site continuously for their own very different purposes. However, what contradicts this long history is the unusually unitary architectural form whose consistency reveals that it was all constructed at the same time, in accordance with a preordained plan.

Only Belluno has ventured to suggest a date, proposing a thirteenth-century origin for the complex at Monfalcone "because it was only in this period that military engineers began to tend towards a defensive scheme on a square plan."[552] In proposing such a date, Belluno has borne in mind the wider fourteenth-century move towards a rectangular plan. However, Belluno did not point out up the unique element of this complex, which is certainly its design.

The castle of Monfalcone does not have a rectangular form of the *castellum* type, nor is it one of those early noble castles built on a polygonal or round base, whose form was determined solely by the individual terrain. Instead it is a construction whose basic concept and design must be compared with that which produced the castle of Tricesimo.

The medieval wall of the castle still has its slit windows, which were also used for small cannon.

Here we find a form that is large and full of strength, and whose effect depends on its clear geometric volume. Certainly at Monfalcone there is no embellishment or architectural decoration, though this is not a sign of poverty or lack of power. Rather, it is the expression of a compact solidity which still impresses the visitor today. The castle of Monfalcone must therefore have been built around 1300, when the building of castles had become a artistic endeavor and it was no

The space inside the walls of the Rocca di Cormons is so small that it was probably formerly roofed over.

longer the case that architectural forms arising from immediate needs were entwined in picturesque casualness. Builders already knew exactly what forms to produce to express the intentions of their patrons.

Some dates allow us to place the birth of the castle in a historical context. In 1259 and 1260 a *Castrum Monfalconis* is recorded for the first time. In accordance with medieval tradition, this must be the name of an inhabited center with a strong outer wall. Around the same time, the patriarch Gregorio di Montelongo granted it the right to hold a market. This privilege was so important to

him that he sacrificed even the claims of Cormons to its security.[553]

This commitment was probably accompanied by the building of the present keep.[554] Any buildings or walls that existed previously had not the slightest importance with regard to the new structure of the castle, which was built from scratch and all at the same time. The solid outer wall, with its remarkable stonework, was a powerful expression of the patriarch's determination to guarantee, at any cost, his possession of Monfalcone, bought at so high a price.

The Rocca (fortress) of Cormons is more difficult to examine. Here we have a construction that reveals little about the original structure. It is not possible to recognize the form of the original entrance, nor the internal arrangement, in part because the little that remains has been distorted by careless reconstruction.[555]

Furthermore, the documentary tradition is more obscure than in the case of Monfalcone. We can never say with certainty, for example, when *castrum* or *castellum* referred to the urban center or the keep. For this reason, studies of the historical tradition must proceed with extreme caution.

The construction of Cormons, despite its much smaller size, shares two crucial points with Monfalcone. On the one hand, there is the clear circular form, unspoiled by any architectural addition. On the other, the castle is here too a sign of dominion, visible from afar and extraordinarily effective. Despite its small dimensions, Cormons, thanks to its position on the highest hill in the vast surrounding area, is more effective than Monfalcone.

The importance of the building is in fact its visual effect alone: the silhouette of the hill of Cormons, crowned by the massive tower-shaped construction, is visible even from the patriarch's seat at the castle of Udine. In this way, the count of Gorizia demonstrated his personal power to the prince, keeping it constantly before him, something the castle of Gorizia could not do because it was hidden behind the hills.

It is highly probable that the castle of Cormons was built at the same time as Monfalcone. The two designs are so similar that they were erected perhaps in contrast with each other. Both were the sign of dominion in a territory; both were placed right under the eyes of their political adversaries. In many other regions of Europe, medieval architectural projects were similarly born of competition of this kind. Zeune recalls the rival families of the counts of Orthenburg, who built ever higher keeps in order to outdo their adversaries, with no thought for the fact that each new castle was further and further away from its source of provisions.[556]

been able to do more, in view of his reduced economic circumstances.

Unlike many other castles, both also had a solidity which made them important military garrisons. At Cormons, however, the most useful element of the structure was the height of the mountain. The circular heart of the castle was so tiny that there was room for only a handful of defenders, while the walls of the bailey do not seem to have been of the best quality.

The Rocca di Cormons, although much smaller than the castle of Monfalcone, had great importance thanks to its strategic position.

The historical struggle between the patriarch and the count of Gorizia could mean that the construction of an extraordinarily up-to-date, effective, and powerful castle might provoke a similar attempt from the enemy, with a view to doing something better.

Thus the smaller Cormons may well have been built before Monfalcone, even if the scanty historical evidence favors a slightly later date. The count thus managed to build a castle which, despite its small size, was extremely conspicuous and effectively fulfilled its function of annoying the patriarch. The count could certainly not have

Monfalcone, on the other hand, could serve as the living quarters for a small garrison, as can be inferred from a series of constructions that made a permanent stay inside it possible. As late as 1514, forty Venetian infantrymen successfully defended it for a long time. There was plenty of space for their accommodation. The surprising number of small wells for hygienic purposes in the area of the walls makes it likely that a strong garrison lived in small houses arranged in a ring around the wall.[557]

The medieval castle cannot have had a strong *palas*. The tower was built only in

1525 and its fortified base served perhaps as a powder magazine.[558] This building, constructed as a tower, testifies to the growing interest of the Venetians in Monfalcone, before the foundation of Palmanova. In that same year, the Venetian lieutenant recommended the enlarging of the Rocca of Monfalcone, justifying this by its strategic position on the border, near the sea.

The ancient castle in fact had a dramatic role in the war between Venice and the League of Cambrai.[559] The Venetians did not get as far as building a larger fortification, but the old structure was extended. The outer wall was strengthened and apertures were inserted for cannon, probably in 1525. Views from later periods give a peaceful image of a picturesque castle, with signs of later rebuilding work, and by now it was only the weakly defended quarters of a small Venetian outpost.

After centuries of gradual deterioration and severe war damage, reconstruction in the 1950s restored to the castle a medieval appearance. However, this radical attempt at conservation has created many problems. Renewing the construction from the aesthetic point of view has marred the castle's historical value, making careful research difficult.

Architectural buildings of the importance of Monfalcone should be preserved in a more careful manner. Their value does not lie in their ability to be an attraction for a Sunday afternoon drive; such buildings contain a considerable part of the history of Friuli, which is still waiting to be discovered. For the sake of both historical knowledge and the general public, it would therefore be better if the funds available were not spent on implausible, or debatable at the least, reconstructions, but were used to make educational use of those ruins that do remain. Instead, the closed atmosphere of the restored castle, with its iron gate, keeps visitors away.

The changing castle

Detailed examination of a number of medieval castles has shown that they were built over time and that they took on their present form above all in recent centuries. An examination of their history after the Middle Ages can therefore be extremely helpful in clarifying a number of issues.

This is a theme to which, so far, little research has been dedicated. In this book we too have often neglected more recent developments in order to concentrate on medieval elements. In Friuli in particular there is continuity between the medieval and the modern castle, a result of, among other things, the personal interest of their patrons in this aspect.

The castle of Villalta may be regarded as encapsulating everything that has been said. Its fascination lies not only in its form and its history. Always considered in the region as a model of the medieval style, it is an outstanding example of the survival of castles after the Middle Ages.

The Castle of Villalta

The castle of Villalta is one of the most typical and best-preserved castles in the region. It owes its fame without doubt to the homogeneity and consistency of its medieval appearance, with its crenellations and towers that are without parallel in Friuli.

Credit for the recent consolidation and restoration of the castle should go to its present owner, Dom Carlos Tasso, who after the damage caused by the 1976 earthquake gave new life to it. But the excellent state of preservation of the castle, which can be admired today, is due also to the efforts of all those who over the centuries managed to keep it alive, with restoration that was always consistent with the original medieval character of the castle, without giving in to the fashions of the times. Medieval buildings survived above all when their owners did not have sufficient financial resources to be able to transform the building into a more comfortable residence, or one more in keeping with the changing tastes and requirements of the day.

With its classic medieval appearance, the castle of Villalta is the result of centuries of history. Built in the 13th century, the castle remains a living building today.

In the case of the castle of Villalta, the della Torre counts, who were among the most powerful and wealthy nobles of the region, have preserved the original character of the complex, even though their resources would have allowed them to make any kind of modernization they wanted. It is therefore of particular interest to reconstruct the various maintenance works and identify the factors that affected the undertakings of the family over so long a period of time.

The castle today

The castle stands on a small hill about fifteen kilometers (nine miles) to the west of Udine, above the hamlet of Villalta. The building is made up of two clearly distinct parts: the castle proper and the burg below, which is entered by a drawbridge and the great entrance tower. To the right and the left, the large courtyard is enclosed by two two-storey buildings for farm use, which at the rear adjoin the outer wall. They have simple façades, such as those found in other aristocratic seats of the seventeenth and eighteenth centuries.

Opposite the entrance, sloping uphill and surrounded by a high and massive wall which creates a clear separation from the other farmhouses of the burg, is a second courtyard. Beyond can be seen the imposing buildings of the lord's quarters. The upper courtyard is accessible only through a narrow crenellated portal, placed at some height, which is reached by a narrow drawbridge. A steep path, carved out of the hill, leads right up to the long mansion, in front of which is an unexpected small open space. Since there is no wall to obstruct the view of the surrounding countryside, this space should be regarded as a terrace rather than a courtyard. To the right is a small round tower whose upper floor, accessible by means of a small staircase, contains a tiny chapel which must have been built at a later date.

The main building is the large block that divides the square in front of it from the rear courtyard. The main façade, visible from far away, not only makes an impact but has some architectural and stylistic elements that are unusual in Friuli castles.

On the first floor are imposing windows with typical Renaissance cornices which, however, are framed with massive blocks of rustication. The first impression is one of a deliberate effort to make elegant urban forms more rustic, in accordance with the sixteenth-century taste for Roman Mannerism, which reached Mantua through Giulio Romano and was introduced into Venice by Michele Sanmicheli and the young Palladio.

This style combined elements that were theoretically and formally irreconcilable. The crude, roughly worked forms were meant to reflect the simple life of the countryside. At Villalta, however, the heavy blocks of squared stone, contrasting with the delicate cornices of the windows, highlight above all the noble, castle-like aspect of the construction.[560]

At the center of the castle is the 6th-century mansion with Mannerist windows, built by the aristocratic della Torre counts.

Portraits of the eminent members of the family hang in three rooms inside the castle of Villalta, helping to exalt their importance.

The second floor has conventional Renaissance windows, with simple round arches and equally simple brick cornices. In contrast with the square windows under the roof, they are placed directly above the apertures of the first floor, thus creating a coherent structure for the façade. The different arrangement of the two floors would seem to suggest that the heavy Mannerist cornices are later additions.[561]

Entering the building, one finds oneself in a broad loggia of four arches which once opened on to the rear courtyard. Two of these arches were later walled up for reasons of stability. To the right of the loggia are rooms used for domestic activities.

The staircase that leads to the *piano nobile*, with its long ramp against the external façade at the back of the mansion, was evidently added with a great deal of difficulty, perhaps because it was once open. The first floor contains a vast hall, well lit by windows placed on opposite walls, and a much smaller room, which has been created by constructing a diagonal dividing wall.[562] Large portraits of the most famous della Torre ancestors used to hang in these rooms on the first floor, constituting a vast wall decoration which was intended to immortalize the statesmen, soldiers, patriarchs, and other eminent members of the family. This vast cycle, composed of paintings of huge dimensions but little artistic merit, celebrated the della Torre family and contributed towards making the castle a family monument.[563]

The second floor, which opens on to the outside with simple windows with round arches, comprises four rooms, both bedrooms and drawing rooms. The whole of the third floor is taken up by one huge loft.

To the left of the palace are four highly irregular buildings which adjoin the outer wall, thus forming a single block, perpendicular to the palace. Next to the main façade, on an almost triangular base, is an imposing structure which gives the impression of being strongly fortified and has large rectangular windows on its façade, an unfortunate eighteenth-century addition. This imposing building includes the old kitchen on the ground floor, an enormous room in which, in past times, those living in the castle spent most of the day. Probably already in the Middle Ages,

the upper floors functioned as reception rooms, as is borne out by the sixteenth-century frescoes which are still visible below the windows.

Next to this building is a tall narrow building, with just one large room. The external wall unites all these parts, even though they are of different heights, and encloses all the rear of the castle. In the courtyard thus created, against the wall, is a high tower that was later joined to the other buildings with a narrow structure.

In the medieval castles of Friuli, the tower was often not incorporated into the outer wall but instead stood alone in the courtyard. At Villalta the situation is less clear: the tower is not really freestanding but nor is it an essential part of the outer wall, as it seems to have been joined on later.

In places the tower has enormous squared rustication, which makes it impossible to distinguish the older parts from the more recent. Indeed, this stonework suggests that the tower was built with salvaged materials. This narrow square tower, each side of which is five meters (sixteen feet) long on the outside and barely less than two (six feet) on the inside, is, as usual, described to visitors today as a prison, while it was probably a larder or a storeroom.

The great hall at the heart of the mansion, formerly known as the portrait gallery of the della Torre family.

The old kitchen of the castle occupies the space of the old medieval palas. It may be the one described by Ippolito Nievo.

The history of the castle

The castle grew gradually, though it is impossible to distinguish the details of the different building phases which took place from time to time after the many acts of destruction it suffered during the course of its history. It is possible only to distinguish between medieval parts and later additions, taking as the criterion the varying thickness of the wall. Before attempting to reconstruct the various phases of building, we need to look first at the historical sources.

The first reference to the castle is in a donation deed which is recorded as having been made at Villaco. In it a certain Heinricus de Villalt is named as a witness. The name Villalt makes it likely that a castle with this name already existed.[564] In 1216 the castle resisted armed attack by the troops of Ezzelino da Romano. Since this was a relatively strong army for the time, it can be assumed that the construction was already very solid.[565]

The fourteenth century was an unhappy period for the Villalta family, which always found itself on the wrong side in the political struggles for power. The castle was destroyed three times. In 1300 the fief was confirmed to the family by patriarch Pietro Gera. However, a short time later he decided to take it back and ordered the Udine militia, under the command of Count Orthenburg, to capture the castle. They failed, and with the help of the count of Gorizia, two further assaults were repelled. On the occasion of the third, on 29 March 1310, however, the castle was captured and "demolished" (*atterato*).

In 1312 Indriuccio di Villalta obtained permission from the patriarch to rebuild the castle and by 1315 the castle was able to resist an assault by the count of Gorizia. The next destruction took place in 1353, after the Villalta family took part in the assassination of the patriarch Bertrando. His successor had the castle razed to the ground.

At the same time, the family palace in Udine was also destroyed and the city council forbade the rebuilding of the castle.[566] Given that only the patriarch had the right to decide such a veto, it must have been simply a question of power, most likely a sign of the council's attempts to extend its dominion over the surrounding territory.

The Villalta family cannot have been too disgruntled with Udine, since in 1380 it moved its residence to the city and obtained citizenship. Perhaps it was just in this way that the political solution to rebuilding the castle was found, despite the veto.

After the family's unhappy experiences over the previous decades, at the end of the fourteenth century it finally decided to take the side of the patriarch. But already in 1381 this turned out to be the wrong side. The Villalta family defended the recently appointed patriarch against his enemies, who, led by Udine and Venice, could also depend on numerous feudal lords. This cost the Villalta family another destruction of the castle, which fell after a siege that used heavy arms and lasted a whole day.

"Twenty-two carts were brought to Villalta for the siege, four bombards with their equipment, and three cases of bolts for the crossbow and four lanterns. Also fourteen iron bars and a barrel of pitch which served to demolish and burn down the castle."[567]

Indriuccio di Villalta was captured and imprisoned in Udine and the castle was completely destroyed. In December 1385, laborers from Udine demolished the walls in six days, with the help of the people of Fagagna and Moruzzo. The tower was also torn down. This demolition of the castle complex took more than two months.[568]

However, in 1389 antagonism between the patriarch and the town of Udine led to the rebuilding of Villalta on the initiative of the patriarch himself.[569] The old Villalta family was by now so impoverished that in 1413 it was not even in a position to pay Carlo della Torre his mother's dowry of 1,400 lire. Instead, they had to give him part of the castle and their landed property. All this marked the beginning of the handing over of the property to the della Torre family, a transition which ended in 1453 with a formal investiture.[570]

In the sixteenth century, the financially secure della Torre family was in a position to rebuild the castle, giving it its present appearance. The reason for this new and radical transformation was a final bout of destruction at the castle, when it was attacked by crowds of peasants in the disturbances of the *giovedì*

The entrance tower built in the late 16th century, when the castle was enlarged and a new burg was created.

grasso (Carnival Thursday) rebellion in 1511. It is probable that on that occasion a fire began, but there does not seem to have been serious damage to the walls.

With the support of Venice, which did not tolerate peasant insurrections, the inhabitants of the surrounding villages were forced to rebuild the castle. In this way, the castle acquired its present shape under the della Torre family in the sixteenth century; it was the della Torre who were the real patrons of the impressive structure we can still admire today.

A second castle?

According to local tradition, there was another castle, earlier than the present one, which is supposed to have stood where the parish church is today. Joppi, who looked for it on a small nearby hill, cites a phrase in the document ceding the castle of 1433, in which mention is made of "the part of the castle adjacent to the Franciscan friary," a small friary donated to the Villalta family. Zucchiatti rejects this argument: since the document concerned the surrounding area too, it is probable that the word *castle* meant not only the buildings themselves but also the area surrounding and belonging to it, with ditches and earthworks, and perhaps the fields beyond. Later the term *villa* was similarly used to indicate an entire property. The "part of the castle adjacent to the Franciscan friary" does not refer, therefore, to another—and in any case, totally undiscovered—castle, but rather to the castle we know.

According to Joppi, this castle would have stood on a hill that is still today referred to with the name *motta*. It is possible that the *motta* may allude to a preceding castle complex, but in this case it seems rather to refer to a burial mound, locally known as *la tùmbule di Foscjàn*.[571]

According to Zucchiatti, even remains of walls found on the top of another hill cannot be considered as the ruins of an older castle. The foundations of the old castle chapel came to light here. As early as the thirteenth century this was referred to as the chapel of St. Leonard.[572]

In my view, the present form of the castle complex should rule out any other theory in

A splendid view of the castle of Villalta from the rear, showing clearly the circular late medieval form. The battlements, though they were remade in the 20th century, help give the complex its majestic appearance.

An axonometric cross section of the square tower of the castle.

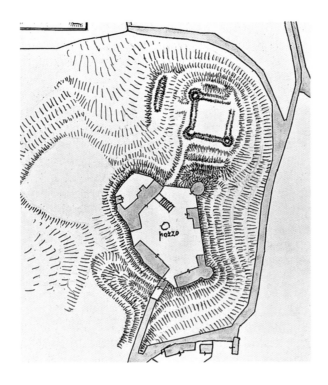

In this plan from the 1930s, the remains of the rectangular-plan 13th-century castle can be seen next to the present castle.

this connection. After the first destruction in the fourteenth century, completely new forms emerged compared to the castle of Villalta, which is on a circular plan. Since Villalta belongs to the earliest type of castle, it is not possible that it can have been built following an earlier castle.

Greater attention should be paid to the possibility that a second castle may have existed alongside the present castle, between 1310 and 1353. This second castle is often cited in documents that distinguish between a "castro veteri in domo nova" (the old castle in the new house) and a "castro veteri prope palatium Domini Endriucci quondam Domini Mainardi di Villalta" (the old castle by the palace of Endriuccio, son of the late Mainardo of Villalta). After the destruction of 1353, this second castle was not rebuilt and hence its stone was made available to the new owner, Carlo della Torre, in 1433; there is a reference to "materials found inside and outside the castle, as well as those of the old castle."[573]

This castle must still have been visible up to the Second World War. Its plan is recorded in a drawing by L. Quarina of the surroundings of the castle in 1939, in which there are indications of a square complex less than a 100 meters (330 feet) behind the tower of the

chapel, where three round corner towers can still be viewed. This record is especially valuable because it passes down to us the plan of an early fourteenth-century castle that was built from ground up instead of using earlier foundations. It is a good example of geometrical precision, a sign of a change of style and of new trends in late medieval secular architecture.

Zucchiatti sees in this castle an attempt to achieve greater defense through a twin system:

> After a century and a half of resistance to assaults and sieges, this castle had won a certain notoriety as an impregnable fortress. The sudden conquest and destruction forced the lords of Villalta to have second thoughts and, no longer feeling safely protected by a single castle, they opted for the twin fortification of the hill.[574]

This improvement, however, does not seem to have been particularly significant from the military point of view, seeing that after a further siege and destruction in 1353 the family did not rebuild the castle. I think it more likely that the creation of a second castle resulted from the fact that at a certain point two brothers each wanted to have his own castle.[575]

Perhaps the second castle was not rebuilt because of the ever more uncertain financial situation. The fact that the older castle was rebuilt, even though the newer one was of much more modern form, would suggest that the latter was structurally weaker.

The medieval castle

The nucleus of the present complex, around the sixteenth-century palace, can certainly be considered an element of the medieval castle. Not all the walls were rebuilt after the final destruction in 1511: clear evidence of this can be found not only in the lancet windows but also in the walls, in places more than a meter (three feet) thick, though it is difficult to determine which parts are medieval and when they were built.

The repeated destruction and rebuilding in the fourteenth century make it impossible to distinguish definite phases. However, we can begin by stating that the great destruction of

1385 left no building standing; even the walls, apart from a few, low ruins, were demolished. Thus the medieval buildings must date from after 1385, but must have used earlier foundations and salvaged material. Even total dismantling could not have completely removed every stone from the castle. After demolition, the main walls at least must have remained standing while in the tower there is evidence of the point at which the walls were renewed. Since the construction of foundations was burdensome and time-consuming, in past centuries recourse was always made to walls already standing. This is why eighteenth-century villas and palaces often have surprising irregularities in their plan.[576]

Bearing in mind all the different occasions of destruction, it would be correct to conclude that the rapid rebuilding in the fourteenth century was carried out mainly on the foundations of older buildings.[577] This is the only explanation, for example, as to why the castle should still today have kept three-quarters of the circuit wall on a circular base. Had the castle we see today been totally rebuilt after one of the bouts of destruction in the fourteenth century, it would have been erected following the rectangular plan beginning to be used in that period.[578] The form of the castle of Villalta clearly reveals its antiquity. It must be supposed that it was a typical medieval fortress built on an artificial mound.

It is not possible to determine whether it was a castle, a motte and bailey castle, or simply a stone tower. All are possible on the basis of its form. The castle of Villalta, like others, may in its early stages been made up of only timber buildings and palisades. The present tower is definitely not part of the wall, which suggests that the original layout must have been different. The tower is perhaps built over the foundations of an older building. It is too small to have been the ancient inhabited tower, the nucleus of a primitive castle, and it must therefore have accompanied a *palas*.

All this points to the castle having been a thirteenth-century complex. At the heart of the ancient structure—and thus also at the center of the mansion built at a later date—a wall can still be distinguished today, which, judging from its thickness, must surely be

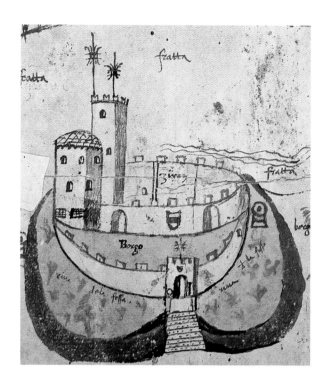

Fifteenth-century drawing showing the castle of Villalta in the late Middle Ages, with the tower, palas, two circuits of walls, and a bailey smaller than today.

medieval, yet its line seems to be inconsistent with the rest of the complex. It is possible that it was precisely here that one of the earliest buildings of the castle was to be found, and that this wall originally belonged to the old center of the castle.

As a rule, a complex of this type would have been surrounded by another circuit of walls, inside which the local population could take refuge with their possessions. Zucchiatti mentions the foundations of a wall outside the outer wall, but it is probable that rather than an enclosure this was a support wall for the steep slope of the hill. It may also have been used, however, as a foundation for the palisades, which on one side of the castle surrounded a larger burg, intended to protect the inhabitants of the village. If we accept these premises, then the appearance of the castle would have changed radically at least once in the late Middle Ages. The parts considered medieval, because their walls have a thickness of over a meter (three feet)—in other words the keep, the tower, and the ouside wall of the palace—could only have been built later.

The upper outer wall, built presumably as a circular stone rampart, was made smaller when the front wall of the present mansion was built. The keep deserves attention: it was

FOLLOWING PAGES: A detailed drawing of the whole castle complex of Villalta.

289

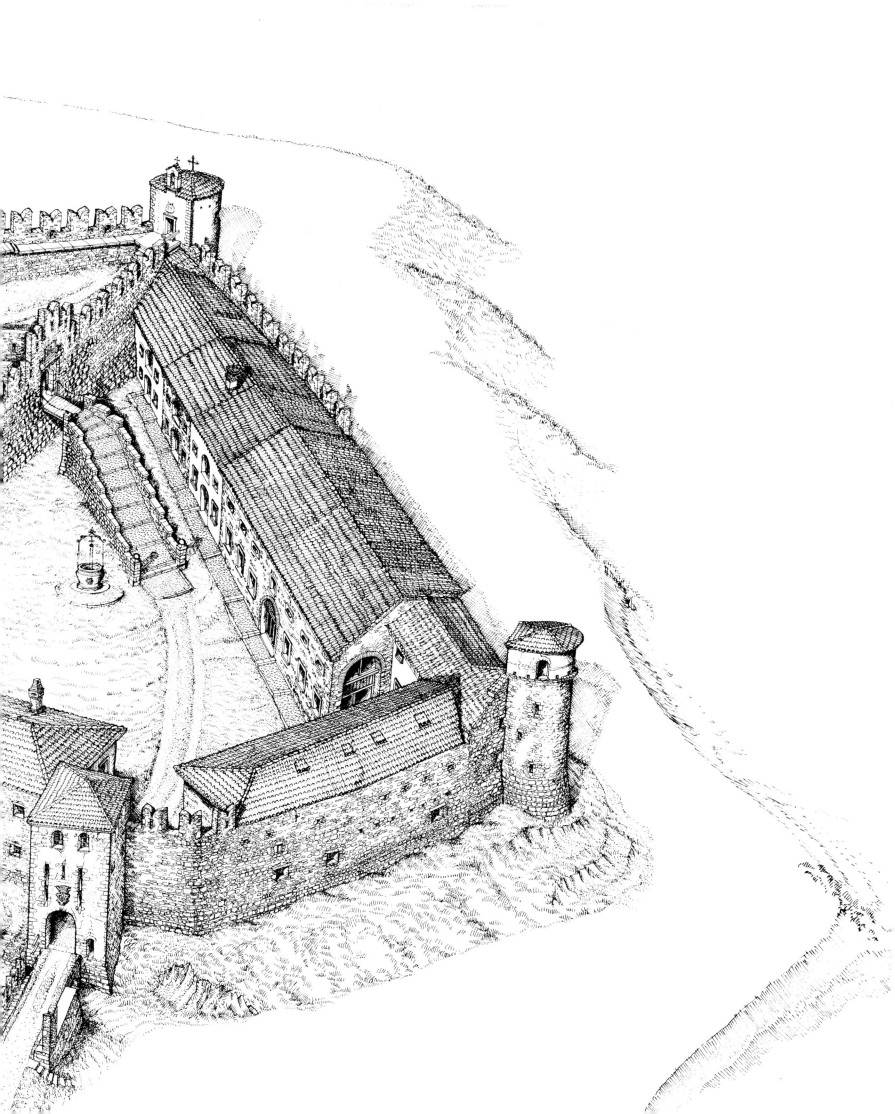

an essential part of the defense walls since it protruded as a bastion and provided lateral protection for the entrance to the castle, of which it was the inhabited part. In this unusual building, two elements of the complex are combined so that a sort of keep is formed: the defense tower and the palace, even if the real function of the defense tower was taken on by the narrow elegant tower.

It remains to be explained when this castle was built. The typical elements, namely the tower and the keep (which is almost an abutment in the wall), should be regarded as alterations following the reconstruction in 1310. Later reconstruction may have made the castle higher each time, but the ground plan probably remained the same.[579]

We have a drawing of this complex dating from 1433, an exceptionally good record, especially if compared with other, much later drawings.[580] In it can be seen two courtyards, the protruding keep, and the tower, which has, however, battlements. Also visible are the two entrance gates to the inner courtyard, which can still be seen today in the wall of the palace; while in the center of the courtyard a line can be seen which may indicate a wall that divided the courtyard in two.[581]

Originally the castle may have had a first burg on the northern side of the square, as is suggested by the presence of a well. Moreover, the northern side of the palace is good-quality work and has been altered. It may have been the original entrance, although to confirm this it would be necessary to carry out an archaeological excavation at the foot of the wall, in the raised hill.

Even if many questions regarding the original medieval form remain unanswered, an approximate plan can nevertheless be drawn. However, the question regarding the structure of the burg remains open. Its vast area, with towers and crenellated walls, today forms an important part of the whole complex. The 1433 drawing already shows a burg surrounded by a circular wall.[582] From the sources we know that the burg was not an empty courtyard but, on the contrary, was densely occupied, as was typical of this sort of settlement:

> Quod in dicto Castro est domus abitationis dicti Domini Francisci in Rocha quae est circumdata muro. Et sunt domus 22

> in burgo similiter circumdato exceptis passibus de quibus superiorum vetustatis temporum. (In the said castle is the dwelling of the aforesaid Francesco [della Torre] in the keep which is surrounded by a wall. There are 22 houses in the burg, which is similarly surrounded by walls except in those parts where the passage of time has destroyed them.)[583]

The drawing shows none of these houses because they were probably humble wooden huts adjoining the outer wall of the burg. The drawing seems to describe only the stone buildings, which leaves the possibility open of a series of wooden buildings in the upper burg as well.

The most intensely debated question is whether the burg today is in its essential form the burg known from the drawing and from the sources, containing twenty-two houses inside its wall. The number of houses gives the impression of a small village. It might thus be thought that in the present-day area of the bailey there was room at that time for all those buildings. This opinion seems to be supported by the fifteenth-century drawing, in which concentric circles of walls can be seen that might correspond to the present complex.

However, the size of houses in the Middle Ages should not be exaggerated: two rooms were sufficient to accommodate a whole family and it would thus have been possible to have 22 houses in a relatively limited area. But if the medieval burg was as large as it is today, it would have been impossible to protect it, because at the end of the fourteenth century the Villalta family would not have been able to assemble a large enough number of armed men to defend more than 200 meters (660 feet) of wall.

The thickness of the walls, which never exceeds 60 centimeters (two feet), proves that the burg was added at a later date. This is also true of the towers and the gate. Above all, the distribution of crenellations and embrasures does not seem to have been determined by the requirements of the Middle Ages, and there are no parapet walks. For this reason, not only the palace but also the burg with its whole outer wall must be classified as belonging to the sixteenth

century, despite their apparently typical medieval features—towers, crenellations, moats, and drawbridges.

The history of the castle as it stands today must therefore be concerned almost exclusively with the work carried out on the instructions of the della Torre family, in a style surprisingly anachronistic for the sixteenth century.

The della Torre family

Among the many feudal families in Friuli, the della Torre family had a preeminent position as early as the Middle Ages. Like almost all the old families in the region, they did not originally come from Friuli. With them began a migration of Longobard families who were to be of importance in the following centuries. The family tower still stands today in Valsassina, in the north of Lombardy.[584]

A certain Martino della Torre, named for the first time in 1147, was probably the founder of the house.[585] The period of della Torre rule in Milan was of particular importance in the history of the family. It lasted, with a few breaks, from 1256, when Pagano della Torre, lord of Valsassina, was named "protector of the people," to 1277, and again, briefly, in 1302.[586]

Later the family divided into a number of branches and settled in many cities of northern Italy. The most successful familial line was the one in Friuli, which could boast four patriarchs among its members. The power of the patriarchs consolidated the position of the della Torre family which, thanks to its many investitures, became one of the wealthiest and most powerful feudal families, especially in the county of Gorizia.[587]

In return for their constant loyalty, the emperor granted the della Torre family new investitures. For centuries, skilled and capable members of the family filled prestigious official positions and offices, coming into possession of many lordships in the region. However, at the end of the seventeenth century, the involvement of the family in public life became increasingly rare. Some particularly disreputable characters became notorious and their disruptive behavior discredited the owners of Villalta for generations. Among these, Count Lucio was notorious for his cruelty and wickedness.

Count Lucio

The life of Count Lucio was made famous by a nineteenth-century novel by Giuseppe Marcotti, *Il Conte Lucio*. It is said of Count Lucio that when in Venice for the Carnival, he appeared on the Thursday before Lent in Piazza San Marco, on a float drawn by six horses, openly flouting the exile imposed on him by the Venetian Senate.

In Treviso Count Lucio had his thugs attack and rob an official courier. When a company of light cavalry was sent to capture him, fighting broke out with Count Lucio's band in the outlying area of Santa Croce. This time the count paid dearly: many of his men were killed and others were taken prisoner and hanged. Count Lucio himself managed to take refuge in Gorizia, outside the Venetian state. On 16 July 1717 the Council of Ten in Venice issued an edict ordering him to give himself up, which was published throughout Venetian territory. They also ordered his

OPPOSITE:
*The castle walls, rebuilt by the
peasants after the damage
done in the "giovedì grasso"
rebellion in 1511, recall the
bastions typical of the time.*

palace in Udine to be razed to the ground and a column recording his crimes to be erected on the site.

When Count Lucio committed another murder, with the help of his Strassoldo relatives, the Council of Ten published an edict ordering his execution "for murder and treason." For its part, the imperial government, at the request of Venice and the victim's relatives, had the guilty parties arrested. This was not easy, since it took a good number of soldiers with two cannons to besiege the castle of Farra. Lucio della Torre, Marianna Strassoldo, and Nicolò Strassoldo were imprisoned in Gradisca, tried, and executed by beheading on 3 July 1723. The Republic of Venice confiscated the family property.

We do not know who lived at Villalta during the following period.[588] However, it must have been a nobleman loyal to Venice, as this is the only explanation for the lion of St. Mark that decorates the entrance above the drawbridge. None of the della Torre family would ever have placed it there. Close examination also reveals the coat of arms of this as yet unidentified occupant of the castle.

Change in the sixteenth century

We do not know much about the reconstruction of the castle after 1511. The castle must have been in poor condition even before this, since in the burg *triginta passus* (thirty paces) of the outer wall had collapsed. We do not know which parts were damaged by the peasants, but it would appear that an earthquake in that same year finished off the job.[589]

With regard to works that had to be carried out by the inhabitants of the villages subject to the castle, in the sixteenth century the della Torre counts continued a process which had already begun with the Villalta family in the previous century. A decree of 1585, the only important document that survives from this time, laid down that the inhabitants of Villalta were responsible for "all construction, repair, and adjustments to the bridge and the lower gate of the castle of Villalta," with their own materials and at their own expense. At the same time, the communities subject to the jurisdiction of Ciconicco and San Vito di Fagagna had "responsiblity for the construc-

tion, repair, and mending of the bridge and the upper gate."[590]

This document makes no mention of the palace itself, as the upkeep of the residence of the feudal lord did not form part of the duties of the subjects. Zucchiatti thought that the della Torre counts accelerated the building episodes of the castle.[591] The leaders of the peasant insurrection, which had alarmed not only the feudal lords but also Venice, were punished severely and the peasants were obliged to rebuild the castle.[592] Over a relatively short time, they were compelled to raise once again the symbol of ancient territorial rights and to make it larger than it had ever been, and had to provide both materials and labor. There were thus no financial problems for the patrons of the works.

The present layout shows clearly that the upper tower and the lower burg are not a single unit. While the main walls of the rebuilt burg are similar to the upper part of the castle, and the burg, with its towers and crenellations, has an authentic medieval appearance, the palace is clearly an intrusion. Its wide and powerful bulk dominates the entire slope. The open space before it cannot be considered a true courtyard but almost a long terrace running parallel to the façade. The wall of enormous square stones which once divided the original burg into two separate units and now terminates on both sides with corners that look like bastions, is not medieval.

The strong walls of the reconstructed castle, which the local people labored to build, gave the castle a fortress-like appearance, although the work carried out on it did not really aim to make it a fortress. One need only examine the rear of the building to understand that the new building merely reflected contemporary taste. This taste can be seen too in many other country residences built at the time: to present towards the village those elements which, as symbols of power, gave the impression of a strongly fortified castle. After a peasant insurrection, it was the natural outcome.[593]

The present burg, however, gives the impression of having been built up against the sixteenth-century castle, though an attempt was made to incorporate it. The new castle built after 1511, while displaying a

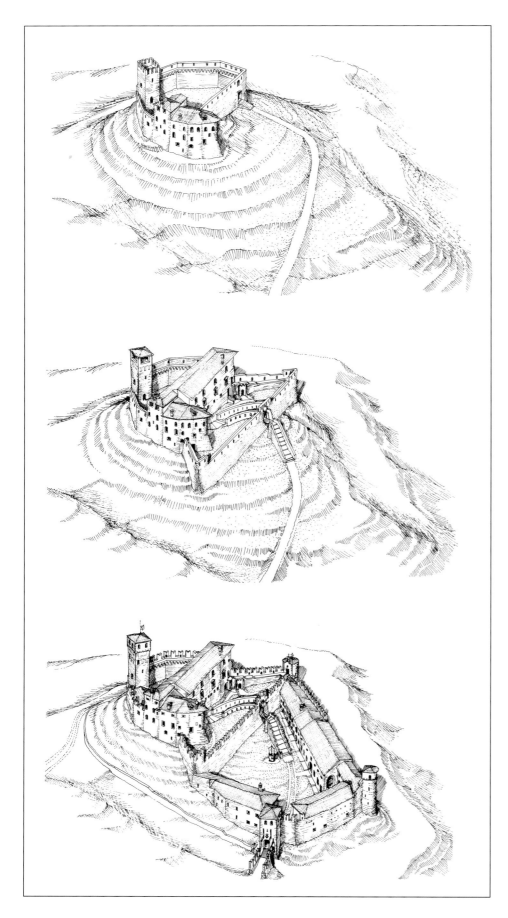

seemingly fortified appearance, did not have a burg. The peasants and servants who had lived there, who had perhaps taken part in the revolt, had to leave the castle, which thus totally lost its medieval functions. Without a military or economic role, the castle was now only a symbol of seignorial power.

The complex was extended, probably in the late sixteenth century, with the addition of the present courtyard. The new forms were again adapted from the medieval parts. With this extension, there was no longer any attempt to impress the peasants, who by now had been pacified for decades.

The symbol of the medieval castle was now raised against a new adversary, the Venetian Republic and its patrician citizens. The opposition of the great feudal families to the Venetian patriciate, represented by an increasingly wealthy aristocracy under the leadership of the Savorgnan family, is one of the key elements of Friuli history after the sixteenth century.

Among the enemies of Venice, who took advantage of any war to show their loyalty to the Hapsburg emperor, in law the supreme head of the region, no family was as committed as the della Torre family. Their stance was repaid generously both in the empire and in the county of Gorizia, which was under Austrian domination.

These political relationships are attested to by the building activities of the families resident in the countryside, where the struggle for power between the old feudal system and the new Venetian landowners was conducted within the seignorial estates. Not by chance, the most striking building to be associated with the claims to power of the feudal lords is the castle of Villalta, the main seat of the della Torre counts during the period of Venetian dominion.

In contrast with the forms of the first rebuilding, after 1511 these returned to an explicitly feudal language. The new burg—in fact no more than an open space—was laid out on the lines of a typical castle courtyard. Behind the tower entrance gate with the family coast of arms, after an imposing drawbridge, is a courtyard enclosed on all sides, whose wall is capped in a number of highly conspicuous points by battlements. The corners of the complex were more ornamen-

tal than defensive, as is often the case in sixteenth-century constructions, such as the well-known Rocca Bernarda. At Villalta, below the roofline there is also a frieze of bricks placed sideways, a popular architectural motif in the sixteenth century. During these works, new crenellations were placed on the corners of the terrace, the small round tower with the chapel was built, and battlements were added to the back wall of the upper courtyard. Thus in the sixteenth century the castle we see today was built. Subsequent changes affected only the court-

stances made it superfluous. After its careful restoration in medieval style by the new owners, with its new, swallow-tailed crenellations, it still remains today the best example of feudal architecture in Friuli.

The small but picturesque castle chapel was created out of one of the 16th-century towers.

yard, where in the nineteenth century domestic buildings were extended up to the imposing dividing wall of the upper castle.

The rundown medieval castle which the family had received by chance as payment of a debt, was thus rebuilt and maintained for a further three centuries as a medieval complex without equal in Friuli. Surviving, despite many changes in taste, as a monument to the family and its status, the castle was abandoned and finally sold in the nineteenth century, when changed political circum-

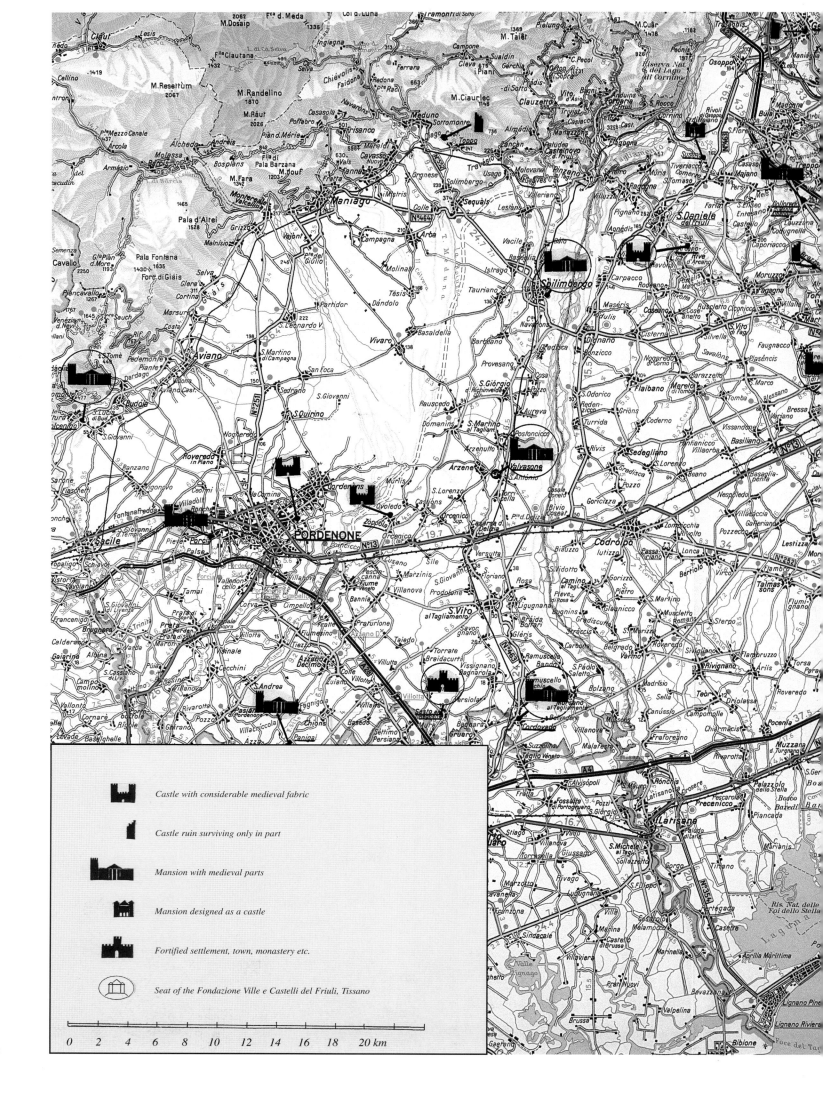

Castle with considerable medieval fabric

Castle ruin surviving only in part

Mansion with medieval parts

Mansion designed as a castle

Fortified settlement, town, monastery etc.

Seat of the Fondazione Ville e Castelli del Friuli, Tissano

0 2 4 6 8 10 12 14 16 18 20 km

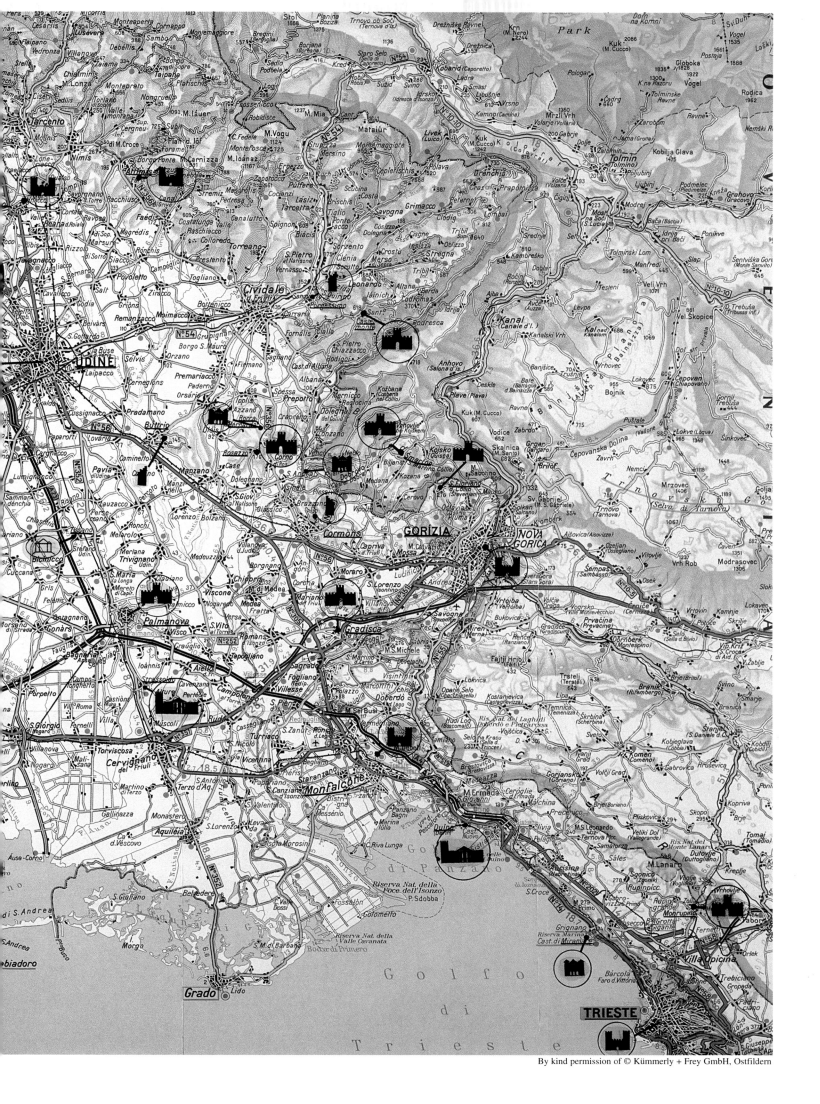

301

Notes

[1] Zeune refers to the painter Wolf Huber who around 1542 created landscape compositions with castles. See Franz Winzinger, *Wolf Huber. Das Gesamtwerk*, vol. 2, Munich Zurich 1979, and J. Zeune, pp. 16, 24. Italian art seems to have taken a different direction in this respect: there are, for example in the Good Government frescoes in the Palazzo Pubblico in Siena and in the frescoes in the chapel of the Palazzo Medici in Florence, a large number of depictions of small fortified rural residences and towers surrounded by walls. These too were obviously a fixed component in painted landscapes, but their forms are not emphasized. It would seem that in general castles in Italy at this period were assimilated in a quite different way. The fortified town house provided the most important model for the architecture of aristocratic palaces. All the same, the German images are important for a study of castles in Friuli, since they are part of the image of the castle of western Europe. This idea was to give rise, with the Romantic movement, to the renewed interest in castles.

[2] Equally impressive is the size of the constructions, found only in the great castles of rulers.

[3] One is reminded of the many decorative forms which terminate in towers and castellations. It is no coincidence that many choirstalls and monstrances recall the forms at Neuschwanstein, while they cannot be said to be representations of medieval castles.

[4] Schock Werner, "Die Burg auf spätmittelalterkichen Darstellungen," in *Burgen und Schlösser*, 1, 1987, pp. 2834.

[5] Domenico Quaglio's fame as a master of the depiction of romantic castles took him as far as Munich, where he was hired by the hereditary prince to complete a "collection of paintings of castles from Bavarian history." His drawings are like those of his contemporaries in their combination of great accuracy of detail with a constant tendency to exaggeration. The mountains are always slightly higher and the ruins more imposing than in reality.

[6] Zeune, p. 30. The top of the main tower of the castle was crowned with a large imperial eagle holding a scroll bearing these solemn words.

[7] Published 1759: "The Wasps. Depravation and corruption destroyed the proud form of a war horse that had been killed beneath its daring rider. Diligent nature uses the ruin of one creature for the life of another. And so a swarm of young wasps flew out of the carcass. 'Oh', cried the wasps, 'what divine origins we have! The proud horse, beloved of Neptune, is our procreator!.' This strange boast was heard by the attentive writer, who thought of the Italians of our day who believe they are nothing less than the descendants of the immortal Romans of antiquity because they were born on their tombs." Gotthold Ephraim Lessing, *Opere*, vol. 1, p. 1005, Munich 1974.

[8] Rainieri Cossar wrote in 1937 that the castle seemed like a stricken colossus, mortally wounded. The central building was struck by four 305 mm. projectiles, breached in several places and everywhere damaged, so that it seemed from one moment to the next that it might collapse with the two large towers. Cracks opened up everywhere with an ever-increasing crescendo. What the war had spared was exposed to the weather and thus risked destruction. First to enter among these collapsing walls, in the confusion of trenches, where coils of barbed wire and grenades were a constant danger, was Giovanni Cossar, who sought to shore up this building of prime importance, which represented "St. Gorizia'." Annalia Delneri, in *Das Görzer Schloss und sein Dorf.* Edizione della Laguna, 1993.

[9] Annalia Delnero, in her study of the history of the castle, gives a useful summary of the debate over reconstruction. Initially the possibility of preserving the building as a ruin was considered, as a memorial to the victims and as a symbol of the high price which had been paid for victory. Soon, however, it was decided to rebuild the castle as "a symbol of the liberated city." "The rebuilding scheme prevailed because it seemed the most appropriate, symbolizing in an immediately recognizable form the determination to encourage the rebirth of a country no longer subject to foreign domination. The degree to which the symbolic meaning of the building was already deeply rooted in the collective consciousness is demonstrated by the unanimity which greeted the decision to turn the castle into a museum of the Risorgimento."

[10] According to Tavano, the lion is probably by Giovanni da Campione and "was certainly moved from Venice in 1508, to be placed on the civic tower. The sculpture was kept in the town for more than four centuries and was placed here in 1919... to commemorate the rebuilding and in a desire to see the Venetian occupation of 1508–9 as a precursor of the return of Gorizia to Italy," Tavano, *Castello di Gorizia*, p. 112. In reality, it seems unlikely that such a large sculpture could be stored for centuries without suffering any damage. Another detail about this unusual high relief carving which seems to have escaped the notice of the uneducated Fascists in their nationalist fervor is that a lion of St. Mark transported in time of war would have held a closed Bible, as can be seen in other lions of the time.

[11] Quoted in S. Tavano, *Il Castello di Gorizia*, Gorizia 1978, p. 68.

[12] Quoted in A. Delneri, *op. cit.*, pp. 18 ff.

[13] In the local newspaper, *Vita isontina*, no. 2, February 1938, quoted in A. Delneri, *op. cit.*, p. 33.

[14] From the report of the commission headed by Cirilli, 1924, quoted in Delneri, *op. cit.*, p. 19.

[15] The material of the windows indicates that they are not of medieval origin. Two of them certainly existed before the First World War and are probably nineteenth-century. Even bearing in mind the importance of the count of Gorizia, all the rooms are too big for a residence of a medieval count.

[16] Hermann Wirth, "Die Burg im Landschaftsbild", in *Burgen und Schlösser*, 3, 1995, p. 161.

[17] Apparently unrelated ditches and mounds can be found over a wide area. At the corner of one of these raised mounds is a small brick tower of unknown function, but clearly not very old.

[18] The drawing can be dated by the handwriting, which appears to be eighteenth-century. The reliability of the drawing can be assumed from two details: the chapel, together with the small side apse is shown in accurate detail, neither schematically nor exaggerated; and the title ("Prospectus Eclesia Veteris San Michaels de Carpeneto") makes it clear that it was not the intention to show a fortification and therefore there was no reason to exaggerate or emphasize the defensive character of the building. The drawing is reproduced in Miotti, vol. 2, p. 90. The reference is incorrect, however: the original is not in the Biblioteca Comunale in Udine and attempts to trace it have been unsuccessful.

[19] It is not clear whether the boundaries of the *cortina* of San Michele were already stone. A similar case is shown in a drawing from 1785, from Mereto di Tomba. This one is provided with captions: next to the entrance, labelled *magna porta*, the structure on its artificial mound shows a wall, labelled *murus*. It seems unlikely that a wooden palisade would be thus described.

[20] Patze, p. 425.

[21] See Czoernig, p. 743.

[22] Czoernig, p. 486. Elsewhere (p. 733) the owner is named as the monastery of Santa Maria in Aquileia. Unfortunately I have found nothing more in the literature on this subject about San Martino, and I do not know the date when the place was referred to as being fortified. It would be interesting to look at the arrangements for feudal dues, which might tell us whether the inhabitants fortified their village themselves and whether they were responsible for its maintenance.

[23] That the strongly fortified Gorizia fell much sooner is due to the fact that the Venetians, underestimating the situation, devoted less energy to attacking San Martino.

[24] Fornasir, in *Maran*, p. 7. For the history of Marano, see the study by Lucas Lüdemann.

[25] From the choice of site, Miotti concludes that it must already have been fortified, but his argument is not convincing. At this period, marshy ground provided better protection than walls, and the excellent walls at Aquileia were certainly of less use than the lagoon of Grado. The patriarch Poppo gave the villa of Marano to the cathedral chapter of Aquileia (Fornasir, *Marano*, p. 7).

[26] Amelio Tagliaferri, "Marano e Maranutto," in Andreina Ciceri and Gianfranco Ellero, *Maran*, Udine 1990, p. 53.

[27] Tagliaferri, in *Maran*, p. 53.

[28] Miotti, p. 46.

[29] Fornasir, p. 8.

[30] Pio Paschini, p. 117.

[31] It seems to me that herein lies the main revival brought about by the Middle Ages to the image of the town. In antiquity, towns would not have had towers, the walls of the towns having only not particularly high projections. Temples and palaces do not appear to have had towers, and the first basilicas did not have bell towers. Towers as symbols of power in the countryside, on the other hand, were already important in Roman times, as will be discussed below.

[32] Biasutti, p. 142 and Miotti, vol. 3, p. 103.

[33] Biasutti, p. 143.

[34] Biasutti, p. 143.

[35] Biasutti, p. 145.

[36] "Turks made a terrible incursion into Friuli in 1499. And from 1508 to 1515 a long and painful war between the Venetian Republic and the German Empire and its allies took place. Then Castelmonte was again reinforced and garrisoned, but was never taken. Another war, known as the war of Gradisca, between the Venetians and the Hapsburgs, took place between 1615 and 1617. This time too the sanctuary was unharmed, although the surrounding villages were put to the sword and the flames." Biasutti, pp. 145 ff.

[37] Miotti, vol. 3, p. 103. However, Biasutti, to whom Miotti refers, gives no information on this matter. A more detailed check is needed.

[38] After 1797 it became the seat of the local council and it is now a shop selling religious items.

[39] Biasutti, p. 60.

[40] Biasutti, pp. 60 ff.

[41] The house was demolished in 1921. Biasutti, *Castelmonte*, pp. 53—55, 121, 127.

[42] For the history of Sesto al Reghena, see Tommaso Gerometta, *L'Abbazia Benedettina di S. Maria in Sylvis*, 1964.

[43] An example is the castle of Sbroiavacca. Gerometta cites it as the owner of the monastery, but the documents published by Miotti on Sbroiavacca show that the monastery belonged to the patriarch who gave it in fief to a noble family who received the land around the castle, in part at least, from the abbey of Sesto. See Gerometta, pp. 36, 37.

[44] *Moggio e le sue valli*, p. 34.

[45] Miotti, vol. 4, p. 369.

[46] Gerometta, p. 67.

[47] Girolamo di Porcia, *Descrizione della Patria del Friuli*, p. 33.

[48] Gerometta (p. 66) calls Sesto a citadelfortress.

[49] Gerometta, p. 66.

[50] *Moggio*, p. 57.

[51] *Moggio*, p. 57.

[52] Marchetti, in *Moggio*, p. 34.

[53] Paschini, pp. 116, 118.

[54] I cannot prove that it was Gerometta who started this story. However, the successive literature always repeats it, with only P. Tigler correctly classifying these architectural forms, in *Reclams Kunstführer Italien*, vol. 2, 2, p. 409.

[55] *Moggio*, p. 33.

[56] Paschini, p. 117.

[57] Paschini, p. 113.

[58] The *palas* was the residence of the lord of the castle.

[59] It resembles the structure of all noble dwellings in the Carnic Alps, with a central corridor and a staircase leading from it. The windows may have been altered at a later date; the same of course may also be true of the plan. The plan and elevation are published in *Moggio Udinese* (Quaderni del Centro Regionale di Catalogazione dei Beni Culturali), Villa Manin, Passariano 1977, "that show the comfort of a nobleman's house" (*Moggio*, p. 57).

[60] Brunner, p. 254.

[61] Brunner, p. 256.

[62] Patze, p. 429.

[63] Brunner.

[64] Aldo Settia, in *Chiese, strade e fortezze nell'Italia medievale*, pp. 99 ff, is sarcastic about the local historians' habit of perpetuating the legend of the eternal threat.

[65] Piper (p. 32) had already written of the limited importance of castles in defending roads.

[66] B. and F. Lorenz, in *Burgen und Schlösser*, 1961, p. 6.

[67] Pichler, p. 147, from *Thesaurus Ecclesiae Aquileinsis*, p. 18.

[68] Pichler, p. 198.

[69] Goez, "Das Leben auf der Ritterburg", in *Mentalität und Alltag im Spätmittelalter*, p. 17.

[70] Hughes, pp. 19 ff.

[71] Zeune, pp. 52 ff.

[72] Ebner, p. 45.

[73] Hinz, p. 35.

[74] Miotti, vol. 5, p. 117.

[75] B. and F. Lorenz, p. 1.

[76] Goez, p. 16.

[77] Goez, p. 16.

[78] Goez, p. 26.

[79] Biasutti, p. 147.

[80] Ebner, pp. 11 ff.

[81] Brunner, p. 39.

[82] Brunner, p. 38.

[83] Brunner, p. 22.

[84] Brunner, p. 23.

[85] Brunner, p. 49.

[86] Brunner, p. 268.

[87] Brunner, p. 86.

[88] Brunner, p. 80.

[89] Brunner, p. 104.

[90] Brunner, p. 240.

[91] Brunner, p. 96.

[92] Patze, p. 436.

[93] Ebner, p .45.

[94] Patze, p. 430.

[95] Ebner, p. 57.

[96] Hinz, p. 128.

[97] "Nulli licuit in Normannia fossatum facere in planam Terram, nisi tale quod de fundo potuisset terram iactare superius sine scabello. Et ibi nulli lucuit facere palium, nisi una regula, et id sine propugnaculis et alatoriis. Et in rupe et in insula nulli licuit facere fortitudinem, et nulli licuit in Normannia castellum facere." Hinz, pp. 130 ff.

[98] In both the Sachenspiegel and the Schwabenspiegel, as well as in the Austrian civil law code of 1237, it is said that all those fortifications with trenches exceeding a certain depth and width, palisades over a certain height, and buildings of more than two floors needed a permit. It was also forbidden to raise mounds or use islands or rocky peaks. Hinz, p. 131.
[99] Patze, p. 432.
[100] Ebner, p. 49.
[101] In northern Germany, the districts had taken over the administration, but were to cede it, in the ninth century, to the counties. See Ebner, p. 51.
[102] Ebner, p. 55.
[103] Ebner, p. 79.
[104] Ebner, p. 57.
[105] Ebner, p. 52.
[106] B. and F. Lorenz, p. 4.
[107] Ebner, p. 59.
[108] For medieval political theories from Augustine to Aquinas, see F. Kern, "La clemenza di Dio," in Brunner, p. 142.
[109] Ebner, p. 80.
[110] B. and F. Lorenz, p. 4.
[111] The power or domain represented by the privileges and rights lodged in the castle. Brunner, p. 256.
[112] Johannes Stumpf, *Gemeiner loblicher Eidgnoschaft Stetten. Lande und Völckeren Chronikwirdiger thaaten beschreybung*, Zurich 1548, vol. 1, p. 103, quoted in Meyer Gaillard, p. 137.
[113] Ebner, p. 19.
[114] M. Mitterauer, "Burg und Adel in Österreich," in *Die Burg im Deutschen Sprachraum*, vol. 2, p. 375.
[115] Meyer Gaillard, p. 128.
[116] Morelli de Rossi, *Fontanabona*.
[117] Satrapa Schill, p. 74.
[118] *Die Nachtigall*, ed. F.H. von der Hagen, in *Gesamtabenteuer*, vol. 2, 1850, no. 25 p. 71–82; Bumke, p. 149.
[119] G. v. Strassburg, in Bumke, p. 149.
[120] Meyer Gaillard, p. 131.
[121] Manzano, p. 390.
[122] Meyer deduces this from the fact that livestock is not mentioned on the lists of feudal tributes.
[123] Meyer Gaillard, p. 131.
[124] Meyer Gaillard, p. 134.
[125] Meyer, p. 135.
[126] Meyer, pp. 134 ff.
[127] Bierbrauer, p. 161.
[128] The examples of Udine and Gorizia show that these towns were situated on the best land of the region. Certainly, the presence of a hill in both cases contributed to making the sites ideal, but the clear relationship between quality of soil and situation of castle continued to be a matter of primary importance even for those feudal castles where production may have been of lesser importance.
[129] Goez, p. 10.
[130] Bumke, p. 20.
[131] Bumke, p. 9.
[132] Bumke, pp. 12 ff.
[133] Goez, p. 13.
[134] Lazzarini, *Brazzacco*, p. 52.
[135] Satrapa Schill.
[136] Satrapa Schill, p. 79.
[137] Meyer, p. 136.
[138] Meyer, p. 202.
[139] Meyer, p. 136. *Seigfried Helbing, der kleine Lucidarius*, ed. Josef Seemüller, Halle, 1886, quoted in Satrapa Schill.
[140] Debts were incurred in the time of Ugo II (1304) and Ugo V (1323), the latter selling for 855 marks "the castle of Zuino" with attached properties to Frederico di Savorgnano. Miotti, vol. 3, p. 185.
141 Pichler, p. 181 ff, Miotti, vol. 3, p. 185.
[142] Pichler, pp. 200, 218.
[143] Bumke, p. 150.
[144] Miotti, vol. 3, p. 332.
[145] Miotti dates the tower to shortly after 1000, apparently with reference to Mor, but this is not necessary. The late mention in documents shortly before 1100 agrees with what we know from western Europe, that in general such constructions were unusual before 1100 (Miotti, vol. 3, p. 331). Grattoni's statement that "there was from Roman times a construction of some importance, given the presence of a protective *vallum*, a stone tower, and a water cistern, all going back to that time" shows a vivid imagination and a cheerful disregard for the historical sources. Until evidence of the existence of Roman defensive structures in the castles is shown, we should not start from the hypothesis of the existence of such watchtowers.
[146] Miotti, vol. 3, pp. 331 ff.
[147] Goez, p. 20. The custom of shutting up prisoners in towers may have become common only later. Both at Moggio and at Tricesimo it appears that the prisons were not situated in the towers until the early modern period.
[148] Zeune, p. 175.
[149] Zeune, p. 171.
[150] Zeune, p. 176; Bumke, vol. 1, p. 153.
[151] Zeune, p. 172.
[152] Zeune, p. 173.
[153] Miotti, vol. 5, p. 318.
[154] Zeune, p. 187.
[155] An *Erker* is a construction of one or more stories, with windows, built on to the façade of a house. Unlike a bay window it does not rest on the ground but protrudes from the level of one of the upper floors.
[156] Zeune, p. 187.
[157] Zeune, p. 186.
[158] Zeune, p. 187.
[159] Bumke, vol. 1, p. 160.
[160] Goez, pp. 20 ff.; Zeune, p. 181.
[161] A work such as the recent *In domus habitationis. L'arredo in Friuli nel tardo Medioevo*, which seeks to trace the history of furnishing, art, and culture of the interior between 1350 and 1500, is an interesting attempt, but of little use insofar as the material presented goes. The large volume shows no furniture from the fourteenth century that could give an idea of the furnishings and daily life in our castles. Furthermore, it draws conclusions about living conditions in the castles from the world of the towns, or even about the secular world from religious art. The authors have done a remarkable job, but it must be said that they are not historians. Unfortunately, however, it is still the fact that in publications and at conferences and exhibitions in the region these same non-specialists are the only ones to take up a position on this subject.
[162] Goez, pp. 22 ff.; Zeune, pp. 170 ff.
[163] Quoted in Miotti, vol. 2, p. 217.
[164] N. Monticoli, *Cronaca delle familglie udinesi*, ed. E. del Torso, Udine 1911, p. 43.
[165] G. Baiutti, p. 50.
[166] Bumke, pp. 26, 27, 29.
[167] Zeune, p. 176.
[168] Bumke, p. 14.
[169] Arnold von Lübeck, in Bumke, p. 159.
[170] Bumke, p. 159. There is a detailed description in Herrad von Landsberg's late twelfth-century *Hortus deliciarum*, where the bed of Solomon is an identical copy of the gift from queen of Hungary's (illustratrated in Bumke, p. 158).
[171] Bergamini, in Miotti, vol. 6, p. 415.
[172] "The frescoes at Sesto al Reghena, commissioned by the abbot Lodovico, from the family of the lords of Frattina, show that the same group (of families with a right to sit in the parliament of Friuli) was in a position to commission specific programs of frescoes, of which these ones are an important example." (Custoza, *In domus habitationis, cit.*, p. 85.)
[173] In the same work on furnishings in Friuli is an article by Casadio on the frescoes of town houses, with the publication of important sources.
[174] Custoza, p. 89. In the same catalogue, Casadio rightly describes the decoration as "a one-off, without parallel" (p. 75). The author's poor understanding of the role of patronage in the Middle Ages is shown by his attempt to define the cathedral at Venzone, a typical example of a the expression in art of the city council itself, as "an artistic expression intimately linked to a strong and deep-rooted chivalric culture," for no better reason than the lordship of Venzone almost a century earlier of a Colloredo (p. 85). The few remaining examples of fifteenth-century furnishings from town houses in Friuli should certainly not be regarded as examples of common decorative forms from that period, as it would be necessary to compare works commissioned by citizens of the towns with those commissioned by the nobility (which is almost impossible) in order to ascertain whether the decoration of the interiors reflects the changes of this fascinating period of radical political and social upheaval.
[175] Bumke, p. 138.
[176] Bumke, p. 153.
[177] Bumke, p. 155.
[178] Bumke, p. 156.
[179] Bumke, p. 157.
[180] Bumke, p. 157.
[181] Zeune, in *op. cit.*, p. 179.
[182] Casadio, *ibid.*, p. 72.
[183] Casadio, *ibid.*, p. 72.
[184] Bumke, p. 24.
[185] Thus, for example, wrote Miotti: "All these [Roman] fortified nuclei... plus a certain number of small protected places that were certainly not lacking, but of which all trace has been lost... subsequently became places of support for the military in the expansion plan that was being outlined beyond the Alps" (Miotti, vol. 7, p. 70).
[186] Otto Piper, pp. 40 ff.
[187] This was already noted a century ago by Otto Piper (p. 37): "our castles had their function during a period shorter than the second half of the Middle Ages... It is quite improbable that some castles should have had a Roman origin which would have been earlier perhaps by about a millennium. Nevertheless, the tendency to ascribe our ancient defensive constructions, especially castles, to the Romans on a vast scale has become widespread to an extent that is hardly explicable in scientific research, particularly of more ancient times and of the population."
[188] Vegetius, *Epitoma rei militaris*, ed. Fritz Wille, Aarau 1988, p. 179.
[189] Quentin Hughes, *Military Architecture*, London 1974.
[190] Giovanni Frau, in Miotti, vol. 6, p. 68. In late antiquity both words have the meaning of settlements placed on high rises, fortified or not (Bierbrauer, p. 165).
[191] Zaccaria, in Miotti, vol. 5, p. 61.
[192] Irzio, *De bello africano*, 37: "In hoc jugo colles sunt excelsi pauci, in quibus singulae turres speculaeque singulae perveteres erant collocatae," and Cicero, *In Verrem*, cited in Piper, p. 58: "Non enim sicut antea consuetudo erat, praedonum adventum significabat ignis e specula sublatis."
[193] Vetters dates these fortifications only to the third and fourth centuries (p. 936).
[194] An example of this is offered by the struggle for power between Septimius Severus and Maximinus, referred to by Herodian.
[195] Only for the security of a spring outside the wall does he recommend the use of a small external guard post, which he himself calls *burgus*, as was the custom at the frontier of the empire: "Quod si ultra ictum teli, in clivo tamen civitatis subiecta si vena catellum parvulum, quem burgumvocant, inter civitatem et fontem convenit fabricari ibique ballistas sagittariosque constitui, ut aqua defendatur ab ostibus." (Vegetius, 4, 10, p. 284).
[196] Herodian, 8, 1, 4, cited by Zaccaria (Miotti, vol. 5, p. 79).
[197] It is surprising that Vegetius never once recorded the fortifications of the *limes*, but this can be explained by the fact that the writing is of much later date.
[198] Vetters, pp. 930 ff.
[199] Bierbrauer, pp. 166 ff.
[200] Zaccaria, p. 80, in Miotti, vol. 5.
[201] I find it inexplicable that, in front of our total ignorance of the situation, Miotti starts with the hypothesis of "an enormous defense work." He has to admit in another place the obvious weakness: "It is easy to argue that that approach, if not defended by an adequate number of armed soldiers, could serve little... This explains without too much difficulty how Alaric with his Visigoths could have overcome at least four times this enormous defense work that only seemed impassable." (Miotti, vol. 5, p. 74). The effective means of late antiquity were indubitably unable to prevent incursions. However, for Vegetius the most basic evil was the bad training in conjunction with the lack of tenacity and will to fight: the troops did not want to bear arms, did not want to build fortified encampments for their stays, and in general were too soft, for which reason no citizen should be enrolled again into the troops.
[202] Thus Roman remains as embryos of castle cannot be shown yet in Friuli. All the citations of related examples also seem uncertain. Lacking any historical documentation, these fortifications seem sensible and logical. "In the light of these finds, we must express serious doubts on the Roman strategic capacity since they would not have taken steps to arm even the courses of our valleys, which lent themselves extremely well to fortification" (Miotti, vol. 7, p. 71). Among the "castles on Roman settings with not uncertain rows of walls," Miotti names the castles of Duino, Udine, Cucagna, Soffumbergo, Villalta, Osoppo, Gemona, and Cassacco (vol. 7, p. 112). For Duino, Villalta, and Cassacco, according to my own present knowledge, this continuity can be excluded. Similar conclusions can be arrived at in the case of Osoppo by comparing it with Invillino. Elsewhere Miotti explains, with some perplexity, the lack of usable remains, ascribing possible destruction to the First World War (vol. 7, p. 78) but at the same time he published the essay of F. Maselli-Scotti which testified to an "absolute lack of pottery evidence for fortified centers" which supposedly formed the "defensive system of the eastern Alps" (vol. 7, p. 292).
[203] "The partly still excellent fortifications of the peninsula and its external territories are due, not least, to the efforts of Theoderic to maintain and, if possible, improve the traditional system. The main fortress was at the same time the most important residence of Ravenna, but considerable sums were also used for the conservation of the walls of Rome" (Wolfram, p. 305).
[204] Wolfram, p. 305.
[205] Claudio Zaccaria (Miotti, vol. 5, p. 61).
[206] Paul the Deacon, in his full history of the Goths, applied himself to this problem in a very prudent way in just nine lines of

his 400-page work: "Furthermore, Theoderic must have undertaken and expanded the organization of the *tractus Italiae per Alpes*, of *castella* at the southern exit of the Alpine countries. In any case, many of the steps taken by the king of the Goths to create fortifications and provision depots in Durance, beyond the Alps and in the Alpi Cozie are well-known." (Wolfram, p. 306).

[207] Vetters, p. 958.

[208] Declaration of Settia in response to a request of mine. The present publications were unknown to him and he considers the known material completely insufficient to attempt a classification.

[209] An important example of the Longobard period is conserved in Castel Seprio near Varese. The building in the form of a castle probably served as the seat of a count. It was defended by solid walls of river pebbles. The rough building has already brought conjectures that it was a wall erected in haste, but I do not think so: the preserved remains of the church, of a substantial size, present a comparable wall, which cannot have been created under pressure of time. The whole structure was what in the documents is indicated as a *castrum*, a fortified village. It almost surely served as a center of government and possessed a lord's manor furnished as always, but the whole structure is so big that it could derive from several buildings that served at least as accommodation for the retinue. Even if the surfaces of the interior were totally empty and the boundary wall thus served mainly as a fortified refuge, it would still not be a castle in the sense that the term came to mean.

[210] "... cuius positio omnis inexpugnabilis existit" (Paul the Deacon, 4, 37).

[211] Over a large basilica of the mid fifth century was erected a new building after a fire before 650. In the eighth century a third church was built for unknown reasons. This, however, was abandoned again in the eighth century, probably as a result of violent action (Bierbrauer, p. 164).

[212] See the studies by Bierbrauer and Fingerlin in the bibliography.

[213] Previously there were two rates of ascent, that already mentioned on the south side and another on the eastern side (Fingerlin, p. 82).

[214] A second tower could not be shown as its foundations had perhaps slipped. "But because of the position it would absolutely not have been necessary:" Fingerlin, p. 82.

[215] Only on the eastern side of the area of the second access were found the remains of a wall that ran from east to west, as well as a rectangular building (Fingerlin, p. 84).

[216] Fingerlin, p. 84.

[217] Fingerlin, pp. 108 ff.

[218] The function is attested to by "traces of trade with distant places."

[219] Bierbrauer, p. 163.

[220] Bierbrauer, p. 167.

[221] Bierbrauer, p. 163.

[222] Bierbrauer, pp. 163 ff.

[223] Ulbert, p. 150.

[224] On the basis of reports of the archaeological excavations by Bierbrauer and Fingerlin, on the mountain of Osoppo a munitions deposit of the Austrian army was exploded, which made it unusable for research. According to Adriano Gransinig, the Italians blew up the modern fortifications on the mountain in order to avoid their falling into enemy hands (*Guerra sulle Alpi Carniche e Giulie*, Tolmezzo 1994).

[225] Invillino cannot be considered part of the Byzantine security system, as L. Schmidt claimed (*Die clausurae Augustanae Germania, II, 1)*, considering the Friuli *castra* to be new structures of the Byzantine administration. For the other *castra* on the edge of the Alps, he admits there was a previous development. This is also sustained by F. Schneider (*Die Entstehung von Burg und Landgemein der Italien*, 1927).

[226] Patze, p. 423.

[227] Such continuity was always assumed for Tricesimo and Julium Carnicum, but up to the present there is no corresponding proof. There is also no evidence of pottery material for the imperial Roman era (F. Maselli-Scotti, in Miotti, p. 281).

[228] Zaccaria, in Miotti, vol. 5, pp. 79 ff.

[229] Bravar, p. 102.

[230] Bravar, p. 102. Perhaps a Roman lighthouse?

[231] A Roman tower protected by a small fence was instead in the middle of the main level area.

[232] In Ebhard it seems still to be lacking; he cites (p. 21) only an unattractive staircase: "Here the triangular space between the main tower, the frontal wall, and the adjacent residential building (only later) was used to place stone stairs squared off and broken in several places, which led to the entrance to the main tower... and up high on the frontal wall."

[233] Particularly fine examples are Wildenburg in Odenwald and Kienzheim in Alsace. At Lahneck it is fixed in the frontal wall in such a way as to protrude at an acute angle in the weak side, at Liebenzell it is completely walled, and at Burgschwallback the main tower, which is round, is in a wall that forms an obtuse angle. *Burg*, in RDK, 150. Ebhard: "as we find similar elements also in castles in the Palatinate and Franconia" (p. 20).

[234] I conducted this research with Joachim Zeune, whose opinion I refer to here.

[235] Even theoretically the idea seems absurd: it would have been unused for centuries in the immediate vicinity of the rather poor castle. Furthermore, it would have been overlooked by it. Any patron around 1100 would have preferred the good building area with the tower in a more defended position on the rock over the sea. There would also have been the worry about someone else taking over such a building. This is as inconceivable as the notion of such a tower having survived without damage after four centuries of barbarian invasions.

[236] This is the corner of a wall of the room today used as a kitchen. Through an opening in the wall, a cavity behind the kitchen is reached, under the frontal wall. Here too the original walls can be recognized, refaced in the Middle Ages. An opening in the wall makes it possible to inspect the outer walls of the southern wing of the tower. In this case, too, I wish to thank Joachim Zeune for his help.

[237] It cannot be excluded that as far as the still recognizable texts are concerned, these are secular figures. From the stylistic point of view, they refer in an obvious way to frescoes showing Byzantine influence in other churches. Bodo Ebhard assumed that there was a chapel, while Bravar spoke of a hall.

[238] Ebhard (p. 17) interprets the remains of the walls above the staircase as fortifications.

[239] Ebhard, p. 17.

[240] This contradicts the possibility that this area was once covered by a larger residence, as might be supposed from its position. The other remains of walls would also confirm the existence of a building in this area, since a boundary wall above the height of the balustrade would have been superfluous.

[241] Here in particular must be named the two great arches, as well as some merlons above the wall at the height of the balustrade. According to Pichler (p. 85), the work would have been carried out at the behest of the last owner of the Torre family, Princess Teresa Hohenlohe-Schillingsfürst.

[242] "Cuius precibus acclinati eidem Friderico patriarchae prenominatum castellum iuris imperii nostri quod dicitur Puziolum pertinens et adiacens in comitatu Foroiuliano": Menis, in Miotti, vol. 6, p. 25.

[243] In 1139 therefore the castle may have already been occupied, which is confirmed by a document on the first border dispute between Duino and Trieste (Pichler, p. 85).

[244] Bravar, p. 105.

[245] B. and F. Lorenz, in *Burger und Schlösser*, 1, 1961, p. 6.

[246] Pichler, pp. 147, 198.

[247] Pichler, p. 84.

[248] Pichler (p. 95) describes it as still surrounded by large buildings, quoting it with the name of Gorizutta.

[249] "Through a door to the north and the suburb [the present garden], substantial defense systems are reached, which protect and cover the main castle. Immediately after the door (*a*)—now only a grill—there is the wide deep moat (*g*) in the middle of extremely high walls. Its depth continues to the right of the road, which here seems like a riverbank. There is access to it, arranged in a rather particular way, going down the stone steps, entering from behind a room (*b*) in the form of a tower, surrounded by walls, then passing through a tunnel dug under the road. The wall which closes the southern part of the moat lines, proceeding toward the east, the suburb along the coast. The wall decorated with merlons at the same time forms the external wall of a prison situated at the back and much higher. Behind a door (*c*), which today consists of a grille, another door leads to rooms underneath whose windows give on to the wall and are barred. On the back of the prison rises a defense building which reaches an imposing height. Its whose presence in this safe place must surprise students of castles: a frontal wall which corresponds to the strict sense of the word and which, in my experience, is found with any frequency only in parts of western Germany and, to a minimal extent, in castles in Austria. In the background, thus, as in the castles of the Palatinate and Franconia, rises the tower in a higher part..." To get there you have to follow the path in the form of a parapet walk, going through the third door (*d*) which is still fortified, until you reach the courtyard.

[250] Pichler, p. 96.

[251] Bravar (p. 109) defines the four-light mullioned window as the oldest part, "part perhaps of a mid fourteenth-century loggia."

[252] "In his report he points out some things missing in the structures (walls not earth filled, moat not very deep) and other points of maintenance (dangerous stairs and half steps, partitions and boarding to be replaced. In short he reports that there is need of certain adjustments and restoration." Bravar, p. 107, in A. Puschini, "Relazioni inedite sui castelli di Trieste e Duino," *Atti e Memorie della Società Alpina delle Giulie*, Trieste 1887, pp. 225–40.

[253] Unfortunately no detailed information exists from which it would be possible to deduce the thickness of the walls and the irregularities of the old parts of the castle.

[254] This is also confirmed by the small excavations made at the southern end of the wall where, apart from the probably Roman remains in the kitchen wall, there is also visible a wall which is certainly medieval and does not run quite parallel to the present outside wall of the frontal wall.

[255] These specialists traveled a lot and, consequently were familiar with many workyards. The fact that the developments in the building of churches were adopted rapidly (cf. the influence of Rheims Cathedral on the basilica of San Francesco in Assisi) is proof of the great mobility of the architects. Villard de Honnecourt's collection of examples from 1225 and 1235 shows how architects offered their services and were engaged even in distant countries like Hungary. See Alexander Antonow, pp. 67 ff.

[256] The price was not mentioned, since cession of the castle in fact seems to have been a settlement of debts (Miotti, vol. 3, p. 188).

[257] Miotti, vol. 3, p. 190.

[258] "He was ordered to arm the castle with great care and study, in order to put it into a state capable of resisting any new aggression." As early as 1509 Sigismund Hofer became his successor. His appointment represents a relatively late example of the normal indications of the sovereign with regard to the building and ownership of castles: "There will not start nor continue wars or attacks (blood feuds are included here), nor will be peace be concluded without our assent. New fortresses will not be erected without our order. Justice will be administered in his district to the poor as to the rich..." (Pichler, pp. 287 ff.).

[259] A little later Matthias Hofer lent money to the Archduke Charles, consolidating in this way the right to the passage of property: "Hofer has devotedly given us a loan of 25,000 Rhenish florins without interest, which must be added to the other sum for which the lord of Duino is committed" (Pichler, p. 302).

[260] See Bravar, p. 98, and Miotti, vol. 3, pp. 191 ff.

[261] Ebhard, however, saw them. Instead of the original pavilion roof, the tower was crowned by an open platform and surrounded by merlons which in all probability were not the original ones. The same is true for the parapet of the frontal wall with spaces between the merlons which go right down to the ground (p. 21). An etching by Valvasor of 1689 shows the castle without merlons.

[262] In her book on the gardens of the region, Francesca Venuto, surprisingly, does not examine this example, neglecting in this way one of the most remarkable castle gardens of the area.

[263] Previously the representation of the myth of the Dark Ages, fostered by Edward Gibbon in his *The History of the Decline and Fall of the Roman Empire*, London 1776–1788. See Franz Georg Maier, "Die Verwandlung der Mittelmeerwelt," in *Fischer Weltgeschichte* (FWG), vol. 9, Frankfurt 1968.

[264] Geary, p. 38.

[265] "The passage to *patrocinium*, that made a tenant farmer out of a peasant, in substance was merely the exchange of one obligation for another. But it is significant that dependence on the landowner (which effectively also offered economic security and protection against fiscal extortion) was felt as a mild passage. Thus this movement did not include only small peasants, but also artisans, even clerks. The strength of attraction and protection of the great landowners from the last years of the fourth century onwards brought about a flight from the towns to the countryside." Maier, FWG, p. 82.

[266] Geary, pp. 37 ff.

[267] Imperial functionaries with the title of *comes* were originally special delegates.

[268] Wolfram, p. 218.

[269] Wolfram, p. 217.

[270] "Here Roman civilization had put down its deepest and strongest roots, and the members of these great families continued the tradition of Roman culture beyond the Imperial era": Geary, p. 39.

[271] Geary, p. 38.

[272] Geary, p. 42.

[273] He had been educated in Byzantium at the imperial court, adopted by the Emperor, and formally installed as regent of Italy. The Roman Sidonius Apollinarius, around 455, praised not only his civilized Roman style of life but even described him as the ideal man who represented all the virtues of the Empire: in his portrait can be seen Greek elegance, Gallic exuberance, and Italian dynamism. He combined public splendor with a scrupulous private home and royal moderation. See Wolfram, *Die Goten*, pp. 208 ff.

[274] Even Gaul came formally under the western Goths as a kingdom tied by a pact. Sidonius Apollinarius speaks significantly of "the peoples of Gaul, who live in Goth territory," and who should remain Roman on the basis of the ancient*foedus* (treaty). In this

sense it is understandable that Sidonius Apollinarius should say that Gaul was in the main part integrated. See Wolfram, pp. 213 ff.
[275] Wolfram, p. 290.
[276] Geary, p. 100.
[277] Maier, p. 331.
[278] Maier, p. 331.
[279] Wolfram, p. 295.
[280] Dhondt, *FWG*, pp. 66, 67.
[281] Wolfram, p. 295.
[282] Maier, p. 328.
[283] Amelio Tagliaferri in *I Longobardi*, p. 102.
[284] Maier, p. 334.
[285] "Even the level of Roman *possessores* did not simply disappear, because with the subsequent conquests systematic suppression of landed property was avoided." Maier, p. 334.
[286] Late Roman *possessores* lived on their estates as much as in towns. In the literature, reference is made to the fact that as a consequence of the great insecurity in the countryside, the town was preferred as a residence, but the opposite is also asserted, that the majority of the aristocracy had long since abandoned the towns and had withdrawn to the safety and autonomy of their large estates.
[287] Eugen Ewig, *Die Merowinger und das Frankenreich*, Stuttgart 1988, p. 94.
[288] The ancient central function of the towns was maintained, in particular by the organization of the church, especially in the case of bishoprics.
[289] Brogiolo, in *I Longobardi*, p. 130.
[290] Menis (*I Longobardi*, p. 342) cites correctly that with the establishment of Longobard rule—and certainly strengthened by their Romanization—towns flourished together with production in the latter period of Longobard rule but trade regained only a small part of its ancient importance.
[291] Azevedo, p. 684.
[292] Azevedo, pp. 677 ff.: "archaeology cannot document any Frankish settlement in the villas, except for a few tombs."
[293] Azevedo, p. 311.
[294] Hinz, p. 138.
[295] Mitterauer, in *Die Burg im deutschen Sprachraum*, p. 375.
[296] Azevedo, p. 667.
[297] Azevedo, p. 671.
[298] Azevedo, p. 688.
[299] Azevedo, p. 678.
[300] Azevedo, p. 672.
[301] Azevedo, p. 684.
[302] In *Bellum Africanum* a villa is called "per magna turribus IV instructa" which removed from Labienus the view of the battle with Caesar near Ruspinae (Vetters, p. 934).
[303] Vetters, p. 934.
[304] Vetters, p. 934. See also Dygve, *Tre ville...*
[305] Unfortunately I have not been able to discover anything about the excavations. See Miotti, p. 79.
[306] Vetters, p. 934.
[307] Azevedo, p. 681.
[308] Hinz, p. 135.
[309] Hinz (p. 142) quotes research by G. Fournier on this subject.
[310] Marcato in *Castello, Comunità e Giurisdizione di Strassoldo*, p. 25: "The lack of placenames of Roman origin at Strassoldo shows that there was an historical moment in which residential settlement was interrupted. Consequently, for an unknown period of time there will have been an absence of stable population there." Probably the region was less marshy in Roman times, before the land sank and the waters of the lagoon rose. However, some everyday Roman objects and coins were found at Cisis (Marzio di Strassoldo, p. 116).
[311] There are many castles on islands whose names have the final syllable *au*, from Mainau to Gubenau, around the present Strassoldo estate. The most ancient names start with *Straso* in 1184, and pass from *Strasson* to *Strassouve*, *de Strasso Strassau*, *Strassolt*, *de Strassou*, *de Strassov*, *de Strasson* to, finally, *de Strasolt*, around 1275, when the present name was established (Marcato, op. cit.). Derivations from *Hau* or *Halt* are less convincing. The consonant shifts in the earlier times correspond exactly to the variations named by Grimm of the word *Aue*: High German *ouwa* and Middle High German *ouwe*, abbreviated to *ou* The ancient definition of Aue as "land surrounded by a course of water, damp land, field, island," corresponds exactly to the topographical situation. See Grimm, *Deutsches Wörterbuch, p. 602.*
[312] Deluisa, *Strassoldo*, p. 24.
[313] In the area there are certainly some placenames of Slav origin which could have arisen in the course of repopulating the territories devastated in Friuli after the Hungarian invasions around 1000. However, there is no concrete indication of the existence of a castle before the end of the twelfth century. Formatti and Tondat (p. 203) thought it "probable that a settlement was present already in the Roman period." M. di Strassoldo finds that there were "building works probably during the Longobard domination or, at the latest, in the tenth century" (*Quaderni*, p. 5), while Rossetti (p. 52) recalls the family tradition according to which in 1035 a Bohemian, Woldariche Strassu received Strassoldo as a fief from the patriarch.
[314] Rossetti, in *Castello, Comunità e Giurisdizione di Strassoldo*, p. 52.
[315] In support of this link is the fact that a lord from Lavariano was called Azo de Azmurgen, an ancient style di Castions and di Campolongetto. See Marzio di Strassoldo, *Castello di Strassoldo*, p. 7.
[316] Marcato, p. 28.
[317] The present church tower, with its typical entrance three meters (10 feet) above ground will have been raised in connection with this *cortina* Going by its form, it is typical medieval work. But cf. Miotti, vol. 2, pp. 189 ff.
[318] Miotti, vol. 2, pp. 189 ff.; Dhondt, in *FWG*, 10, p. 67.
[319] Marzio di Strassoldo, *Castello di Strassoldo*, p. 7. The continuity of the property and the family for 400 years is naturally unsure. Uniquely, external indications favor the acceptance of this link: the extensive property which originally belonged to the fief was allodial, the noble origin of the family, whose investiture cannot be attributed to the times of the patriarch, and the declaration of the family in the thirteenth century that it lived in accordance with Longobard law.
[320] According to Soloniero di Strassoldo, in the sixteenth century, the castle was built in 1211. See Miotti, vol. 2, p. 312, citing A. Benvenuti.
[321] Miotti asserts: "Raised almost at the intersection of two of the most important roads of the Friuli plain... considerable strategic value was provided by the site, which justified the presence of a large fortress." Miotti, vol. 2, p. 312. Rossetti (p. 50) held that Strassoldo was a bulwark against the Hungarians.
[322] If in 1381 destruction took place as a result of the battles over the nomination of the patriarch, Filippo d'Alecon, it is uncertain how this can have happened as the consequence of the Venetian siege during the conquest of Friuli, which took place between 1418 and 1420. We know nothing of the fate of the castle during the Turkish invasions, though it could have been defended perhaps because of its hidden and protected position.
[323] From the very beginning, two towers are named in all the documents on Strassoldo. The source here, however, is not clear.
[324] Di Strassoldo, *Castello, Comunità e Giurisdizione di Strassoldo*, p. 117
[325] The act of division, in the Archivio di Stato in Gorizia, was published for the first time in 1904 by Grion in *Pagine Friulane* and was summarized by F. Swida in *Archeografo Triestino*, 15, p. 206.
[326] Di Strassoldo, *op. cit.*, p. 118.
[327] As usual, the dating is based on a series of reasonings. In Friuli in the tenth century defensive castles certainly existed for protection against the Hungarian invasions. A castle of this type certainly existed at Strassoldo, an important fortress on an important crossroads. It can certainly also be said that the biggest and most crooked tower at Strassoldo belonged to the oldest part of the castle, and for this reason must automatically date back to the tenth century. The sources for this reasoning are mainly from Miotti. Yet even he speaks of the building of the castle taking place in 1211; the second part of the article unfortunately is not by him and gives rise to a series of unfounded suppositions, as indicated above.
[328] The gate was discovered during rebuilding works carried out on the instructions of Countess Elisabetta di Strassoldo. The assumption put forward many times, according to which the building was, because of the lack of internal walls, placed on a type of keep, is misleading (Rossetti, p. 62). Present-day popular misconceptions with regard to the size of the lady of the castle's apartment are strong. A storeroom on the ground floor, a hall, and places to sleep for the servants on the first floor, men on the second and women on the third floors, and above, perhaps, a platform for defense: these were the dimensions of a tower in the thirteenth and fourteenth centuries.
[329] Prison cells were not originally found in these secret towers. The inadequate hygienic situation, which made it impossible to clean a hole of this sort, means they cannot have been used for this, especially if the rooms above were being used or lived in.
[330] Extensive rebuilding works were carried in the upper castle after 1322. The act of division speaks repeatedly of the rebuilding works which were foreseen and necessary, in particular in the area of the outer wall and the gates.
[331] In the area of the lower castle, the walls built towards the middle of the fourteenth century were made of brick while the older walls were made in stone, brought probably from Aquileia. The building materials needed were identified by Vittorio Foramitti.
[332] The situation is further complicated by a declaration by the feudatory owner in 1587. In this, the description of the different parts seems to make sense only if the tower mentioned only once is moved to a corner diametrically opposite to the present one. Even if massive foundations were found there, this would mean that the tenth-century tower would have been the result of work carried out around 1600.
[333] "A simple oversight, mechanically repeated from author to author, has contributed to exaggerated the importance of the Hungarian catastrophe in the minds of local historians, and to encourage their conviction of its profound and irreversible influence on the economy, the populationm, and the institutions of the whole region. The hypothesis that the patriarch was engaged in successful campaigns (Menis) against the Hungarians has been supported on the basis of meager clues and controversial interpretations. Nor is it clear what military force the patriarch would have been had..." Aldo Settia, *Chiese e fortezze nel popolamento del Friuli*, p. 103.
[334] It has been proved that the chapel tower was raised in a later period. Nevertheless, it appears improbable that this would have originally been a watchtower. Neither its entrance, which obviously dates from the modern period, today walled up, nor its rather thin walls make this hypothesis plausible (Nicolette, in Miotti, p. 315; Deluisa, p. 35). The so-called Lombard cross, too, on the back of the apse was not executed before the late Middle Ages. There is no doubt that in this period the forms developed by the Longobards were still widespread.
[335] Di Strassoldo, p. 21.
[336] Foramitti.
[337] The act of division suggests houses next to one another, in which the brothers lived one next to the other. The common use of an intermediary part is still to be determined; it would have been used as a reception area where celebrations and banquets were held.
[338] Di Strassoldo, *op. cit.*, p. 118.
[339] From the *Cronaca* of Niccolò Maria di Strassoldo (Joppi, cited by Foramitti, p. 205).
[340] "The walling of Strassoldo was begun. It was made of walls with merlons, and the gate of the bridge which goes to the new village and the gate of the courtyard." Marzio di Strassoldo, (*op. cit.*, p. 124; Foramitti, p. 205.
[341] Rossetti, p. 66; Marzio di Strassoldo, in *Castello, Comunità e Giurisdizione di Strassoldo*, p. 125.
[342] Di Strassoldo, *op. cit.*
[343] See Marzio di Strassoldo, *op. cit.* With the rise of agriculture in the eighteenth century, Strassoldo gained further improvement in its economic situation, which continued in the nineteenth century with the building of mills.
[344] In the eighteenth century there was a casemate. From its description can be understood only that probably it was in ruins. It could also have been a prison, which in recent times has always been supposed to have been in the tower of the castle. The term *casemate*, meaning secret, represents too slight an indication for such an interpretation and thus also for the remains of the tower. Support for the presence of the tower can be found in the eighteenth-century plans on which the walls and also the high part of the tower are marked dark (Museo Provinciale, Gorizia, Archivio Stati Provinciali, Sez. II).
[345] This can be learnt from the eighteenth-century plan, which also shows the tower.
[346] Of course attempts have been made to recognize in this tower the massive tower mentioned above, which elsewhere is defined as an open tower, called the casemate. But this is not possible because it is just this building that is defined as the large house and must be the old *domus magna* (big house). The text of the act of division is quoted according to Vittorio Foramitti and Nicola Tondat's transcription: "Joseffo q.s. Fantutio Strasoldo, Paulo et Oratio fratelli possedemo li infrascrittibeni posti nella giurisdizione del castello di Strassoldo... La giurisditione che per nostro caratto ne tocca del castello di Strassoldo inferiore,c o il Torazzo detto già palazzo comune fra noi consorti di sotto... Hieronimo, Nicolò Maria, Ludovico et Francesco fratelli q.s. Pietro di Strasoldo... La portione che a noi tocca della torre discoperta posta nel ziron del castello di sotto detta la casa matta. Aurelio, Giacomo, Giulio et Silvio fratelli q.d. Lodovico di Strasoldo... La portione a noi spettante della casa grande posta nel castello di sotto di Strasoldo nel zirone, dettala casa matta discoperta." (The brothers Joseffo of the late Fantutio of Strassoldo, Paolo, and Orazio possess the goods written herein placed within the jurisdiction of the castle of Strassoldo... The jurisdiction that for our portion concerns the lower castle of Strassoldo, with the great tower previously called communal building among us all listed below... Hieronimo, Nicolò Maria, Ludovico, and Francesco, sons of the late Pietro di Strassoldo... The portion owing to us of the open tower in the courtyard of the lower castle, called the casemate. Aurelio, Giacomo, Giulio, and Silvio, brothers of the late Lodovico di Strassoldo... the portion owing to us of the big

house placed in the lower castle of Strassoldo in the courtyard, called the uncovered casemate.)
[347] If the windows were authentic, the building would have another floor.
[348] Ettore Strassoldo recorded that the signature of the document for the building of Palmanova took place in his house. In fact, we know that in 1587 the house of a certain Ettore backed on to the church as well as "con il signori di Zuane et Lucretio fratelli Strasoldi, col signor Bortolomio, et con l'acqua grande" (and on to the property of Giovanni and Lucrezio di Strasoldo, brothers, the property of Bartolomeo, and the great water). From this it is certain that Ettore lived to the east of the present upper castle. Since Giovanni and Lucrezio lived next to him, and knowing that entry into the castle was on the left, it must be the southeastern corner. Giovanni and Lucrezio, however, lived in the northern part and there possessed a tower and a house. The questions inherent in this tower have already been dealt with exhaustively. In this case, too, there are numerous queries generating a series of mysteries.
[349] Favoring this theory, according to which the old parts were incorporated, are the stories passed down by the family, which indicate this area as the oldest part. In 1587 a certain Michele di Strassoldo was the owner of a house which was bordered with a ditch to the west and to the north, with the courtyard to the south and with the present road leading to the church to the east. This outlines finally the place of the present wing with respect to the church (Foramitti).
[350] The church was rebuilt between 1719 and 1736, though few of the old structures will have been used (Foramitti, p. 207).
[351] The lower part with the chancery has a thick wall at the back. The upper wing seems to have used part of the old outer wall. In each house the buildings were much lower, showing evidence of old plasterwork, an unequivocal sign that two floors were added at a later date. Only to the chancery was added a single floor. This extension must have taken place in the nineteenth century. The remains of the plasterwork were analyzed by Foramitti.
[352] The year 1728 is carved on a stone (Mancini Lapenna, p. 9). The relatively late link between the women's gallery and façade and the staircase in the main house, and the wide passage, give the impression that the work was carried out at the same time. This sixteenth-century building is unanimously dated to 1587. However, this is contradicted by the 1587 description, in which no mention is made of a chapel.
[353] See the works by Billig and Antonow cited in the bibliography.
[354] According to Hinz, in the mid nineteenth century, A. de Chaumont, with his studies on antiquities, set in motion modern studies on castles of this type that are indicated (by a French term, *motte*, *château à motte*, in Latin *mota*, which had taken the place of the older German term, *Turmhügel*, a fortified tower on a hill. See Hinz, p. 11.
[355] The various texts published on the etymology of the term were collected by M. de Bouard. A Germanic root of the term has been rejected by almost everyone; a Latin origin, however, has never been proved. It is presumed that the term was coined in the area where the greatest number of mottes are to be found. The French term *motte* seems, however, to indicate above all the construction of a mound or artificial hill, of which the covering in turf was of the maximum importance. In western Switzerland, in particular in Bernese dialect, the term *Mutte* exists to indicate clumps of turf. The close connection between the creation of the mound and defensive ramparts and the verb *einmotten* have also to be seen in this context. In the language of the documents, the term is used only from 1100 onwards. Hinz is of the opinion that scholarly writers tended to substitute the popular term with its corresponding Latin expression. He is uncertain whether the lack of a term reflected the fact there were few castles of this type. See M. de Bouard, *Château Gaillard*, vol. 2, Cologne/Graz 1967, pp. 19 ff., and Hinz, p. 15.
[356] Hinz (p. 75) also cites mottes whose phases of enlargement have been documented from the archaeological point of view (Husterknupp, Borssaele, Gaisenberg, and Duffield).
[357] Hinz, p. 42.
[358] Hinz, p. 25.
[359] Hinz published the results of a series of excavations that give evidence of a clear stratification of the terrain. The author recalls, however, that in some cases the stratification could be clarified by comparing different zones of the excavation.
[360] A number of other medieval castles on the plains which today have disappeared were built on prehistoric mounds that only in relatively recent times were called with the name of motte (Settia, *Motte*, p. 379).
[361] Even if Vetters assumes that many lords, in times of peace, lived outside the motte if this was built on land that was insalubrious and swampy, the fact that it acted as a fixed residence was the main characteristic of the motte and all the other castles of the nobility which followed it. Right from the outset it was not important if the motte was formed as an allodium or in a relationship of subordination to a lord of superior rank. See also Hinz, p. 23.
[362] Hinz, p. 39, according to Walter von Clusa, *Historia Ardensium*.
[363] Hinz (p. 39) cites an example: In his *vita* (life) of bishop Johannes von Trouenne, Johann von Colmieu writes "intra vallum domum vel, qua omnia despiciat, arcem in medio aedificare."
[364] In this case too it is possible to make comparisons with Strassoldo, where both for the upper and lower castle we find a separate building given over to use as a kitchen mentioned in documents dating from the fourteenth century.
[365] Already in 641, one of the few documents of the period mentions a castle in wood with a rampart and palisades over the installation, in which the king of the Franks, Sigisbert, had to take refuge: "Radolfus haec cernens, castrum ligneum monitum super Unstrude fluvio in Toringia construens, exercitum undique quantum plus potuit, collegens, cum uxorem et liberis in hunc castrum ad se definsendam stabilisit." Vetters, *Von der Spätantiken zum Mittelalter im Ostalpenraum*, 1965, p. 949.
[366] In this respect Hinz (p. 35) recalls that the king of Hungary, as late as the thirteenth century, permitted the Teutonic Knights to replace their wooden castles with those in stone. We do not know, however, if wood was forbidden as building material because it was less strong or simply because it was not aristocratic enough.
[367] Aldo Settia, who, like no other, has studied documents relating to castles in Italy, informed me in a discussion that in Italy the term *balfredum* normally indicates a somewhat temporary structure, not excluding that at times it could have referred to a mobile tower. In Friuli, however, the Germanic influence was so great that even he would say that it was a tower important in the western European sense of a watchtower; this would then be confirmed by the particular value that it had in the subdivision.
[368] "... altum ut nunc est suis propriis sumptibus et expensis cum bono et idoneo fundamento, verumtamen quod si illud murum per magistros muratores videretur fore bonum et habere congruum et bonum fundamentum, quod sit ut nunc est permitti possit, salvo quod si caderet propter aliquod pondus suppositum aut alio modo, quod idem cui dicta pars acciderit suis sumptibus et expensio reddificare teneatur de novo cum bono fundamento et muro."
[369] While wooden castles were certainly much more widespread in Germany still in the eleventh and twelfth centuries, in Italy this type of construction had probably already been abandoned (Antonow, p. 61).
[370] In his study on the transition from building in wood to building in stone in Saxony, Gerhard Billig holds, for example, that according to the results of archaeological excavations, this change took place only slowly in the thirteenth century and that this was, however, a regional characteristic (*Burgenforschung aus Sachsen*, 1994, p. 8)
371 Gerhard Billig, *Burgenforschung aus Sachsen*,3/4, 1994, p. 8.
[372] Vinicio Tomadin, *Colloredo*, p. 49.
[373] At Lürken have been found workshops for blacksmiths and for the production of ceramics (Hinz, p. 47, and F. Tischler, *Niederrheinisches Jahrbuch*, 3, 1951, pp. 52 ff).
[374] Hinz, p. 46.
[375] Settia, *Villaggio-Dimora*, pp. 219 ff.
[376] As a model for the *burgus*, Schuchard (p. 198) identified the keep type of large tower, which even when near the *limes* was placed on a flat mound. See also Hinz, p. 90: the mounds of the *burgi* were not in the least like mottes. They were more or less surrounded by moats which had to let the water flow and were caused by the extracted earth that was slightly higher. The *centenari*, however, which too were considered precursors of the keep, were made up of a single story and were similar to normal castles. We have to wonder if it was in this sense that Vetters too intended it.
[377] Hinz, p. 92. See R. Fellmann, *Die Principia des Legionslagers Vindonissa und das Zentralgebäude der römischen Lager und Kastelle*, Bruges 1958.
[378] In this way parts of the Roman castles were used later as old Gallic fortified centers.
[379] It is evidently seen as a new architectural form which does not have precursors in the late Roman period prior to the Merovingian period.
[380] Hinz, p. 121.
[381] "Posuimus fundamenta in capella quam in tumulo vallis munitofecimus in Habrica." In this regard, according to Settia the use of the participle *erectus*, and its variant *inflactus vel tumefactus* in another copy, shows that the mound was created artificially. This is the oldest reference to the building of a motte. Settia, *Motte*, p. 372.
[382] "Dum premeret patriam rabies miserabilis istem/Nec non et omnigenum populatio maxima rerum/Leudoinus sancta Motinenensis presul in aula/His tumulum portis et erectis aggere vallis/Firmavit, positis circum latitantibus armis/Non contra dominos erectus corda serenos/Sed cives proprios cupiens defendere tectos." Settia, op. cit., p. 371.
[383] Settia, op. cit., p. 375. In France, the term *motte* is encountered mainly in the placenames of the north. In England, however, the term was not used in popular language and is found only in documents (Hinz, p. 16). This confirms the thesis that mottes had a close connection with the Norman conquest; it would also explain their diffusion in southern Italy.
[384] Settia, op. cit., p. 380.
[385] Settia, op. cit., p. 376.
[386] Settia, op. cit., p. 377.
[387] Settia, op. cit., p. 376.
[388] Even more than in the names of the families who commissioned the building of the castles, Germanic influence is proved by the numerous terms deriving from German: *Burghut*, *Morgengabe*, *Bergfried*, *Fehde*.
[389] Lazzarini, *Castelli del Friuli. Brazzacco*, p. 52, referring to A. Joppi, Not. com.
[390] Lazzarini, p. 55, referring to Ciconi, *cit* Archivio Comunale, Udine.
[391] Of particular interest is the steep cone about 200 meters (220 yards) south of the upper castle. Today it is part of a large garden arranged so close to the outer wall that little remains of the ditches and ramparts. The embankment is surprisingly steep as over time the rains should have flattened it. For this reason one tends to favor the hypothesis that there must have been a solid nucleus in its interior. The high ground today has a diameter of about 20 meters (65 feet) and more or less the same height.
[392] The archaeological excavations, unfortunately interrupted, on the outside of the wall brought to light a quantity of accumulated material of about one meter deep. The layers, however, were composed of material that is found in periods that go up to the Middle Ages and it was not possible to excavate right to the bottom. See Vinicio Tomadin, *Brazzacco*.
[393] Vinicio Tomadin speaks cautiously of a radical transformation of the high ground, without, however, being able to locate it with precision.
[394] It should be noted that the term *motte* is used only once in the document, while the whole structure is defined as *castellum* This confirms that here we are not dealing with an old abandoned motte found somewhere near the castle.
[395] Cited by Miotti, vol. 3, p. 258. The sources are the *Regesti per facilitare una breve istoria dei Castelli Friulani*, a manuscript written in 1922 (Archivio Frangipane, Ioannis), a copy of which is in the Biblioteca Civica, Udine, by Luigi Frangipane. Like his predecessors in the nineteenth century, the author unfortunately never says where the document is that he refers to in the abbreviation with a single phrase.
[396] Research for documents has had little success. Frangipane's sources by now are in parts of archives that have been lost and the material preserved in the library of Udine, according to the directors of the library, would require years to be examined and put in order. In the Archivio di Stato in Venice such material may only be examined if it is not on the top shelves which, for reasons of safety, the staff no longer touch. As the situation of archive material is so chaotic that it is impossible to know in which archive to look, or whether the documents are too old or simply located too high up to be able to access them, there remains only the small satisfaction of the old document summaries.
[397] Miotti, vol. 3, p. 258, citing Frangipane. The same reference, however, can be found in Manzano, who cites the sources of Nicoletti, perhaps the only one to have actually seen the document. The solution to the mystery of the whereabouts of this important document died with him more than a hundred years ago.
[398] Miotti, vol. 3, p. 258. The source is the *Regesti per facilitare una breve istoria dei Castelli Friulani*, cited in note 397.
[399] Miotti, vol. 3, p. 258, quoting Frangipane. The same reference, however, can be found in Manzano, who cites the sources of Nicoletti; see note 397.
[400] Miotti, quoting Frangipane, who quoted Manzano, who quoted a document in the Archivio Enrico di Zucco.
[401] Manzano, 13 October 1353, according to the Spilimbergo Chronicle: "The occupants of Gramogliano, besieged by the army of the patriarch of Aquileia, surrendered on condition that they give the castle to the patriarch and could leave safely with all their belongings. Thus three days later the aforementioned castle was razed to the ground."
[402] Manzano, according to *Rerum Goritiensis*, Archivio Comunale, Gorizia, Attems.
[403] This position could be an element in favor of the existence of a castle in this zone. Steep walls, strengthening the slope and supporting a thesis of this type, have recently been brought to light. The poor state of conservation of the walls makes it implausible that this was the wall of a medieval castle. Almost without mortar, stones found all over the place and of different sizes were used here. In particular, the corner wall shows that it was made by

inexpert hands. Favoring the thesis that the castle would have been in a different place, it could be added that, over and beyond the strange location of the chapel, the fact that the documents mention continuous changes of ownership cannot be ignored. According to them, repeated mention is made of a tower which was sold but should already be in the possession of another or had belonged to an earlier owner, producing a confusion that can only be resolved with the existence of two different towers. Against this hypothesis, however, is the fact that in no document is an upper or lower castle spoken of. A subdivision of the castle, therefore, never took place.

[404] Miotti believed that he had recognized medieval remains in the cellar wall. On the basis of the type of building work, however, this must almost certainly be excluded.

[405] At Spessa there are three similar striking corner towers, while the towers of Rocca Bernarda are found opposite on a mound. These can be placed in relation to the building of the entire system, dating from the 1560s.

[406] The present owner speaks of foundations and aqueducts that can be found under the meadows. In the cellar there is furthermore a fine floor made of small bricks, about four centimeters wide and twelve centimeters long, in herringbone pattern, The use of clay panels is also surprising: as well as being enormous, they were produced with a white clay which according to Vinicio Tomadin is not to be found in this region. These types of floors were made only in the Roman period.

[407] I do not know the basis for this date.

[408] Settia, *Il castello da villaggio fortificato a dimora signorile*, p. 225.

[409] Cited Biller, p. 127: "Ein castel heizet daz, da ein turm stat, unde mit einer mure umbefangin ist und sich diu zwei beschirmint under einanderen."

[410] Biller, p. 126.

[411] Hinz, *Motte*, p. 71.

[412] The watchtower at Strassoldo is a small narrow bell tower with walls so thin that it cannot be older than 300 years. The two-light mullioned windows at Gorizia and Arcano, indicated as evidence of the residential function in their related plans, not only look the same but have equally modern imitations which are less than a 100 years old. The same thing can be said of the 1930s parapet walk at the castle of Gorizia or about the walls that only very recently were raised at Arcano, obviously for decorative reasons. The few walls that can be seen at the old castle of Duino are found in the only room that can be defined as a defense passage, equally of the late nineteenth century, and they were quite superfluous in that place (see the chapter on the castle of Duino). As far as the keep is concerned, this is normally the same as the *palas*. But at Colloredo the term circular keep has been used to define the whole area of the outer wall which over time has been extended, while other cases which have not undergone this development are still preserved with their original form. Therefore, the three types—Colloredo, Arcano, and Brazzacco—made distinct by Nicoletti-König, were originally one only, a modest building attached to the outer wall, as is still visible today at Brazzacco even when the complex was not the original *palas* and was not even found in its place. The practically insuperable difficulty of reconstructing the architectural history of castles in Friuli makes it naturally risky—and ultimately absurd—to attempt to establish a typology on the basis of their shapes. In fact, to base oneself solely on the aspect visible today generally gives a false picture of castles, because here rules are being proposed which only today derive from aesthetic categories. Nicoletti-König is an architect and therefore cannot be reproached because she is interested only in the external aspect, and does not take the historical development into consideration. What is most regrettable is the fact that amateur publications are distributed with a claim to historical validity and represent a basis for all the knowledge about castles in Friuli. Thus a presupposition is created for a totally distorted image of a discipline that can only very slowly be put right.

[413] In this case what is being spread is the standard popular belief, defining the *castrum* always as a four-sided form and emphasizing, instead, the *castellum* as a fortress of modest dimensions, having more than anything a function of control and guard. In this way, the function of the *castellum* or the *castrum* (used synonymously as fortified settlements) is almost totally neglected. This, however, is something that critics have accepted for a long time. *Castella. Cento due opere fortificate del Friuli Venezia Giulia*, Udine 1995, pp. 33–43.

[414] The term *casa forte* (fortified house), like keep, is used in a wide sense and therefore does not help much. They are useful only in those cases where they need to be distinguished from the term castle when it concerns a house walled in stone that served as a lord's manor and had no defense walls or gates.

[415] Miotti, vol. 5, p. 143.

[416] The good state of conservation of the castle is due to the decision of the family in the eighteenth century to build a manor at the

foot of the small castle mound, although this did not mean that they gave up the building's function as a stately home. They decided to move the agricultural wing to the old castle and at the same time to leave there the chancery, in other words, the center of feudal power, with its apartment for the secretary. In this respect, vast restoration works were carried out in the sixteenth century which, two hundred years later, were continued with the first reconstruction in Romantic style. As a result, today many parts of the walls as well as all the windows must certainly be regarded as non-medieval substitutions. In its structure, however, the castle still gives a medieval impression.

[417] Only a sixteenth-century document refers to a tower which existed in the thirteenth century and was five paces wide, which seems too small. See Lazzarini, *Castelli del Friuli*, p. 75.

[418] Its name is mentioned for the first time in a document of 1186. See Miotti.

[419] In contrast to lower Brazzacco, which is certainly a castle attested in the Middle Ages, but whose modest remains today have little interest.

[420] From the archaeological excavations it can been seen that the hill was raised by using rubble. As mentioned previously, as the excavations were stopped too soon, it is not possible to determine the measurements of this elevation nor to establish whether the hill is the motte indicated in the sources.

[421] Lazzarini, *Castelli del Friuli*, p. 55

[422] The bringing forward of the foundation date of the castle to the period of the Hungarian invasions is based on a similarity of names, as is implied by Mor and Paschini for the first time. Miotti suggested that Braitan's defense structure was near Pozzuolo. Great satisfaction at the thesis of a passage from Braitan to Brazzà was shown in particular by Alvise Savorgnan di Brazza in *Castello di Brazzacco* (Collana Castelli Storici 7), Cassacco 1983, p. 5. The excavations of July 1992, under the direction of Vinicio Tomadin and Donatella D'Angelanon, however, provided proof of a settlement prior to the mid fourteenth century, even if it should be added that the excavations could not be completed. See Tomadin, *Brazzacco*.

[423] Lazzarini, p. 75.

[424] Lazzarini, p. 76.

[425] Lazzarini, p. 75.

[426] Miotti, vol. 2, p. 67.

[427] It is also obvious that the outer wall in front of this house was substantially reinforced by exactly the width of the house itself, as if here there had been once another building about which, however, nothing can be said. One explanation may be that the present house was built in a place where there were no other buildings, and used only the external walls of buildings already in existence. This makes sense when not only is there a wish to remove a lot of rubble, but a gradual re-use of the stone of the demolished building can also be made.

[428] All the other parts of the outer wall were built in a unitary way and just for this reason the addition of great blocks at a later date is obvious.

[429] Speculation on the presence of a Roman road has no sense here since it could never have led to the highest peak of the area. It does not even find any continuation on this limited castle system in any land register.

[430] In the literature on the subject, it is unanimously considered that the west wing is the oldest inhabited part, without, however, giving any reason. The remains of a tower should be sought by excavating in the area of the courtyard, because the subsequent constructions would not have been built over its remains. A castle of this size without a tower, on the other hand, is unthinkable. It is equally unthinkable that it could have been only in the area of the burg.

[431] The extent to which these buildings were founded on medieval parts should be examined in detail. It seems rather hasty to date all the present towers, together with the second circuit of wall in this form, to the early fourteenth century, as occurs, for example, in the drawings by Paolo Zuliani in Vinicio Tomadin, *Indagine archeologica*, 1994. The excavations published in the same volume have proved that under the Nievo wing the outline of the walls and the outer walls was once completely different, as can be seen in other castles too. The widespread reconstruction of medieval castles on the basis of remains that are still visible—or rather that were visible before the 1976 earthquake—is therefore naive and not at all productive. It can only be hoped that the reconstruction of the castle that is still under discussion—useless and even negative from a historical-artistic point of view—will be at least accompanied by a serious archaeological study of the whole area, since the only result of the reconstruction will be the destruction at enormous cost of all the historical remains that still exist.

[432] I am basing myself on an excellent representation of architectural history by Angelo Morelli de Rossi, in *Castello di Fontanabona*.

[433] Morelli de Rossi, p. 32.

[434] This date was reported by Miotti. Morelli de Rossi indicates 1196 as the first date, however. This would confirm that the castle was built in the last decade of the twelfth century.

[435] According to Zeune, the overabundance of classical elements in the door, in particular the picturesque mechanism for a blind, gives the impression of not being medieval but part of a later readaptation.Corresponding to this is also the remarkable difference in protection between the old Salcano door, with its high ramps, and the low unprotected access of the modern door which could have been blasted open by any small cannon.

[436] Annalia Delneri, p. 22.

[437] Piper, pp. 182 ff.

[438] The age of the building is proved by the joins in the stonework at the side and by the particular type of workmanship on the walls.

[439] Archivio Grattoni-d'Arcano, Fagagna.

[440] If the entrance was indeed here, unfortunately not certain because it has had its present form only since the seventeenth century.

[441] The fact that the present building shows no signs of medieval walls is therefore not proof against finding the tower in this place.

[442] Miotti, vol. 2, p. 40.

[443] Reference is made to this in an inventory of 1461: "In camera turri, in qua solit erat dormire..." Archivio Grattoni-d'Arcano, Fagagna.

[444] Maurizio Grattoni, in *Castella*, p. 48.

[445] See Miotti, vol. 2, p. 38.

[446] Even the arches on the door are not medieval; the outside one, going by the form, is already of modern date and the pointed Gothic arch on the inside reveals by the technique of its construction that it was remade with older stones, without it being possible to say what, if anything, had been in its place.The little low walls of the boundary were incorporated for their picturesque interest, probably on the foundations of medieval timber walls.

[447] In the family archive, reference is always made to single buildings when inventories were made on the occasion of divisions for inheritance.

[448] Maurizio Grattoni, who knows most about the history of the castle, considers it to be trapdoor, however, with a note that for a long time not all *Erker* were also latrines, just as today it is generally thought that not all *Erker* discovered in the nineteenth century were for military use. In the case of Arcano, all that is needed is to fix a corresponding place that ends in the ditches between the upper castle and the village. One would expect to find trapdoors above all where enemies could have passed, in other words, near the door. This is obviously not the case at Arcano. The latrines were preferably inside the residence to avoid having to go a long way.

[449] The wealth of material such as descriptions and inventories in the possession of Maurizio Grattoni would make it possible, perhaps, in this case to risk a dating if these could be put to an analytical reconstruction. It might be observed that the present residential structure with this length of 16 or even 17 meters was built in the seventeenth century.

[450] Miotti thought they were thirteenth- or fourteenth-century (vol. 2, p. 42).

[451] However, it must be borne in mind that the immediate vicinity of the opening of the original *Erker* argues against a medieval date for the window, never mind what function the *Erker* may have had. Probably the affinity between these windows and those at Gorizia is not by chance; style, materials, and shape are practically identical. They must have been made therefore at the beginning of the twentieth century.

[452] Maurizio Grattoni found the references to this in the documents in his family archive.

[453] Perogalli, pp. 30 ff.

[454] *Burg*, in *RDK*, p. 128.

[455] It is thus somewhat less surprising that Miotti, in all his often adventurous arguments in favor of the Roman origins of Friuli castles, neglects this aspect, if one considers that all the as yet distorted attempts at a typological classification of Friuli castles have become the best-known and important phenomenon of the international debate.

[456] This development is shown very clearly by K.H. Clasen.

[457] "It was probably built at the beginning of the eleventh century to defend the road from the ford on the Tagliamento that led towards Pordenone, threatened by the disastrous Hungarian incursions." *Castella*, p. 146.

[458] Benedetti, p. 7.

[459] Concerning this dating, I refer readers to the chapter on the history of the castle (pp. 228–37).

[460] See Stanislaus von Moos, "Der Palast als Festung," in Martin Warnke, *Politische Architektur in Europa*, Cologne 1984.

[461] See Miotti, vol. 4, p. 463, and Grattoni, in *Castella*, p. 146.

[462] Analyzing the way in which they were built, it can be deduced that these walls were not made with old materials. A semicircular

stone ridge, today used for a flowerbed, at the back of the country house, is in the same way a relic of a building of the modern era which cannot have been a defense tower.
463 It is real pity that the upper floors were not rebuilt after the earthquake in 1976, since the high center of the castle was of great significance with regard to the overall effect of the façade and the formal uniformity of the complex.
464 The whole part under the tower was rewalled, using a set of old bricks under the arch frieze that protruded for a height of about two meters. The protruding part which seems to outline a balustrade in the shape of crenellations may be new. An analysis of the wall structure would, however, throw light on the original state. A wing added in subsequent centuries seems to cover a part of the small tower which, if it was found to be authentic, would extend along the added wall.
465 There is no trace of mortar here, while the room above the door, where the grille should be hung, has a similar window, as has the façade.
466 Grattoni refers to Pomponio Amalteo as the painter of the frescoes, without quoting his source: *Castella, p. 146.*
467 Andrra Benedetti, *Il Castello di Zoppola*, (Nozze Lotti-Galante), Zoppola 1970.
468 Benedetti, p. 11, citing Diplomatarium Portusnaonense, no. 109, Vienna 1865.
469 Benedetti, p. 21.
470 Miotti, vol. 4, p. 465.
471 What stands out is only the thickness of the walls which is inconsistent with the ground floor to the left and the right of the tower. On the one hand, this is explained by the door which once existed here. An examinations should be made to see if, on the other hand, an entrance existed in an earlier period. In this way, the aesthetic problem would be resolved if an entrance was not found in the center. It might be important that two lines existed here in the sixteenth century. Such a hypothesis would also explain why the residential part was divided into two such distinct parts and placed in diametrically opposite positions at the end of the courtyard.
472 We still do not know, however, why the wall near the tower shows such obvious joins up to the roof. It is already surprising that the tower was not built in the outer wall, but behind it, but this can be explained by the fact that was built after the wall. Nevertheless, it should have had a visual connection with the main facade, which emerges from the top of the remaining facade. It is probable therefore that its height was increased in a later period, when the facade was already at its present height.
473 G. Bergamini, M. Buora, *Il Castello di Udine*, p. 117.
474 Benedetti, p. 18.
475 In the same way, the tower is attributed to the fifteenth century by the Touring Club Italiano guide, *Friuli-Venezia Giulia*, p. 459.
476 Girolamo di Porcia.
477 In the course of the refacing to enlarge the complex with the Baroque building in Istrian limestone on its right, the back of the tower had to be raised by about two meters (six feet) to have it in line with the slope of the roof of the nearby construction.
478 Forniz, in Miotti, vol. 4, pp. 252 ff.
479 However, in this they failed repeatedly. They had to take Treviso citizenship, promise to live in accordance with its laws, and commit themselves to the dominion of the patriarch. See Forniz, *Il palazzo nuovo*.
480 Girolamo di Porcia, pp. 36 ff.
481 The present walls around the front garden were built to attempt to limit the damage caused by the building of a connecting road. Nineteenth-century drawings, photographs, and plans, however, show how the space in front of the castle was completely free.
482 The sloping pedestal in squared stone was probably built at the same time as the windows above it, toward the end of the sixteenth century, perhaps even together with the building of the large palazzo on the right.
483 Forniz, *Il Campanile*, p. 13.
484 This was determined in the sixteenth century with an extraordinary family tree that was approved by the emperor on the payment of a modest offering. The key to this historical acrobatics is the similarity of the name Porcia to the Latin *Porcius*, the consul of Cato, Marcus Porcius.
485 Forniz, in Miotti, vol. 4, p. 250.
486 Only Custoza recounts numerous armed conflicts, defining Porcia as the protagonist of Friuli's history, without, however, indicating his sources (*Castella, p. 104).*
487 Forniz, pp. 15 ff.
488 Anonymous chronicler (Miotti, vol. 4, p. 255): "a mansion of modern new construction cost more than 50,000 ducats, for which the quarried stone alone would cost more than 15,000 ducats."
489 Quoted by Miotti, vol. 4, p. 255.
490 See Forniz, op. cit.
491 Miotti, vol. 4, p. 338.
492 Miotti, vol. 4, p. 425.
493 Gilolamo di Porcia, p. 50.
494 Giuseppe di Ragogna, in Miotti, vol. 4, p. 426. Miotti (p. 425) does not believe in the prehistoric origin of the tower but nevertheless finds "more or less certain the Roman origin of the *castrum turris*."
495 Miotti, vol. 4, p. 426.
496 Thus these blocks of stone are not of Roman or other origin, and the walling is not without mortar, as Ragogna wrote.
497 Miotti, vol. 4, 425, quoting Paschini, II p. 66.
498 "There are no words to express fully the bitter regret for such an error, seeing the unpleasant results of the reconstruction which can be observed today," wrote Piero Marchesi in *Torre di Pordenone, castello e territorio* (Quaderni del Centro Regionale di Catalogazione Passariano), 1967.
499 Nevertheless it is odd that both the photo and the fresco in Palazzo Damiani Galvani in Pordenone show a perfectly rectangular line of the walls, even though this does not correspond to the remains brought to light by the excavations.
500 Giovanni de Portis was, from 1276, the owner of the castle that was almost completely renovated by the family in 1304 at huge expense.
501 In this case we have to be careful with the dating, because Romanesque forms continued for a long time in Friuli and in all the Middle Ages notable delays in time can be observed.
502 The position of the walled windows makes it unlikely that all the other two-light windows were exactly in the place where larger windows of a later date are now found. The walls inside the building, furthermore, are so thin that with their seventy-centimeter thickness they show the typical measurements of modern constructions.
503 See the drawing of Gaetano Sturolo of 1772 in the Museo Archeologico Nazionale di Cividale, which shows a whole series of such castles. Cf. V. Tomadin, *Il Castello di Zuccola*, p. 65.
504 Piper, p. 429.
505 Built in the first decade of the fourteenth century. The square building, which is 52.4 meters long (172 feet), encloses an equally square courtyard "on whose four sides was placed on the building a gallery on two floors, with a vaulted ceiling, open towards the interior." O. Piper, p. 600.
506 Miotti, vol. 2, p. 348.
507 Cited Miotti, vol. 7, p. 346.
508 Ibid., p. 346
509 Ibid., p. 346.
510 Cited *Statuti di Tricesimo*, Tricesimo 1992, p. 5.
511 Ibid.
512 Miotti, vol. 2, p. 349, note 29.
513. It could not otherwise be explained how the nonetheless substantial buildings of the burg with their towers could have been reduced by the artist to a limited rural wing, as can be seen on the back of the drawing. This could also be confirmed by the drawing of the mansion, in which from one side a hint of a staircase seems to be recognizable while of course the position of the windows on the façade does not seem to fit this theory at all. Here too, however, it is important not to take a drawing of a time as a view with documentary value. Finally, it is understandable that an artist should have put the far more beautiful windows of the main façade in place of the unattractive ones at the back.
514 Certainly the quoted court official, di Rivosa, was treated particularly well by the patriarch, a reason for which, for example, he was expressly freed from any payment to the stewards of Tricesimo; but it is just this fact that makes it clear that he cannot also, at the same time, be the steward.
515 Manzano had repeated the already heavily condensed formulation of a version published in the nineteenth century by Bianchi, a typical instance of the gradual change in meaning through dangerous, second-hand quotation. In the text by Manzano, the *casa forte* was a dwelling with strong walls but in Bianchi's it had only one strong wall.
516 There is, however, another reason for rejecting the existence of a larger castle structure in the place now occupied by that ugly church. If before its construction there had really still been walls of the older castle, or there had been at least at the time of Paghini's drawing, then they should have been evident in the Napoleonic or the Austrian land survey map. Instead, in both surveys that rectangular field is declared as an orchard, very likely surrounded by a wall that was passed on from the plan of 1647. The walls of a castle would here have required a boundary completely different from the terrain. They would have been emphasized with a different color and would have had to present another indication under the number of the field. Tax was calculated on the basis of the usefulness of the land: a field with ruins would have had a property value much lower than that of the orchard registered here. For these reasons we must, in all respect, contradict Miotti on this point. The remains of walls that he saw on this land were presumably the remains of one of the typical outer walls, with or without battlements, which surrounded so many villa kitchen gardens in the seventeenth and eighteenth centuries. This is testified also by Paghini's drawing, which cannot be interpreted otherwise.
517 The Palladian building inside the present burg is a dubious modern imitation. It is quite incomprehensible why the specialists, usually so pedantic, in the case of so important a building have allowed a falsification of these dimensions. The area of the burg may well be considered from then to have been destroyed and lost, like all the area of the front courtyard, which was extended inside and covered with a terrace. At first sight this is not seen from the outside, but it has seriously compromised the effect of the whole structure. Furthermore, the area of the courtyard has in this way been removed forever from any possibility for archaeological research.
518 Archivio di Stato di Venezia, Commissione Feudi, B.55, Raccolta Petenà.
519 Inside, however, the burg was built in a very different way from today. Not only the court official di Rivosa had a feudal dwelling here, but in the Napoleonic land survey some houses in ruins are noted that subsequently disappeared.
520 The investiture of the court official di Rivosa dates to 1328, and the responsiblity of Tommasutto di Pertenstain to renew the fortifications to 1332.
521 In 1289 the district of Tricesimo was devastated by a count of Gorizia. In 1345 his successor assaulted the castle of Tricesimo and forced it to surrender.
522 Since in this case the unusual form could coincide with the recourse to the specialist from Padua, perhaps it is here that the origin of the forms may be found. The steward, Tommasutto di Pertenstain, was clearly of Germanic origin.
523 Of course, there is the possibility that some two-light windows were lost when the new windows were put in. Nevertheless, the two-light windows that have been preserved are at such a different height from the present windows that traces should be visible.
524 Miotti, vol. 2, p. 348.
525 On 14 March 1501 the lieutenant of the Savorgnan, Nicolò de Superbis, obtained the investiture for Tricesimo (Miotti, vol. 2, p. 348).
526 Giovanni di Prampero left the castle to his heirs in 1509, but according to Miotti's assumption (op. cit., p. 348), on the basis of the building contracts dated 1504, there must have been an owner of the castle already by this date.
527 The sale took place in the presence of the Venetian authorities, as is passed down by their documents: "for a sum of little more than 2,000 ducats, from the Magistrato delle Rason Vecchi". Giorgio Baiutti, *Castello di Cassacco*, Udine 1987, p. 41.
528 A document cited by Miotti from 1504 gives information on building contracts with the aim on the part of Giovanni di Prampero to enlarge the main building. It is not clear from the document which particular works were carried out.
529 It is not easy to decide whether the second window already belonged to a side wall or was still part of the façade. The artist does not seem to have been particularly interested in architecture or particularly skilled in this field. Yet this picture has indubitable historical value. A false picture of the house could not be kept in the chapel of the same house. The representation must therefore intend to give a faithful rendering, unlike those from the standard views of the castle in the Romantic period.
530 The plan of a building raised on older bearing walls can be seen, for example, in the castle of Polcenigo, where the regular façade does not relate to the tortuous plan.
531 Bödefeld and Hinz go so far as to say that the Renaissance in the Veneto "was accepted as an exotic, distant fashion." *Du Mont Kunst-Reiseführer. Die Villen im Veneto*, Cologne 1987, p. 84.
532 The finest vaults in Friuli are found not only in the palaces of Gorizia and Gradisca, but also in a number of villas, such as, for example, Cronberg near Gorizia and in the ancient seat of the Strassoldo di Grafenberg family in Gorizia. In this latter case, I have, however, seen references to the fact that these vaults, like many others, were the invention of the last owner, Count Wilhelm Coronini.
533 Of course there is the doubt that such a tower existed, because it is absent from the sixteenth-century picture in the chapel and also from those starting from 1750 when the great *panorama* of Tricesimo was made. No traces were found subsequently, even in the recent excavations in the courtyard, according to Miotti. But since in this place a horrible construction in reinforced concrete was built, eyewitnesses of the works would have to be found in order to draw useful conclusions. The 1647 drawing is so precise, however, that I have no doubts. Even the possibility of a commissioned embellishment cannot be considered, because it was done under the supervisory authorities of Venice who would have had no interest in a false tower.
534 This is how I interpret the writing in the Venetian document: Archiveio di Stato, Venice, Commissione Feudi, B. 55, Raccolta Petenà.

[535] See A. Chastel, "La villa en France au XVI siècle," *Bollettino CISA*, 11, 1969, p. 258.
[536] G. Baiutti, p. 43.
[537] "Rendered almost uninhabitable and almost destroyed... and impossible to restore because of their weakness." Baiutti, p. 43.
[538] The model used was perhaps the truss on the back of the castle of Udine which there, however, completes perfectly the Mannerist concept of the façade.
[539] Next to the main doorway there was earlier a small exit walled up from the outside, which today is still recognizable from the inside. In this way, the doors of the central hall which led to the side rooms were moved. A round arch can still be recognized in the wall, on which a fresco of the sixteenth century has been discovered. Miotti (vol. 2, p. 350) dates the fresco to the mid fifteenth century and draws the conclusion that the wall, as part of a tower that existed earlier here, was incorporated into the building of the *palas* This is impossible because the *palas*. had already been built in the fourteenth century and had new internal walls at the beginning of the sixteenth century.
[540] In 1288 it was called *palatium inferius* (lower palace) and in 1289 *palatium novum vel grande* (new, or big, palace). See G. Bergamini, M. Buora, *Il castello di Udine* The most ancient part was frequently identified with the triangular tower that, according to documentary information, must have been here. If it is indeed the case that a rare type of construction was there, it must be thought that this presents the minimum useable surface area in relation to the area occupied by the walls, a reason for its rare use. In conclusion, therefore, it is to be excluded that larger reception rooms were be found in such a construction. In the Germanic area, triangular main towers are known: Grenzau near Koblenz, Rauhneck in lower Austria, and Schalleg, Gonobitz, and Waldstein in Steiermark (Piper, pp. 181 ff.).
[541] G. Bergamini, M. Buora, p. 43.
[542] This was the basis for a reconstruction of the castle by A. Burelli and S. Gri, which shows a broad base of a two-floor building, overlooked by a building in the form of a cube which seems to have been erected on its terraced roof. Apart from the technical problems that such a construction would have created, it seems also, for other reasons, to have been created out of free fantasy, and the seal cannot in this case authorize us to believe that the mansion was built in two parts in the form of terraces. See G. Bergamini, M. Buora, p. 45.
[543] *I Castelli abbandonati*, p. 109.
[544] All four outside walls were of the same thickness, up to a third of the long external wall, whose thickness was about double. The internal wall built on to this was of the same thickness. It possibly formed, together with the outside wall, the part of the structure that was reinforced in the rebuilding of 1308.
[545] *I Castelli abbandonati*, p. 111.
[546] I am not in possession of the text of the document. If the market really was named, it cannot have been drawn up before 1262, as Belluno claims. Miotti, vol. 3, 295; Belluno, 112.
[547] Miotti (vol. 3, p. 295) also approves of this with regard to Monfalcone: "Let us suppose that speaking of *castrum* is not an allusion to the stronghold, rather to the dwelling places already protected by walls."
[548] The patriarch's residence must have been in the immediate vicinity of the cathedral. There are no references to buildings on the castle hill which were more important than the small keep reinforced solely by a long outer wall. To transfer residences to the hilltops and build there constructions like castles did not correspond to the custom of late antiquity. I know no example of this and there is no reason to think that Cormons was an exception.
[549] In the opinion of the small guidebook produced by the Consorzio per la Salvaguardia dei Castelli Storici del Friuli Venezia Giulia, the keep of Monfalcone is the result of at least 2,000 years of activity: "Previously the seat of a motte, then a Roman lookout post guarding the Via Gemina... the site was certainly that of a fortification during the rule of Theoderic." These theories may well be false, like those that follow, according to which it was built as "a defensive stronghold of the patriarchate of Aquileia towards the county of Duino." It must be said clearly that Duino was not a county. Nor did the poor lords of Duino represent a real threat while they were not allied to Gorizia. At Cormons we find something similar: "It seems that the very first fortification was on Monte Quarin, in the appurtenance of the Gorizia family, where the original castle Cormons was placed from pre-Roman times onwards, which then became a Celtic center and afterwards a Roman *castrum*."
[550] "The various builders, obliged perhaps by the chronic scarcity of resources or conditioned by their awareness of the provisional nature of what they were doing, were unusually consistent in an architectural expression based on an economic functionalism, leaving no room for indulgence. No decorative compromises or pictorial references were left on its vast and bare surfaces, no moldings of any sort or protruding elements. There is room only for the essential, expressed and achieved with minimal means. It is just for this reason that the keep is markedly different from many other contemporary or similar monuments." Belluno, pp. 113 ff.
[551] The tiny tower-shaped building at Cormons was obviously added later.
[552] He continues: "The suggestion of pre-Roman outer walls of pebbles, which can still be glimpsed between the flanks of the hill, should not have been foreign to this concept of a central scheme." Belluno, p. 114.
[553] Belluno places the foundation of the market in the year 1262. According to Miotti, however, the need to give peace to the market and the town, contributed to the peace with the Count of Gorizia in 1260. The details, therefore, need to be checked. Belluno, p. 112.
[554] According to Belluno (p. 112), the keep was then rebuilt. If this dating is right, it must have been a very early example of this new way of thinking in the architecture of castles.
[555] The present entrance is in this form of modern date. It is not clear whether earlier there was something here. Miotti recognized the ancient entrance in the arch appearing barely above the present level of the ground, but this is false. Here, without doubt, the opening is of the latrine whose well still exists in the walls. This latrine is important evidence for dating. It shows that here right down to the foundations was a medieval structure, that it was inhabited, and that it was still higher than it is now. Unfortunately no more can be said. The problem of the meaning of the strange tower-formed building connected to it is also difficult. The surface of the Rocca is so small that the wish for an addition is understandable. But since it is of such a ridiculous size, it cannot really have served as an extension. Going by its size, it was more probably the space for a tower-shaped staircase, but perhaps it was built with reference to the original entrance, which may have been very high, in that part of the walls which is now missing, or was replaced in a completely arbitrary manner.
[556] Zeune in *Die Burg als zeitgemässes Statussymbol*, pp. 27 ff.
[557] That these peripheral constructions were not built in the Venetian period only can be inferred from the joining of the stonework of the strengthening of the outer wall, which points to having been inserted later between internal partition walls.
[558] Miotti, vol. 3, p. 299.
[559] "The land of Monfalcone... being near the sea and easily saved... I consider necessary, and for the security of that land, that a keep should be made, in the place of the small keep which in the past wars was ruined by the enemy." Miotti, vol. 3, p. 299.
[560] These are windows with rich cornices and a small triangular gable like a crown, typical of Renaissance architecture. The cornice, however, is faced with imposing blocks of ashlar work which constitute a new cornice. The lintel of the window, for example, is not placed in the logical position compared to the triangular gable placed above, which rises, in accordance with traditional architectural rules, above a window architrave which, however, is not suitable for the imposing keystone. To put together elements so theoretically irreconcilable was part of the intellectual games and insecurities of Mannerism. The attempt to make it seem rustic, however, has a significance that concerns the content and is introduced to indicate, in this way, a type of rural architecture in which crude, rough forms are supposed to mirror the simple life of the countryside.
[561] In this case, however, it does not seem very logical not to have rethought all the façade as a unit. It seems to be a clearly architectural motif, borrowed from artisans who were not in a position to adapt themselves better to the structure of the whole facade.
[562] This wall, with no parallel on the ground floor nor on the second floor, has a sloping position tipping surprisingly towards the external part on the right.
[563] The pictures are clearly influenced by Venetian sixteenth-century models. In theory, therefore, they could have been carried out at the same time as the mansion. However, I believe, seeing the low quality of the paintings, that they date from the seventeenth century.
[564] Both Miotti and Zucchiatti see this Heinricus as the founding father of the Villalta family. It is true that the name Villalta does not seem to be so unusual as not to have been used a number of times in this period. Nevertheless, later documents cited by Miotti seem to place this Heinricus and his descendents in such a close relationship with Friuli history that here it is possible to start out with a link between the name and the castle. See T. Miotti, vol. 2, pp. 467–73.
[565] V. Zucchiatti, p. 12.
[566] Miotti, vol. 2, p. 476.
[567] Zucchiatti, pp. 34–35; Miotti, vol. 2, p. 467.
[568] The chronicle of the destruction is described in detail by Zucchiatti, pp. 35 ff.
[569] The reconstruction was started under the patriarch d'Alençon and completed under Giovanni di Moravia: T. Miotti, vol. 2, p. 469.
[570] Miotti, vol. 2, p. 469.
[571] Zucchiatti, p. 10; Joppi, *Disegni di prospettive dei castelli, terre e città del Friuli, secolo DVII*, Ms. 208, Fondo Joppi, Biblioteca Civica, Udine.
[572] Zucchiatti, p. 9.
[573] Zucchiatti, pp. 23 and 27.
[574] Zucchiatti, p. 22.
[575] The names of the owners of both castles are also different, as is shown in the documents presented by Zucchiatti.
[576] The mansion of the Count of Polcenigo which, according to documents, was rebuilt from the foundations, is a case in point. A look at the present plan shows, however, that a large part of the remains of the medieval walls was reused, even if this led to great irregularities inside. See C. Ulmer, *Ville friulane*, Udine 1993, p. 268.
[577] In the part of the base that is under ground, a door suggested to Zucchiatti that the present-day hill had become so high only by means of adding earth at different times. The remains of the castle that had been destroyed several times must have remained *in loco* and thus the high ground gradually grew by about three meters. I find this unlikely, since in those times most of the material was used for rebuilding and the remains of small stones and filling material would have been insufficient to raise the ground by three meters (10 feet). I would suggest that the material amassed was made up mainly of earth and pebbles, as was typical of castles on mounds in the Middle Ages. The base of the tower therefore should be studied again with this in mind. According to Miotti, the great rustication blocks in the lower part are characteristically Roman in the working of the stones. This leads us to believe that there may have been an earlier building here.
[578] Significantly, the drawing of 1939 of the second castle, built at the beginning of the fourteenth century, presents in its still recognizable bearing walls a totally regular plan.
[579] It would be more obvious to determine the main transformations after the destruction of 1385. It must be said, however, that the part of the medieval castle which is still recognizable could hardly have been built on the threshold of the modern era. Moreover, the destruction of 1511 was not total, as is testified by the numerous round arches that have been walled up and by the remains of walls in the base of the tower, which derive from an earlier period and must have been used in 1385 as a basis for reconstruction. For the rest, it must not be forgotten that the rebuilding of 1385 was not carried out by the family but by the patriarch, and in great haste. It is therefore just for this reason that it is assumed that particular novelties were not introduced here, but that only the reconstruction of the ancient complex needed to be carried out as quickly as possible and thus some of the simple preceding forms were probably renewed.
[580] Miotti still adheres to the date of 1480, later written on the drawing. I agree with Zucchiatti, however, who has studied the question of dating in depth.
[581] If this was a dividing wall, the most probable explanation was that it was a division between two brothers, in the same way as the two entrances could be explained. In a later division in 1700, the castle was divided into two parts, following this same line.
[582] Even if this drawing is precise in the details that can easily be verified, the wall of the burg is only indicative and therefore not fully reliable. The imprecision in the walls is reflected also in their height because they are not represented in their real dimensions. As far as the front wall of the present mansion is concerned, we can say with certainty that the medieval parts reached the second floor, since the thin sixteenth-century walls began only above. These drawings have to be treated with care. For example, drawings later than this are so unreliable that even the present-day complex cannot be found in them; they are often the result of imagination. and demonstrate meager artistic skill.
[583] Trans. Zucchiatti, op. cit., p. 18.
[584] According to Litta and Lazzarini-del Puppo in the twelfth century, the brothers Ariprando and Galvanio, in a double marriage with the two heiresses from the Valsassina family, took possession of this lordship. Such a version, however, renders impossible the theory that the name derives from the tower of Valsassina.
[585] The frequency of the name della Torre, del Torre, and associated names is explained by the medieval custom of giving names to families in relation to their seat of residence. The tower was a typical seignorial residence and until each was given a name to distinguish it from others, the common name was repeated with few variations. The example of the dei Torre family of Cividale comes to mind, as they had their tower in Piazza Ristori, still recognizable today. It seems that this residence was sufficient to give the name to the family, as was the case with other families who only placed their coat of arms over their doors.

[586] *Storia di Milano*, (Fondazione Treccani degli Alfieri), Milan 1954, vol. 4, p. 289.

[587] C. von Czoernig *Gorizia*, Milan 1969 (original title *Das Land Görz und Gradisca*, Vienna 1873), p. 677.

[588] It would be in line with the Republic's normal practice if the castle with its fief had been sold to the highest bidder, but no archival sources for this have yet been found. The della Torre family managed, during the Napoleonic occupation, to get the property back, which contradicts the notion of its being possessed by another family during the intervening sixty years.

[589] Zucchiatti, p. 29.

[590] Zucchiatti, p. 38.

[591] Zucchiatti, p. 12.

[592] The head of the Council of Ten, A. Loredan, 16 March 1511: Zucchiatti, p. 12: "Having appeared in our presence, the interventions in name of the heirs of the here-mentioned gentleman Aloysio de la Torre, requesting of me the restoration of the jurisdiction for themselves and restitution of the things taken with violence during the recent trouble... We shall proceed with such a severe form of punishment against the disobedient that the penalty shall be a lasting example to them and to all those who may presume to rebel against the orders of their superiors."

[593] The Villa della Torre in Vipulzano shows similar solutions. Concepts of this type can be found in the celebrated Villa Farnese at Caprarola, made familiar in the works of Peruzzi and the publications of Serlio. See S. von Moos, *Turm und Bollwerk*, pp. 131 ff.; C. Ulmer, pp. 139 ff.

Bibliography

Albrecht, U., *Von der Burg zum Schloss*, Worms 1986.

Antonow, A., *Planung und Bau von Burgen im süddeutschen Raum*, Frankfurt 1983.

Antonow, A., *Burgen des südwestdeutschen Raums unter besonderer Berücksichtigung der Schildmauer*, Bühl 1977.

Antonow, A., *Planung und Bau von Burgen im süddeutschen Raum*, Frankfurt 1993.

Baiutti, G., *Castello di Cassacco* (Collana Castelli Storici del Consorzio per la Salvaguardia dei Castelli Storici del Friuli Venezia Giulia), Cassacco 1987.

Bandmann, G., *Mittelalterliche Architektur als Bedeutungsträger*, Berlin 1951.

Belluno, E., "La Rocca di Monfalcone", *Antichità Altoadriatiche, 10.*

Benedetti, A., *Il Castello di Zoppola* (Nozze Lotti-Galante), Zoppola 1970.

Bergamini, G., Buora, M., *Il Castello di Udine*, Udine.

Bering, K., *Herrschaftsbewusstsein und Herrschaftszeichen. Zur Rezeption staufischer Architekturformen in der Baupropaganda des 13. und 14. Jahrhunderts*, Essen 1988.

Bersu, G., *spätrömische Besfestigung Bürgle bei Gundremmingen, Münchner Beiträge zur Vor- und Frühgeschichte*, 10, Munich 1964.

Biasutti, G., *Castelmonte*, ed. A. Blasotti, Castelmonte 1987.

Bierbrauer, V., *Invillino-Ibligo in Friaul. Veröffentlichung der Kommission zur archäologischen Erforschung des spätrömischen Raetien der Bayerischen Akademie der Wissenschaften, 2 vols.*, Münchner Beiträge zur Vor- und Frühgeschichte, 34, Munich 1988.

Biller, T., "Das bastonierte Schloss als Bautypus des 16. Jahrhunderts", *Schriftenreihe Festungsforschung*, 3, Wesel 1984.

Biller, T., "Rechteckburgen im nordöstlichen Harzvorland. Zur Entwicklung der norddeutschen Burgen im 14. Jahrhundert", *Burgen und Schlösser*, 1, 1986.

Biller, T., *Die Adelsburg in Deutschland*, Munich 1993.

Billig, G., "Der Übergang von der Holz- zur Steinbauweise im Burgenbild von Sachsen", *Burgenforschung aus Sachsen*, 3/4, Waltersdorf 1993.

Bognetti, G.P., *Castelseprio*, Castelseprio 1968.

Bosio, L., "Le fortificazioni tardoantiche del territorio di Aquileia", in *Il territorio di Aquileia nell'Antichità, Antichità Altoadriatiche*, 15, 1979.

Bravar, G., "Il Castello di Duino", *Antichità Altoadriatiche, 10.*

Bruhns, L., *Hohenstaufenschlösser*, Leipzig 1937.

Brunner, O., *Land und Herrschaft. Grundfragen der territorialen Verfassungsgeschichte Österreichs im Mittelalter*, Darmstadt 1990.

Bumke, J., *Höfische Kultur, Literatur und Gesellschaft im hohen Mittelalter*, Munich 1997.

Burgen der Salierzeit, ed. H.W. Böhme (*Römisch Germanisches Zentralmuseum, Monographien, 25, 26*), Sigmaringen 1991.

"Burgen im deutschen Sprachraum. Ihre rechts- und verfassungsgeschichtliche Bedeutung", ed. H. Patze, 2 vols., *Konstanzer Arbeitskreis für mittelalterliche Geschichte, Vorträge und Forschungen*, 19, Sigmaringen 1976.

Caciagli, G., *Il castello in Italia*, Florence 1975 (2nd. edn 1979)

Cagiano de Azevedo, M., "I palazzi tardoantichi ealtomedievali", in *Atti del XVI Congresso di Storia dell'Architettura* (Athens 1969), Rome 1977.

Cagiano de Azevedo, M., "Ville rustiche tardoantiche e installazioni agricole altomedievali", in *Agricoltura e mondo rurale in occidente nell'alto Medioevo. Settimane di studio del Centro Italiano di Studi sull'alto Medioevo*, 13, Spoleto 1965.

Castella. Centodue opere fortificate del Friuli Venezia Giulia (Consorzio per la Salvaguardia dei Castelli Storici del Friuli Venezia Giulia), Udine 1995.

Castello, Comunità e Giurisdizione di Strassoldo. Ottocento anni di storia, ed. M. Strassoldo, Strassoldo 1990.

Chateau Gaillard. Études de Casteollogie médiévale, 13, Actes du colloque international tenu a Wageningen, 1986

Christlein, R., "Das spätrömische Kastell Boitro zu Passau-Innstadt. Formen der Kontinuität am Donaulimes", in *Von der Spätantike zum frühen Mittelalter*, ed. J. Werner, *Konstanzer Arbeitskreis für mittelalterliche Geschichte*, 25, Sigmaringen 1979.

Clasen, K.H., *Burg*, in *Reallexikon zur deutschen Kunstgeschichte*, 3, Stuttgart 1954.

Coulson, C., "Structural symbolism in medieval castle architecture", *Journal of the British Archaeological Association*, 132, 1979.

Czerwinsky, P., *Die Schlacht und Turnierdarstellung in den deutschen höfischen Romanen des 12. und 13. Jahrhunderts*, Berlin 1976.

Czoernig, C. von, *Das Land Görz und Gradisca*, Vienna 1873.

Dannenbauer, H., *Adel, Burg und Herrschaft bei den Germanen*, Darmstadt 1956.

Delbrück, H., *Geschichte der Kriegkunst, in Das Mittelalter*, 3, Berlin 1907.

Delneri, A., *Il Castello di Gorizia e il suo borgo*, Monfalcone 1993.

Deluisa, L., *Strassoldo, nell'agro di Aquileia*, Udine 1993.

Dhondt, J., "Das frühe Mittelalter", in *Fischer Weltgeschichte*, 10, Frankfurt 1968.

Domini, S., *La Rocca di Monfalcone* (*Collana Castelli Storici del Consorzio per la Salvaguardia dei Castelli Storici del Friuli Venezia Giulia), Cassacco 1983*.

Duby, G., *The Chivalrous Society*, London 1977

Dürst, H., *Rittertum*, Lenzburg 1964.

Ebhard, B., *Der Wehrbau Europas im Mittelalter. Versuch einer Gesamtdarstellung der europäischen Burgen*, vol. 1, Berlin 1939, vol. 2, Stollhamm 1958.

Ebhard B., *Deutsche Burgen als Zeugen deutscher Geschichte*, Berlin 1925.

Ebhard B., *Deutsche Burgen*, Berlin 1907.

Ebhard B., *Die Burgen Italiens*, 6 vols., Berlin 1917.

Ebner, H., *Die Burg als Forschungsproblem mittelalterlicher Verfassungsgeschichte*, in *Burgen im deutschen Sprachraum. Ihre rechts- und verfassungsgeschichtliche Bedeutung*, ed. H. Patze, 2 vols., in *Konstanzer Arbeitskreis für mittelalterliche Geschichte, Vorträge und Forschungen*, 19, Sigmaringen 1976.

Egger, R., "Der Alpenraum in der Zeit des Übergangs von der Antike zum Mittelalter", in *Vorträge und Forschungen*, 1965.

Ewig, E., *Die Merowinger und das Frankenreich*, Stuttgart 1988.

Fiaccadori, G., Grattoni d'Arcano, M., *In domo habitationis. L'arredo in Friuli nel tardo Medioevo*, Udine 1997.

Fingerling, G., Garbsch, J., Werner, J., "Die Ausgrabungen im langobardischen Kastell Ibligo-Invillino, Friaul", *Germania*, 46, 1968.

Fleckenstein, J., "Über Ritter und Rittertum. Zur Erforschung einer mittelalterlichen Lebensform", *Mittelalterforschung (Forschung und Information)*, 29, Berlin 1981.

Foramitti, V., Tondat, N., "I Castelli e il Borgo di Strassoldo. Proposta per un restauro", tesi di laurea, lstituto Universitario di Architettura, Venezia, 1989/90. Synopsis in *Restauro: tecniche e progetto, saggi e ricerche sulla costruzione dell'architettura a Venezia*, ed. Giuseppe Cristinelli, 1994.

Forniz, A., *II campanile della chiesa di San Giorgio a Porcia*, Sacile 1962.

Forniz, A., *L'abitazione antica e il Palazzo nuovo del vescovo nel castello di Porcia*, Udine 1969.

Förtsch, R., *Archäologischer Kommentar zu den Villenbriefen des jüngeren Plinius*, Mainz 1993.

Frankovich, R., *I Castelli del contado fiorentino nei secoli XII e XIII*, Florence 1976.

Geary, P., *Die Merowinger*, Munich 1996.

Gerometta, T., *L'abbazia benedettina di Santa Maria in Silvis*, 1964.

Gerometta, T., *Burgen und feste Plätze*, in *Glossarium Artis. Wörterbuch zur Kunst*, 1, Tübingen 1977.

Goetz, W., "Das Leben auf der Ritterburg", in *Mentalität und Alltag im Spätmittelalter*, ed. C. Meckseper, E. Schraut, Göttingen 1991.

Gransinigh, A., *Guerra sulle Alpi Carniche e Giulie*, Tolmezzo 1994.

Grimm, P., *Die vor- und frügeschichtlichen Burgwälle der Bezirke Halle und Magdeburg*, Berlin 1958.

Hahn, H., Renger-Patzsch, A., *Hohenstaufenburgen in Süditalien*, Munich 1961.

Hale, J.R., *Renaissance Fortification. Art or Engineering*, Norwich 1977.

Haseloff, A., *Die Bauten der Hohenstaufen in Unter-italien*, vol. 1, Leipzig 1919/20.

Heine, H.W., "Frühe Burgen und Pfalzen in Niedersachsen, von den Anfängen bis zum frühen Mittelalter", in *Wegweise zur Vor- und Frühgeschichte Nieder-sachsens*, 17, Hildesheim 1991.

Hinz, H., *Motte und Donjon*, Cologne 1981.

Hinz, H., "Motte und Donjon. Zur Frühgeschichte der mittelalterlichen Adelsburg", in *Zeitschrift für Archäologie des Mittelalters*, ed. W. Janssen, H. Steuer, Cologne 1981.

Hofer, P., "Die Haut des Bauwerks. Methoden zur Alterbestimmung nicht datierter Architektur", in *Geschichte und Theorie der Architektur*, 1, Stuttgart 1968.

Holz, W., *Kleine Kunstgeschichte der deutschen Burg*, Darmstadt 1965.

Hübner, W., "Die frühmittelalterlichen Wehranlagen in Südwestdeutschland nach archäologischen Quellen", in *Burgen im deutschen Sprachraum. Ihre rechts- und verfassungsgeschichtliche Bedeutung*, ed. H. Patze.

Hughes, Q., *Military Architecture*, London 1974.

I castelli abbandonati, guida ai più suggestivi ruderi di castelli del Friuli Venezia Giulia (Istituto Italiano dei Castelli, sezione del Friuli Venezia Giulia), Monfalcone 1994.

Janssen, W., "Niederungsburgen im Rheinland, vom Holzbau zur Steinburg", in *Burgen aus Holz und Stein. Schweizer Beiträge zur Kulturgeschichte und Archäologie des Mittelalters*, 5, Olten-Freiburg 1979.

Keen, M., *Chivalry*, London 1984.

Kerber, D., "Landesherrliche Residenzburgen im späten Mittelalter", in *Die Burg als kulturgeschichtliches Phänomen. Veröffentlichungen der Deutschen Burgenvereinigung*, Stuttgart 1994.

Kiess, W., *Die Burgen in ihrer Funktion als Wohnbauten*, Stuttgart 1961.

Klaar, A., "Grundfragen der Typenbildung der

hochmittelalterlichen Burg", in *Bericht über den 9. österreichischen Historikertag in Linz*, Vienna 1968.

Lazzarini, A., *Castelli del Friuli*, various editions, Udine.

I longobardi, exhib. cat., Villa Manin and Cividale, 1990, ed. G.C. Menis, Milan 1990.

Lorenz, B., Lorenz, E., "Die funktionelle und rechtsgeschichtliche Entwicklung des Befestigungswesens in Deutschland bis zum Ausgange des Mittelalters", in *Burgen und Schlösser*, 1961.

Maier, F.G., "Die Verwandlung der Mittelmeerwelt", in *Fischer Weltgeschichte*, 9, Frankfurt 1968.

Mancini Lapenna, F., *Strassoldo. Guida storico-artistica*, Strassoldo 1982.

Manzano, F. di, *Compendio di storia friulana*, Udine 1876 (repr. 1976).

Maran, ed. A. Ciceri, G. Ellero (Società Filologica Friulana), 1990.

Marcato, C., "La storia e l'ambiente attraverso i toponimi", in *Castello, Comunità e Giurisdizione di Strassoldo. Ottocento anni di storia*, ed. M. Strassoldo, Strassoldo 1990.

Maselli Scotti, E., "Problemi suscitati dai recenti scavi di Duino", *Atti dei Civici Musei di Storia e Arte di Trieste*, XIII/l, 1983.

Maurer, H.M., "Bauformen der hochmittelalterlichen Adelsburg in Südwestdeutschland", *Zeitschrift für Geschichte des Oberrheins*, 115, N.F. 76, 1967.

Maurer, H.M., "Die Entstehung der hochmittelalterlichen Adelsburg in Südwestdeutschland", *Zeitschrift für Geschichte des Oberrheins*, 117, N.F. 78, 1969.

Meyer, W., Die Burg repräsentatives Statussymbol. Ein Beitrag zum Verständnis der mittelalterlichen Adelsburg, Zeitschrift für schweiz. Archäologie und Kunstgeschichte, 33, 1976.

Meyer, W., "Die mittelalterliche Burg als Wirtschaftszentrum", *Château Gaillard*, XlII, 1986.

Meyer, W., *Europas Wehrbau*, Frankfurt 1973.

Miotti, T., *Castelli del Friuli*, 7 vols., Udine 1976-1988.

Mitterauer, M., "Burg und Adel in Österreich", in H. Patze, *Die Burgen im deutschen Sprachraum*, vol. 2, Sigmaringen 1976.

Moggio e le sue valli, ed. P. Treu, G. Fior, Tolmezzo 1978.

Moggio Udinese (Quaderni del Centro Regionale di Catalogazione dei Beni Culturali), Villa Manin di Passariano 1977.

Mor, C.G., "Castello d'Ibliggine", *Ce fastu?*, 38, 1962.

Morelli de Rossi, A., *Castello di Fontanabona* (Collana Castelli Storici del Consorzio per la Salvaguardia dei Castelli Storici del Friuli Venezia Giulia), Cassacco.

Nebbia, U., *Castelli d'Italia*, Novara 1955.

Paschini, P., *Storia del Friuli*, Udine 1953.

Paschini, P., "L'abbazia di Rosazzo sino al periodo della commenda", in *Memorie storiche forogiuliesi*, 1956 and 1957.

Patze, H., *Die Burgen im deutschen Sprachraum. Ihre rechts- und verfassungsgeschichtliche Bedeutung*, 2 vols., Sigmaringen 1976.

Perogalli, C., *Castelli della pianura lombarda*, Milan 1960.

Pichler, R., *Il Castello di Duino*, Trento 1882.

Piper, 0., *Burgenkunde*, Munich-Leipzig 1905

Porcia, G., *Descrizione della Patria del Friuli*, repr. Udine 1897.

Quarina, L., "Castellieri e tombe a tumulo in provincia di Udine", *Ce fastu?*, 19, 1943

Rodaro, N., *Castello di Udine* (Collana Castelli Storici del Consorzio per la Salvaguardia dei Castelli Storici del Friuli Venezla Giulia), Cassacco.

Rossetti A., "L'evoluzione urbanistica ed architettonica di Stassoldo dalle origini ai giorni nostri", in *Castello, Comunità e Giurisdizlone di Strassoldo. Ottocento anni di storia*, ed. M. Strassoldo, Strassoldo 1990.

Satrapa-Schill, A., *Das Leben und die Versorgung auf mittelalterlichen Höhenburgen*, Phil. Diss., Stuttgart 1978

Satrapa-Schill, A., "Das Leben und die Versorgung aufmittelalterlichen Höhenburgen", in *Burgen und Schlösser*, Stuttgart 1979.

Savorgnan di Brazzà, A., *Il Castello Brazzacco* (Collana Castelli Storici del Consorzio per la Salvaguardia dei Castlli Storici del Friuli Venezia Giulia), Cassacco 1983.

Schneider, F., *Die Entstehung von Burg und Landgemeinde in Italien*, Berlin 1924.

Schock, W., "Die Burg auf spätmittelalterlichen Darstellungen", in *Burgen und Schlösser*, 1987.

Schuchardt, C., *Die Burg im Wandel der Zeiten*, Potsdam 1931.

Settia, A., "Il castello da villaggio fortificato a dimora signorile", in *Castelli, storia e archeologia*, conference proceedings, Cuneo 1981.

Settia, A., "Incastellamento e decastellamento nell'Italia padana fra X e XI secolo", *Bollettino Storico Bibliografico Subalpino*, 79 (74), 1976.

Settia, A., "Fortificazioni collettive nei villaggi medievali dell'alta Italia. Ricetti, ville forti, recinti", *Bollettino Storico Bibliografico Subalpino*, 74, 1976.

Settia, A., *La struttura materiale del castello nei secoli XI e XII*, Turin 1979.

Settia, A., *Chiese, strade e fortezze nell'Italia medievale*, Rome 1991.

Settia, A., "Motte e castelli nelle fonti scritte dell'Italia settentrionale", *Mélanges d'archéologie et d'histoire médiévales, en honneur du Doyen Michel de Boüard*, Geneva 1982.

Spiegel, H., *Schutzbauten und Wehrbauten. Einführung in die Baugeschichte der Herrensitze, der Burgen, der Schutzbauten und der Wehrbauten. Grundlage einer Typologie*, (Schriften zur Burgenkunde des Deutschen Burgeninstituts Heft 4), Deutsche Burgenvereinigung, Nuremberg 1970.

Statuti di Tricesimo, ed. Ivonne Pastore, Tricesimo 1992.

Strassoldo, M., *Castello di Stassoldo* (Collana Castelli Storici del Consorzio per la Salvaguardia dei Castelli Storici del Friuli Venezia Giulia Cassacco 1982.

Strassoldo, M., *Lineamenti di vita economica dal Medioeva, in* Castello, Comunità e Giurisdizione di Strassoldo. Ottocento anni di storia, ed. M. Strassoldo, Strassoldo 1990.

Szameit, E., *Der Krottenturm bei Zwentendorf. Über die Weiterverwendung zweier spätantikerWehrbauten des österreichischen Donaulimes im Mittelalter. Zwentendorf und Tulln, in Burgen der Salierzeit*, ed. H.W. Böhme (Römisch Germanisches Zentralmuseum, Monographien 25, 26), Sigmaringen 1991.

Tabarelli, G.M., Conti, F., *Castelli del Trentino*, Milan 1974.

Tagliaferri, A., "Marano e Maranutto", in*Marano*, ed. A. Ciceri, G. Ellero (Società Filologica Friulana), 1990.

Tavano, S., *Il Castello di Gorizia*, Gorizia 1978.

Tomadin, V., "Il Castello di Colloredo di Monte Albano", in *Testimonianze archeologiche*, Colloredo di Monte Albano.

Tomadin, V., *Indagine archeologica nell'ala Nievo del Castello di Colloredo di Montalbano*, Colloredo, 1994.

Tomadin, V., "Relazione preliminare sullo scavo nel Castello di Brazzà", *Quaderni Friulani di Archeologia, Società Friulana d'Archeologia*, 3, 1993.

Tresésin-Tricesimo, ed. A. Ciceri, T. Miotti, Società Filologica Friulana, Udine 1982.

Tuulse, A., *Burgen des Abendlandes*, Vienna-Munich 1958.

Ulbert, T., "Zur Siedlungskontinuität im südöstlichen Alpenraum am Beispiel Vranje", in *Von der Spätantike zum frühen Mittelalter*, ed. J. Werner (Konstanzer Arbeitskreis für mittelalterliche Geschichte, 25), Sigmaringen 1979.

Uslar, R. von, "Studien zu frühgeschichtlichen Befestigungen zwischen Nordsee und Alpen", *Beiheft*, 11, 1964.

Vegetius, *Epitoma rei militaris*, London 1885.

Vetters, H., "Die Kontinuität von der Antike zum Mittelalter im Ostalpenraum", in *Vorträge und Forschungen*, 10, 1965.

Vetters, H., "Von der Spätantiken zur Frühmittelalterlichen Festungsbaukunst", in *Ordinamenti Militari in Occidente nell'alto Medioevo. Settimane di studio del Centro italiano di Studi sull'alto Medioevo*, 15, Spoleto 1968.

Werner, J., "Zu den alemannischen Burgen des 4. und 5. Jahrhunderts", *Speculum Historiale*, 1965.

Werner, K.F., "Heeresorganisation und Kriegführung im deutschen Königreich des 10. und 11. Jahrhunderts", in *Settimane di Studio del Centro Italiano di Studi sull'alto Medioevo*, 15, Spoleto 1968.

Wildeman, T., *Rheinische Wasser-burgen und wasseruhmwehrte Schlossbauten*, Neuss 1959.

Wirth, H., "Die Burg im Landschaftsbild", in *Burgen und Schlösser*, 3, 1995

Wolfram, H., *Die Goten*, Munich 1990.

Zeune, J., *Burgen, Symbole der Macht*, Regensburg 1996.

Zeune, J., "Die Burg als zeitgemässes Statussymbol. Drei Fallstudien aus Kärnten", in *Die Burg als kulturgeschichtliches Phänomen. Veröffentlichungen der Deutschen Burgenvereinigung*, Stuttgart 1994.

Zucchiatti, V., "Cenni storici sulla costituzione del castello di Villalta", *Istituto italiano dei Castelli, Sezione del Friuli Venezia Giulia, Studi e Ricerche*, 8, 1989.

Index

Acknowledgements

We would like to thank all those who have helped us with their expertise and their time. First of all, our gratitude is extended to Monsignor Alfredo Battisti, Archbishop of Udine, the Archdiocesan Curia of Udine, the Reverend Don Sergio Di Giusto at the Pieve of Tricesimo, the Reverend Don Carlo Costantini, parish priest of Pozzuolo del Friuli, Professor Don Sandro Piussi, head librarian of the Biblioteca Pietro Bertolla in the archdiocesan seminary in Udine, and Dr. Cristina Moro.

For their valuable advice we would like to thank Dr. Giuseppe Bergamini, director of the museum and art gallery in Udine, Dr. Maurizio Buora, Dr. Massimo Lavarone, Dr. Romano Vecchiet, head librarian at the Biblioteca Civica Vincenzo Joppi in Udine, Dr. Francesca Tamburlini, the Biblioteca Guarneriana of San Daniele, the Consorzio per la Salvaguardia dei Castelli Storici del Friuli Venezia Giulia, the Archivio Capitolare in Udine, the Museo Archeologico in Cividale, Vittorio Foramitti, Professor Maurizio Grattoni d'Arcano, Luca Marcuzzi, Professor Vittoria Masutti, Licio Pavan, Professor Aldo Settia, Professor Vinicio Tomadin, and Dr. Joachim Zeune.

We would also like to thank the Comunità Collinare del Friuli Venezia Giulia, the state archives in Udine, Pordenone, Gorizia, and Venice, the staff in the museums and libraries who have helped us, and the Amministrazione Provinciale of Trento. We are grateful to Franco Vignuda for his courteous collaboration.

We are particularly grateful to those people who opened their homes and castles to us and provided valuable information: Count and Countess Marzio di Strassoldo Grafenberg, Count Giorgio di Strassoldo Grafenberg, Countess Elisabetta di Strassoldo Grafenberg and her daughter Lella Williams-Strassoldo, Dom Carlos Tasso de Saxe-Coburg e Braganca, Prince Gherardo di Porcia e Brugnera, Count Paolo di Porcia e Brugnera, Count Guecello di Porcia e Brugnera, Count Antonino di Colloredo Mels, Counts Francesco and Antonio Beretta di Colugna, Prince Charles della Torre e Tasso, Counts Vincenzo, Carlo, and Gian Prospero Panciera di Zoppola Gambara, Count and Countess Christoph della Torre-Valsassina, Angelo Morelli de Rossi and Countess Anna Maria Frangipane Morelli de Rossi, Dr. Filippo Martinengo, General Guido d'Attimis-Maniago Marchiò, Dr. Detalmo Pirzio Biroli and Roberto Pirzio Biroli, Domenico Taverna, and the Bardelli family.

We are grateful to Chiara Gini, Peter Guldin, and Lucas Lüdemann, who have been closely involved in the production of this volume.

Christoph Ulmer
Gianni d'Affara

The Italian publishers would like to thank the Cassa di Risparmio di Udine e Pordenone for their assistance in the production of this book.

Antonio Stella
President of Magnus Edizioni S.p.A.

Photographic Acknowledgements

All the photographs are by Gianni d'Affara with the exception of:
Marcello Bertoni, pp. 64, 65
Centre Guillaume le Conquerant, Tapisserie de Bayeux, pp. 175–77, 180–81
Elio and Stefano Ciol, pp. 69, 141
Luciano Pedicini, pp. 107, 144, 145
Antonio Quattrone, pp. 11, 83
Istituto Fotografico Scala, pp. 31, 66-67, 70–71, 179

The following photographs are published with the permission of the Ministero per i Beni Culturali e Ambientali:
Archivio di Stato, Udine, Napoleonic Land Survey, pp. 202, 213
Archivio di Stato, Pordenone, Napoleonic Land Survey, pp. 40, 187, 225, 239
Archivio di Stato, Gorizia, Napoleonic Land Survey, p. 205
Archivio di Stato, Venice, p. 59
Museo Archeologico Nazionale, Cividale del Friuli, p. 271

Publication of the aerial photographs in this
volume has been authorized by the SMA
(permits 12-084, dated 23.5.95,
and 12-105 dated 29.6.95)